# PERSONALITY FROM BIOLOGICAL, COGNITIVE, AND SOCIAL PERSPECTIVES

## WARSAW LECTURES IN PERSONALITY AND SOCIAL PSYCHOLOGY
Published in cooperation with the Warsaw School of Social Sciences and Humanities, Warsaw, Poland

**Volume 1**
**PERSONALITY FROM BIOLOGICAL, COGNITIVE, AND SOCIAL PERSPECTIVES**
Edited by Tomasz Maruszewski, Małgorzata Fajkowska, and Michael W. Eysenck

*Forthcoming . . .*

**Volume 2**
**PERSONALITY, EMOTION, AND COGNITION**
Edited by Michael W. Eysenck, Małgorzata Fajkowska, and Tomasz Maruszewski

**Volume 3**
**PERSONALITY DYNAMICS: EMBODIMENT, MEANING CONSTRUCTION, AND THE SOCIAL WORLD**
Edited by Daniel Cervone, Michael W. Eysenck, Małgorzata Fajkowska, and Tomasz Maruszewski

# PERSONALITY FROM BIOLOGICAL, COGNITIVE, AND SOCIAL PERSPECTIVES

Edited by

## Tomasz Maruszewski
*Polish Academy of Sciences and
Warsaw School of Social Sciences and Humanities
Warsaw, Poland*

## Małgorzata Fajkowska
*Warsaw School of Social Sciences and Humanities and
Polish Academy of Sciences
Warsaw, Poland*

## Michael W. Eysenck
*Roehampton University
Whitelands College
London, United Kingdom*

ELIOT WERNER PUBLICATIONS, INC.
CLINTON CORNERS, NEW YORK

Library of Congress Cataloging-in-Publication Data

Personality from biological, cognitive, and social perspectves / edited by Tomasz
Maruszewski, Malgorzata Fajkowska, and Michael W. Eysenck.
p. cm. — (Warsaw lectures in personality and social psychology ; v. 1)
Includes bibliographical references and index.
ISBN-13: 978-0-9797731-5-0
ISBN-10: 0-9797731-5-6
1. Personality. 2. Cognition. I. Maruszewski, Tomasz. II. Fajkowska, Malgorzata.
III. Eysenck, Michael W.
BF698.P3657 2009
155.2—dc222009030078

2009030078

ISBN-10: 0-9797731-5-6
ISBN-13: 978-0-9797731-5-0

Copyright © 2010 Eliot Werner Publications, Inc.
PO Box 268, Clinton Corners, New York 12514
http://www.eliotwerner.com

Printed in the United States of America

# Contributors

**Kris Baetens** • Department of Psychology, Vrije Universiteit Brussel, Brussels, Belgium

**Marek Cielecki** • Warsaw School of Social Sciences and Humanities, Warsaw, Poland

**Joanna Dreszer** • Laboratory of Neuropsychology, Nencki Institute of Experimental Biology, Warsaw, Poland; Nicolaus Copernicus University, Torun, Poland

**Michael W. Eysenck** • Department of Psychology, Roehampton University, Whitelands College, London, United Kingdom

**Małgorzata Fajkowska** • Institute of Psychology, Polish Academy of Sciences, Warsaw, Poland; Warsaw School of Social Sciences and Humanities, Warsaw, Poland

**Urszula Jakubowska** • Institute of Psychology, Polish Academy of Sciences, Warsaw, Poland

**Miroslaw Kofta** • Faculty of Psychology, University of Warsaw, Warsaw, Poland

**Monika Lewandowska** • Laboratory of Neuropsychology, Nencki Institute of Experimental Biology, Warsaw, Poland

**Tomasz Maruszewski** • Warsaw School of Social Sciences and Humanities, Warsaw, Poland; Institute of Psychology, Polish Academy of Sciences, Warsaw, Poland

**Justyna Medygral** • Laboratory of Neuropsychology, Nencki Institute of Experimental Biology, Warsaw, Poland

**Risto Näätänen** • Department of Psychology, University of Tartu, Tartu, Estonia; Centre for Functionally Integrative Neuroscience, University of Aarhus, Aarhus, Denmark; Cognitive Brain Research Unit, Department of Psychology, University of Helsinki, Helsinki, Finland

**Wlodzimierz Oniszczenko** • Faculty of Psychology, University of Warsaw, Warsaw, Poland

**Grzegorz Osinski** • Nicolaus Copernicus University, Torun, Poland

**Katarzyna Paprzycka** • Department of Philosophy, University of Warsaw, Warsaw, Poland

**Kinga Piber-Dabrowska** • Interdisciplinary Center for Applied Cognitive Studies, Warsaw School of Social Sciences and Humanities, Warsaw, Poland

**Ernst Pöppel** • Institute for Medical Psychology and Human Science Centre, Munich University, Munich, Germany; Parmenides Centre for the Study of Thinking, Elba, Italy, and Munich, Germany

**Grzegorz Sedek** • Institute of Psychology, Polish Academy of Sciences, Warsaw, Poland

**Jan Strelau** • Warsaw School of Social Sciences and Humanities, Warsaw, Poland

**Elzbieta Szelag** • Laboratory of Neuropsychology, Nencki Institute of Experimental Biology, Warsaw, Poland; Warsaw School of Social Sciences and Humanities, Warsaw, Poland

**Aneta Szymaszek** • Laboratory of Neuropsychology, Nencki Institute of Experimental Biology, Warsaw, Poland; Warsaw School of Social Sciences and Humanities, Warsaw, Poland

**Frank Van Overwalle** • Department of Psychology, Vrije Universiteit Brussel, Brussels, Belgium

# Foreword

This volume grows out of the first Biennial Symposium on Personality and Social Psychology organized by the Warsaw School of Social Sciences and Humanities. Since the conference was a great success, it is fair to claim that the chapters inspired by this meeting will be of significant value in understanding the role of personality in human behavior.

This volume includes papers embedded in various personality theories. The diversity of approaches to personality research is the price that we pay for its growth, and the integration of findings seems to be a challenging goal to reach. In this regard, in the introduction the editors propose their view of personality in a way that makes the field an integrative discipline. Actually, the volume covers three areas of research that examine the different types of relationships between behavior and personality. However, the authors of these papers do not always elaborate on the way in which they understand personality. In some cases this understanding of personality can be indirectly surmised on the basis of the research tools applied. Sometimes it seems that the researchers work on the elementary individual differences in cognitive functioning that are only underpinnings (together with many other influences) of personality formation. It turns out that research conducted with reference to basic processes is extremely important from a theoretical and practical point of view—for example, in speech therapy or in understanding the difficulties of maintaining self-identity by elderly members of society.

The initial chapters address general problems, in particular the relationship between biological and personality variables. Subsequent chapters concern some traits of personality (or their bases) and behavior on a variety of levels, including the processes of attention and memory, processes of inferences, and complex social behavior.

Two kinds of research conducted on personality with respect to behavior are also presented in this volume. First, within the social cognitive frame, researchers limit themselves to measuring individual styles of cognitive functioning with experimental procedures. This approach entails looking at relationships between cognitive styles and processes as phenomena located on the same level of functioning, which is one's cognitive functioning. Second, with questionnaires assessment, investigators survey relationships among personality traits (coherent across situations and stable over time) and complex social behaviors. Metaphorically, close proximity between cognitive tendencies and cognitive processes produces more conclusive results, whereas no direct correspondence among overt, complex actions and isolated personality traits limits the clarity of the achieved findings.

The concise delineation of the theoretical framework presented by the editors helps integrate various data from very different studies. The theoretical assumption outlined in the introduction also suggests the necessity of conducting studies by taking into account very complex personality phenomena, as well as the very complex external conditions in which people act.

It is my firm conviction that this volume edited by Tomasz Maruszewski, Małgorzata Fajkowska, and Michael W. Eysenck is a stimulating book that represents an important contribution to the field. Therefore it gives me great pleasure to recommend this volume to fellow researchers, teachers, and students as an advanced text in courses on personality and social psychology.

*Andrzej Eliasz, Rector*
*Warsaw School of Social Sciences and Humanities*

# Contents

### Chapter 6 • The Mismatch Negativity: A Unique Window on Central Auditory Processing ....................... 115

*Risto Näätänen*

## PART III.
## SOCIAL CONTEXT:
## FROM WITHIN PERSONS TO AMONG PERSONS

### Chapter 7 • Environmental and Genetic Determinants of Sociopolitical Attitudes ............................. 129

*Urszula Jakubowska and Wlodzimierz Oniszczenko*

### Chapter 8 • The Cognitive Nature of Prejudiced Individuals ....... 145

*Kinga Piber-Dabrowska, Grzegorz Sedek, and Miroslaw Kofta*

**Chapter 9 • ERP Time Course and Brain Areas of Spontaneous
                and Intentional Social Inferences .................... 173**

*Frank Van Overwalle and Kris Baetens*

# PERSONALITY FROM BIOLOGICAL, COGNITIVE, AND SOCIAL PERSPECTIVES

# An Integrative View of Personality

## Tomasz Maruszewski
## Małgorzata Fajkowska
## Michael W. Eysenck

### PAST AND PRESENT

Historically personality psychology has been known as a field of substantial conceptual disagreements and competing theories and research traditions. Although a lack of consensus still exists, there are nevertheless significant areas of agreement in the field (e.g., Brody & Ehrlichman, 1998; Caprara & Cervone, 2000; Maltby, Day, & Macaskill, 2007). We are convinced that consensus is reflected in the following beliefs: the dispositional approach has its limitations; personality is a complex, dynamic system; and personality functioning may be explained by reference to a system of interacting dispositional tendencies and cognitive, affective, and social mechanisms.

The important point is that the limitations of the dispositional approach are reflected in the debate between dispositional and situational theorists concerning the relative roles of personality traits and situational specificity in determining individual behavior (e.g., Brody, 1988; Epstein, 1983; Funder, 2001, 2008; Mischel, 1968; Shoda, Mischel, & Wright, 1994). After decades of the person-situation debate, which represents a significant phase in the development of personality theory, empirical evidence has led most researchers to conceptualize personality traits as latent dispositions that influence the behavior of individuals in many different situations and for extended periods of time (e.g., Brody & Ehrlichman, 1998). However, the

*Personality from Biological, Cognitive, and Social Perspectives* edited by Tomasz Maruszewski, Małgorzata Fajkowska, and Michael W. Eysenck. Eliot Werner Publications, Clinton Corners, New York, 2010.

situational factors mediating or moderating the association between latent traits and reactions or behaviors (e.g., Chamorro-Premuzic, 2007; Strelau, 2008) serve to reduce the predictive value of latent traits. Accordingly, it led us to questions about the cross-situational consistency of traits (e.g., Eliasz, 1995) and intraindividual coherence (e.g., Caprara & Cervone, 2000; Eliasz 1981; Fajkowska & Eysenck, 2008). Moreover, it gives rise to the verification of the trait concept and attempts to interpret it as an inner, multilevel mechanism that determines the coherent stability of behavior—in other words, its trans-situational variability and stability over time (Eliasz, 2004; Fajkowska, in preparation).

We assume that personality is a complex, dynamic system of psychological structures, mechanisms, and processes. This self-organized and self-regulating system is a result of nonlinear interactions between its elements or subsystems (see Caprara & Cervone, 2000; Fajkowska-Stanik, 2001; von Bertalanffy, 1950, 1968). In other words, the key feature of any complex and dynamic system (here personality) is its tendency to be ordered and stable. This is achieved gradually through development and the "final form" is not wholly predictable (Fajkowska, in preparation). Thus intraindividual coherence might be understood as the interplay between psychological processes and mechanisms (biological and social factors) that allows sustaining a continuous sense of personal identity and individuality (Caprara & Cervone, 2000). The phenomenon of personality coherence incorporates three issues: integration of personality processes, coherence in overt psychological response, and continuity in phenomenological experience (Caprara & Cervone, 2000). In addition, the coherence of personality can be better understood in the context of intraindividual and interindividual differences. The analysis of person-to-person variations and intraindividual variations helps identify mechanisms that explain not only much of this variability, but also the stability and continuity of functioning (Fajkowska, in preparation). It should be stressed that we regard individual differences—as well as patterns of intraindividual variability and coherence—as involving a set of dispositional tendencies together with affective, cognitive, and social mechanisms (cf. Fajkowska, in preparation).

In short, we claim that contemporary research on personality should rest on three major assumptions, which potentially provide foundations on which to build in the years ahead: (a) personality is a complex system, resulting from the interactions among biological and psychological mechanisms and the interplay of dispositional cognitive, affective, and social subsystems; (b) there is coherence and continuity of individual behavior; and (c) these factors imply the need to use measures from different response systems.

## PERSONALITY FROM AN INTEGRATIVE PERSPECTIVE

The reference points described above do not unduly constrain theoretical and empirical enquiries. These assumptions allow us to benefit from the trait-theoretical frameworks that highlight intraindividual and interindividual differences in relatively stable psychological characteristics (with underlying biological influences or mechanisms). They also enable us to benefit from the affective and social cognitive perspectives, which tend to investigate psychological mechanisms associated with the interpretation and regulatory capacities of individuals. Moreover, they also let us take advantage of approaches to personality defined as the self-system shaped by personal experiences. The personal experiences form the integrated information system, which at the same time serves as a frame for receiving the new information (see Falkowski, Maruszewski, & Nęcka, 2008; Maruszewski, 2001). In essence, the development of the self-system is possible thanks to one's life experience (see Allen, 2006; McAdams, 1999).

We believe that the challenge of diversity (e.g., in approaches and methods) makes personality psychology an integrative discipline. As we look at the contents of this book, we should be optimistic about the growth of this branch of knowledge. Why is that? In this volume we try to show that personality can be studied in terms of distinctive characteristic behavior patterns (dispositions) or psychological processes, but can also be analyzed within an integrated and unifying framework (see Mischel & Shoda, 2008).

## WHAT'S AHEAD IN THIS BOOK

In response to the theoretical assumptions formulated above, we would like to present this book, which provides theoretical and empirical evidence that variation in neural reactivity—as well as at the level of genotypes—is related to individual differences in personality. More recently advances in noninvasive brain mapping and molecular biology and genetics have made it possible to associate personality traits with individual differences in brain structure and function, and to identify common variations in genes related to personality traits (e.g., Canli, 2008). Hence the evident biological mechanisms of personality have their connections with cognitive, affective, and social systems of individual functioning. Consequently, we focus on the biological (physiological and neurological), psychological (behavioral and self-descriptive), and interpersonal (relational and communicative) factors contributing to personality functioning.

The volume is organized in three parts and nine chapters. As can be seen, the authors of the chapters have different backgrounds, nationalities, career paths, and scientific interests. Their scientific interests include the determinants or mechanisms, dynamics, structure, and expression of personality.

### Part I: "On Some Biological Contributions to Personality"

Part I begins with a philosophical chapter by Katarzyna Paprzycka on reductionism and reductivism in philosophy of mind. She presents the current state of debate regarding the question of whether psychology is in principle reducible to "more fundamental" sciences such as neurobiology. According to her, reductionism occurs in two forms: metaphysical and methodological. Metaphysical reductionism is a speculative view, according to which all psychological (and other higher level) theories—including personality approaches—will eventually be reduced to "more fundamental" theories. Methodological reductionism (reductivism) can be formulated as a methodological directive: of two theories that are equally good in all other respects, we should choose the one that promises to be more easily reducible to a "more fundamental" theory. The survey of arguments against reductionism should at least deter scientists from accepting reductionism too quickly. Moreover, she argues that reductivism should be rejected even by reductionists.

However, Wilson (1998) sees reductionism as the natural mode of science and claims that in the end complexity—rather than simplicity—is what interests scientists. Reductionism is the way to understand complexity. The love of complexity without reductionism makes art, while with reductionism it makes science. At each level of personality organization, the phenomena may require new principles and laws that cannot be predicted from those at more general levels. But only a simpleminded reductionism would expect one personality or behavioral trait to be associated with a particular biological factor. Given the constant mutual interactions between the biological and environmental pathways, reductionism of one to the other is impossible (see Zuckerman, 2003). In other words, it is necessary to decompose personality to its elements (e.g., traits) and different levels of its manifestation (e.g., cognitive, social) to know the complexity of individual functioning.

Accordingly, Jan Strelau claims that the answer to the question "How far are we in searching for the biological background of personality?" depends on the theoretical conceptualization of a biological background of personality and personality per se. Strelau states that there is now plentiful evidence coming from behavior genetics and molecular biology, which have shown that the genetic background is very appropriate to most phenomena considered as "personality." However, the cognitive-oriented and trait-oriented approaches split into two separate fields in the search for the neurophysiological mechanisms underlying personality. To make this point, he argues that the main focus of the cognitive-oriented personality approach is to analyze the biological mechanisms underlying different aspects of memory functioning, which are crucial for explaining personal identity. In turn, the trait-oriented personality approach regards personality as reflecting differences in the reactivity level of neurobiochemical mechanisms underlying specific traits. It is adequately reflected in investigations of temperament. The studies selected by Strelau make it clear that we are still far from identifying the relevant mechanisms responsible for individual differences in personality. That is because the biological bases of personality traits are a result of many interactions and transactions among the separate biological and psychological mechanisms, including the influence of environment (broadly defined).

The chapter by Strelau presents personality dispositions and processing dynamics as competing approaches, or at least as two distinctive sides of one system. The next chapter, "A Neurocognitive Model of the Self" by Marek Cielecki, focuses on a more cumulative approach to personality. Personality psychology is an unusually broad field because it covers a wide spectrum of phenomena and levels of analysis; thus personality processes would be impoverished without a concept of self. The self makes personality coherent and is associated with neural, cognitive, affective, and social mechanisms (see Robins, Tracy, & Trześniewski, 2008). In his chapter Cielceki demonstrates that the basic notions of self-theories can be defined in neurocognitive terms. Moreover, the contemporary models of self converge in distinguishing its internal, external, and integrated facets (e.g., private, public, and collective). Accordingly, three standards of self-regulation are continuously posited by personality and social psychology (self-identity, self-esteem, and control). That trichotomy is underlined by the structure of the (human) brain with the right hemisphere serving the basic survival functions and directing the person inward, the left hemisphere providing the liaison to the (social) environment and directing outward, and the corpus callosum enabling an integration of these conflicting tendencies.

The next chapter deals with self-variability and stability on the neural level. The high variability of neuronal processes on the cellular level gives rise to a specific problem—that is, how to create and maintain the identity of a percept, a thought, or the self. In "Perceptual Identity and Personal Self: Neurobiological Reflections," Ernst Pöppel claims that temporal integration mechanisms on several levels appear to be used to overcome neuronal variability. In particular, an automatic integration mechanism of a few seconds (approximately 2–3 seconds) is used for identity creation and short-term maintenance. This temporal stage is also used for subjective self-reference. In studying the content of episodic memory in several hundred participants of different age groups, another phenomenon was discovered that may at least partly explain the shaping of personal identity throughout the entire life span: important images of our personal past are characterized by the fact that one sees oneself in one's own memory. This observation implies that our episodic memory is altered in a way to allow such self-reference. It is possible that patients with neurodegenerative diseases who suffer from memory problems may also partly lose their identity, since they no longer have access to images of their own past, which are stored in their episodic memory.

## Part II: "Nourishment of Personality: Information and External Conditions"

The chapter "Time and Cognition from the Aging Brain Perspective: Individual Differences" by Elzbieta Szelag, Joanna Dreszer, Monika Lewandowska, Justyna Medygral, Grzegorz Osinski, and Aneta Szymaszek opens Part II of the book. These authors have come up with neuropsychological evidence suggesting that temporal information processing provides one of the most fundamental principles underlying complex higher cortical functions like language, attention, memory, or motor control. This chapter reviews their own results of studies concerning individual differences in both cognitive functioning and timing. Based on these results, they claim that both cognitive functioning and timing decline with age, with considerable deterioration starting in individuals aged 60 and older. Another finding indicates that adolescents of superior intelligence show better performance than those of average intelligence. The close relationship between cognition and timing is therefore shown to constitute a potentially new theoretical background for future neurorehabilitation programs.

The next chapter in this section is "The Mismatch Negativity: A Unique Window on Central Auditory Processing." Risto Näätänen demonstrates the effects of changes on repetitive auditory stimulation. He offers a hypothesis that auditory event-related potentials can be present even when attention is not engaged and may be viewed as indices of sound discrimination accuracy. The mismatch negativity as a research tool makes it possible to record central auditory processing and different forms of auditory memory. Näätänen presents the research procedure in a very detailed manner to persuade readers that it is one possible way to reconstruct brain activity connected with changes in the repetitive auditory stimulation. Much of the available evidence focuses on fairly basic cognitive processes and suggests that auditory mismatch negativity reflects a "primitive sensory intelligence." However, there are also some findings (e.g., on language) suggesting that auditory mismatch negativity occurs in the context of complex processing.

## Part III: "Social Context: From Within Persons to Among Persons"

Part III is composed of three chapters. The first deals with the topic of the major determinants of sociopolitical attitudes, the second with prejudiced personality, and the third one provides strong and convincing evidence concerning some of the key processes involved in spontaneous and intentional social inferences.

Thus Urszula Jakubowska and Wlodzimierz Oniszczenko, in their chapter "Environmental and Genetic Determinants of Sociopolitical Attitudes," present empirical results clearly indicating that some sociopolitical attitudes (e.g., toward homosexuals, race, the death penalty, divorce, and abortion) may be inherited. They assumed that personality is a possible mediator in the heritability of attitudes. The results from the authors' twin studies on the relationships between personality traits with a large genetic component (as stated in the Big Five approach) and sociopolitical attitudes are rather inconclusive. Many of these findings also point to low and statistically insignificant correlations—or no correlations at all—between personality traits and sociopolitical attitudes. Jakubowska and Oniszczenko very carefully conclude that sociopolitical attitudes are influenced mainly by environment, and that biological mechanisms of inheritance of personality and sociopolitical attitudes are just as enigmatic.

In their chapter "The Cognitive Nature of Prejudiced Individuals," Kinga Piber-Dabrowska, Grzegorz Sedek, and Miroslaw Kofta argue that the integrative approach—which combines the cognitive perspective and personality mechanisms—might potentially improve research on prejudice. They show that prejudice is not a general psychological phenomenon, which can be attributed to all members of given social group, but rather a set of specific cognitive mechanisms that are characteristic of prejudiced individuals. For instance, across the series of their own studies, they demonstrate the effect of prejudice on perception and reasoning associated with ingroup members (the social cliques and linear orders procedures). In other words, negative prejudice may potentially facilitate the processing of information about outgroup persons, but also may impair the memory and reasoning processes about ingroup members. Additionally specific cognitive limitations were found among negatively prejudiced participants across various paradigms (social cliques models; mental arrays; classic Stroop test). This pattern of findings is highly distinctive for the results on positive prejudice.

Previous research in social cognition has revealed that people often infer the trait implications of others' behaviors, and that they can do so spontaneously without being aware of or intending to make these inferences. Such behavioral research, however, is silent about the neural processes that underlie trait inferences. Frank Van Overwalle and Kris Baetens, in their chapter "ERP Time Course and Brain Areas of Spontaneous and Intentional Social Inferences," try to answer an important question: can event-related brain potentials (ERPs) provide support for the occurrence of spontaneous trait inferences, and how do these differ from intentional trait inferences? In two studies they measured ERPs while participants read sentences describing the behavior of a target person from whom a strong or opposite trait could be inferred, under instructions to read the material or make trait inferences. In comparison with sentences that were consistent with the implied trait, when the sentences were inconsistent, an event-related P300 waveform was observed. This indicates that trait inferences were made previously while reading the sentences, irrespective of the participants' spontaneous or intentional goals. Overall the P300 shows considerable parallels between spontaneous and intentional inferences, indicating that the type and timing of the inconsistency process is very similar. In contrast, source localization (LORETA) of ERPs suggests that spontaneous inferences show greater activation in the temporo-parietal junction compared to intentional inferences. Memory measures taken after the presentation of the stimulus material showed significant correlations, with the P300 and the LORETA activation predominantly following spontaneous instructions, indicating that these neural components are valid neural indices of spontaneous inferences.

* * * * * *

The primary goal of the Warsaw Lectures in Personality and Social Psychology is not to provide a comprehensive review of research on personality, but instead to reflect on selected, advanced themes in the field. As a result, the potential readership consists of professionals and graduate students in personality functioning and individual differences. Our second goal is to convince readers that personality and brain or genetic research are exciting and endlessly fascinating endeavors. We hope that after reading this volume, you will share these sentiments and join us in looking forward to the publication of *Personality, Cognition, and Emotion*, the second volume of the series.

8    Tomasz Maruszewski et al.

# REFERENCES

Allen, B. P. (2006). *Personality theories: Development, growth, and diversity* (5th ed.). Boston: Pearson/Allyn & Bacon.

Brody, N. (1988). *Personality: In search of individuality.* New York: Harcourt Brace Jovanovich.

Brody, N., & Ehrlichman, H. (1998). *Personality psychology: The science of individuality.* Englewood Cliffs, NJ: Prentice-Hall.

Canli, T. (2008). Toward a "molecuar psychology" of personality. In O. P. John, R. W. Robins, & L. A. Pervin (Eds.), *Handbook of personality: Theory and research* (3rd ed., pp. 311–327). New York: Guilford Press.

Caprara, G. V., & Cervone, D. (2000). *Personality: Determinants, dynamics, and potentials.* Cambridge, UK: Cambridge University Press.

Chamorro-Premuzic, T. (2007). *Personality and individual differences.* Oxford, UK: Blackwell.

Eliasz, A. (1981). *Temperament a system regulacji stymulacji* [Temperament and system of regulation of stimulation]. Warsaw: Państwowe Wydawnictwo Naukowe.

Eliasz, A. (1995). Podmiotowe i środowiskowe czynniki utrudniające efektywną regulację stymulacji [Personal and environmental factors disturbing the effective regulation of stimulation]. *Czasopismo Psychologiczne, 1*, 129–141.

Eliasz, A. (2004). Transakcyjny Model Temperamentu: Analiza właściwości temperamentu z perspektywy nomotetycznego oraz idiograficznego badania osobowości [Transactional Model of Temperament: The analysis of temperament from the nomothetic and idiographic perspective of personality]. In Z. Chlewiński & A. Sękowski (Eds.), *Psychologia w perspektywie XXI wieku* (pp. 49–95). Lublin, Poland: Towarzystwo Naukowe KUL.

Epstein, S. (1983). The stability of confusion: A reply to Mischel and Peake. *Psychological Review, 90*, 179–194.

Fajkowska, M. (in preparation). *A Complex-System Approach to Personality and Indvidual Differences.* Clinton Corners, NY: Eliot Werner Publications.

Fajkowska, M., & Eysenck, M. W. (2008). Personality and cognitive performance. *Polish Psychological Bulletin, 39*, 178–191.

Fajkowska-Stanik, M. (2001). *Transseksualizm i rodzina. Przekaz pokoleniowy wzorow relacyjnych w rodzinach transseksualnych kobiet* [Transsexualism and families: Transgenerational transmission of relational patterns in families of transsexual women]. Warsaw: Wydawnictwo Instytutu Psychologii PAN.

Falkowski, A., Maruszewski, T., & Nęcka, E. (2008). Procesy poznawcze [Cognitive processes]. In J. Strelau & D. Doliński (Eds.), *Psychologia. Podręcznik akademicki* (Vol. 1, pp. 339–510). Gdańsk, Poland: Gdańskie Wydawnictwo Naukowe.

Funder, D. C. (2001). Personality. *Annual Review of Psychology, 52*, 197–221.

Funder, D. C. (2008). Persons, situations, and person-situation interactions. In O. P. John, R. W. Robins, & L. A. Pervin (Eds.), *Handbook of personality: Theory and research* (3rd ed., pp. 568–580). New York: Guilford Press.

Maltby, J., Day, L., & Macaskill, A. (2007). *Personality, individual differences and intelligence.* London: Prentice-Hall.

Maruszewski, T. (2001). *Psychologia poznania* [Cognitive psychology]. Gdańsk, Poland: Gdańskie Wydawnictwo Naukowe.

McAdams, D. P. (1999). Personal narratives and the life story. In L. A. Pervin & O. P. John (Eds.), *Handbook of personality: Theory and research* (2nd ed., pp. 478–500). New York: Guilford Press.

Mischel, W. (1968). *Personality and assessment*. New York: Wiley.

Mischel, W., & Shoda, Y. (2008). Toward a unified theory of personality: Integrating dispositions and processing dynamics within the cognitive-affective processing system. In O. P. John, R. W. Robins, & L. A. Pervin (Eds.), *Handbook of personality: Theory and research* (3rd ed., pp. 208–241). New York: Guilford Press.

Robins, R. W., Tracy, J. L., & Trzesniewski, K. H. (2008). Naturalizing the self. In O. P. John, R. W. Robins, & L. A. Pervin (Eds.), *Handbook of personality: Theory and research* (3rd ed., pp. 421–447). New York: Guilford Press.

Shoda, Y., Mischel, W., & Wright, J. C. (1994). Intraindividual stabiliy in the organization and pattering of behavior: Incorporating psychological situations into the idiographic analysis of personality. *Journal of Personality and Social Psychology, 67,* 674–687.

Strelau, J. (2008). *Temperament as a regulator of behavior: After fifty years of research.* Clinton Corners, NY: Eliot Werner Publications.

von Bertalanffy L. (1950). An outline of general systems therapy. *British Journal of the Philosophy of Science, 1,* 134–165.

von Bertalanffy L. (1968). *General systems theory*. New York: George Braziller.

Wilson, E. O. (1998). *Consilience: The unity of knowledge*. New York: Vintage Books.

Zuckerman, M. (2003). Biological bases of personality. In T. Millon, M. J. Lerner, & I. B. Weiner (Eds.), *Handbook of Personality: Vol. 5. Personality and social psychology* (pp. 85–117). New York: Wiley.

PART I

# On Some Biological Contributions to Personality

# CHAPTER 1

# Is Neurobiology of Personality Inevitable?
## A Philosophical Perspective

## Katarzyna Paprzycka

### INTRODUCTION

As a philosopher, I should take no stand on any empirical matter concerning personality research. In fact, it would be an overstatement to even consider such questions as whether neurobiology of personality is possible. I want to address a different question: whether neurobiology of personality, or indeed neurobiology of any field traditionally covered by psychology, is inevitable. This question has been tackled by philosophers, especially philosophers of mind concerned with the question of reductionism.

Reductionism embraces the thesis that all psychological theories, laws, and explanations are in the end reducible to neuroscientific ones. We might not be at a stage of scientific development to see that this is so, but if we wait long enough, we will ultimately be able to derive all psychological theories, laws, and explanations from neuroscience. Reductionists thus hold that to the extent that personality research has its place in science, it must be grounded in neuroscience. Neuroscience of personality is in this sense inevitable.

There is but a short step from the belief that neuroscience of personality is inevitable to the belief that it is the only worthwhile pursuit for personality research. Let us call the view that embraces this latter step "reductivism." According to reductivism, we should now prefer research in neurobiology of personality over research in pure psychology of personality.

*Personality from Biological, Cognitive, and Social Perspectives* edited by Tomasz Maruszewski, Małgorzata Fajkowska, and Michael W. Eysenck. Eliot Werner Publications, Clinton Corners, New York, 2010.

The primary aim of this chapter is to draw a clear distinction between these two types of positions: reductionism (and antireductionism) on one hand, and reductivism (and antireductivism) on the other. In the first part of the paper, I outline the current state of the debate between the proponents of reductionism and antireductionism. While the debate is ongoing and there are periods where one of the sides seems to be winning, it might be worthwhile to simply adopt the position of agnosticism on this issue and let the scientists work out the ultimate shape of the sciences. Still, philosophical arguments in these matters are important because they help to undercut the opinion that reductionism is the only possible position, a point of view that is gaining more adherents (especially in neuroscience-friendly circles). In the second part of the paper, I will criticize reductivism as detrimental to the development of science. I will argue that even supporters of reductionism have every reason to deny reductivism.

## REDUCTIONISM AND REDUCTIVISM

Reductionism, together with the contrary position of antireductionism, are speculative positions about the ultimate shape of science. Reductionists claim that there is one basic science (most reductionists believe it to be physics) to which all other sciences are reducible. The theories, laws, and explanations of the other sciences are going to be (in the final, unachievable limit) derived from physical theories, laws, and explanations. In particular, reductionists claim that psychology (in its final form) is going to be reduced to the neurosciences (in their final form). In a deep sense, reductionists believe that there is only one science (the unity of science thesis).

According to antireductionism, on the other hand, the observable diversity of sciences reflects a deep fact about the diversification of reality. Some antireductionists believe that reality is ontologically diverse (dualists, pluralists). Other antireductionists are monists—in fact, most are physicalists (they believe that everything that exists is physical)—but they nonetheless believe that there are many autonomous levels at which such physical reality can be explained. According to antireductionists, even at the end of the day, in the unachievable limit, there will be many sciences, not one science. In particular, many antireductionists believe that psychology is (and will remain) an autonomous science, irreducible to the neurosciences.

Those two positions are speculative philosophical positions concerned, as I emphasized, with the final (and so unachievable) state of science. Philosophers are used to thinking about abstract matters and the debate about how the mind is related to the body has been at the center of speculative philosophical attention since Descartes. In recent years, because of rapid developments in the neurosciences, abstract philosophical debates are also being tackled by scientists in concrete empirical research. While this is fruitful in detailed discussions of empirical problems, where philosophers have let their speculation free, it is potentially dangerous in more abstract matters that have traditionally been at the subject of philosophy.

Reductivism is the view that we should, right now, prefer neuroscientific research over psychological research that is unrelated to the neurosciences. Reductivism might appear to be a simple consequence of accepting reductionism. If one is a reductionist (i.e., believes, among other things, that psychology will be reduced to neuroscience), then reductivism might appear to be reasonable (i.e., we should prefer the more fundamental research). I will claim later that this is only an appearance: not only does reductivism not follow from reductionism, but in fact it would be irrational for any reductionist to be a reductivist.

## REDUCTIONISM AND ANTIREDUCTIONISM

At the beginning of the twentieth century, there was a consensus among philosophers that we would know everything about the mind if we knew everything about the brain. Indeed, most philosophers believed that if we knew everything about the world of microparticles, we would indeed know everything about the world. They thought that there is only one world (monism), the physical world (physicalism). It seemed reasonable to suppose that there is one ultimate theory describing and explaining the functioning of this world (the unity of science thesis) and that it will be some future physical theory. As a matter of fact, there are many theories in physics; there are also many sciences. This fact does not contradict the unity of science thesis. Because science has a hierarchical structure (there are many levels at which scientists investigate reality), higher level theories are reducible to lower level theories (reductionism). Reductionists have also supported their view by pointing out some examples of reduction (e.g., the reduction of qualitative thermodynamics to statistical thermodynamics, or the reduction of classical genetics to molecular genetics). With more research (it was believed) sociology will eventually be reduced to psychology, psychology to biology, biology to chemistry, and chemistry is already to a large extent reduced to physics.

It might be thought that reductionism is the only natural view to hold. With the development of science, it will appear only more inevitable. However, most philosophers thinking about the issue have reached precisely the opposite conclusion. It is a striking fact that while most philosophers at the beginning of the twentieth century were reductionists, most philosophers at the beginning of the twenty-first century are antireductionists. Many arguments for antireductionism have been voiced. I will focus on three groups.

I should warn the reader, however, that each of the arguments is a wellspring of huge debates, some of which are highly technical in nature. This survey of the arguments is merely meant to delineate a general direction for further discussion rather than to give any conclusive arguments.

## Methodological Arguments

The main thrust of the methodological arguments for antireductionism is to show that while the world is one, it cannot be fully understood by one theory — or more precisely, at one theoretical level.

Hillary Putnam (1975a) points out that the same phenomenon can be explained on different levels. Moreover, the laws that are invoked by such explanations need not be reducible to the laws of physics. Imagine a cylindrical wooden peg made of Quercus rubra being pushed through a square hole in a wall made of concrete. Suppose that the circumference of the circular cross-section of the peg is equal to the circumference of the hole. The fact that the peg will not go through the hole can be explained quite simply by the laws of geometry. One could, of course, also explain this fact by appealing to the laws of microphysics. One would then have to treat the peg and the wall as a structure of atoms, calculate the forces between them, and consider how the force applied to the peg affects the initial system of forces. This tedious explanation would also allow us to understand why the wooden peg did not go through the hole in the concrete. However, this explanation is in some ways less adequate than the geometrical one. If we changed the peg for one with a bigger radius (and made of Pinus nigra) and tried to push such a peg through a correspondingly bigger hole in a wall made of steel, our geometrical explanation would remain valid while we would have to start work on the microphysical explanation from scratch. This example is also meant to illustrate that higher level explanations may be epistemically independent from lower level ones. The laws of geometry are certainly irreducible to the laws of physics.

Of course this is not to say that physical facts are irrelevant even in this example. The fact that the two objects — the peg and the wall with the hole — are solids with certain physical properties makes the geometrical explanations applicable in such cases. Imagine the attempt to insert a concrete peg through a hole in a wall made of stretchable silicon, or imagine the attempt to insert a metal peg through a wooden wall with great impact force. However, what such examples demonstrate is that there are certain boundary conditions on the applicability of the geometrical explanations. Within those conditions the geometrical explanation is really the best explanation we have of the fact that a cylindrical peg will not go through the square hole whose circumference is equal to that of the peg.

Second, it has been argued (Davidson, 1980a, 1980b; Fodor, 1974) that higher level sciences cut reality at different joints. It is thus hard to hope that higher level laws are going to be derived from lower level ones. To make the point vivid, Fodor (1974) puts forward the example of the Copernicus-Gresham law of monetary exchange. From a physical point of view, money is an extremely heterogeneous category. Money can be made of various types of metals, pieces of paper, and electronic signals, and it may be realized in yet other ways in the future. These physical objects have different physical properties. It seems irrational to expect that the laws of physics would suffice to generate any economic law concerning money.

In some methodological approaches (Cartwright, 1983; Nowak, 1971, 1980), the very understanding of the structure of a scientific theory offers a way of seeing how two scientific theories can be about the same reality but come up with different irreducible laws. In such approaches scientific theory is to be understood not as a set of claims (Nagel, 1961), but rather as a hierarchical structure of claims. Such a hierarchy has at its top the simplest idealizational laws, which capture the relationship between the most important factors in play in a given phenomenon. At lower levels the laws are concretized and modified to include the influence of the less important factors until—at the bottom of the hierarchy—factual claims (or their approximations) are reached that capture the relationship between all the factors in play in all their complexity. Given such an understanding of the nature of theory, there emerges the possibility that even if the factual claims of a theory (psychological, say) can be derived from the factual claims of another theory (biological, say), it does not follow that the idealizational laws of the former can be derived from the idealizational laws of the latter because the two theories can take different factors to be most important (Dupré, 1993; Paprzycka, 2004). In this way there is a possibility that one science captures different regularities than those captured in another science, even if both talk about the same reality.

Finally, the doubts concerning reductionism arise also in philosophy of science. It turned out that the cases cited as paradigmatic examples of reduction fail to satisfy the requirements that methodologists place on reductions. It has been pointed out, for example, that Galileo's law of free fall is simply incompatible with Newton's theory of gravitation. It has also been pointed out that some biological theories, such as the theory of evolution or population genetics, are in their very nature irreducible to chemical theories. The theory of evolution captures reality at an entirely different level: the force of natural selection has simply no correlate in the macro- or microreality of physical forces.

## The Argument from Ignorance of Philosophy of Mind

One of the causes (though not reasons) why reductionism seems a natural view to hold is the erroneous assumption that there are only two positions one can hold about the mind: dualism and reductive materialism. Dualism is the view that there are material and mortal bodies as well as immaterial and immortal souls. Reductive materialism involves the claim that there are no souls but brains and that the right way to study minds is to study brains. One of the main tasks of philosophy of mind since the 1960s has been to investigate the different ways in which the mind-body relationship can be conceptualized while accepting materialism—that is, without invoking special mental substances. There are three basic views; each has its advantages and disadvantages. I will review their basic theses without attempting to evaluate them. I want to emphasize, however, that there is no warranted transition between the belief that mind is somehow related to the brain (and not to some special mental substance) and the belief that psychology must be reduced to neuroscience. There are materialisms that accept the reduction thesis and there are materialisms that do not.

The (type) identity theory (Smart, 1959), also called reductive materialism, can be captured by the slogan "mind = brain." According to the theory, every mental event is identical to some brain event (and more precisely every type of mental event is identical to some type of brain event). Feeling pain, we are told, is identical to C-fiber firing. We are not in a position to discover all such identities, but identity theorists believe that the progress of neuroscience will increase our knowledge in this regard. The identity theory leads to reductionism: if mental events are identical to brain events, then the knowledge of such identities — together with the knowledge of appropriate neuroscientific laws — would enable us to derive psychological laws (though see Paprzycka, 2004).

The identity theory may appear the most natural and obvious theory to hold; it may even bear the mark of being scientific. This is why it is so astounding that the theory is incompatible with some obvious scientific data and that it renders artificial intelligence (AI) impossible. Let's begin with the second point. The main task of AI research is to construct a thinking machine. A thinking machine must possess some thoughts, among others a certain arbitrary thought $T$, on which it must be able to operate well. According to the identity theory, thought $T$ is identical to some brain state $B$. This suffices to show that no machine (which does not possess a brain) could be in the brain state $B$, and so that no machine could have thought $T$, and so that no machine could think. If mental events are identical to brain events, then only beings that have brains can have minds. Artificial intelligence is thus impossible. There are of course many controversies concerning the possibility of artificial intelligence, but such a declaration from a philosophical armchair seems only to speak against the point of sitting — in this case against the identity theory.

For similar reasons any kind of prostheses or chips designed to replace or improve mental functions would seem to be impossible. If some thought or perception is identical with some brain event, then a being whose brain has been incapacitated in such a way that the brain event can no longer occur cannot have that thought or perception. Again, this seems unacceptable in view of scientific facts.

Functionalism (Putnam, 1975b) is the position that can accommodate the above objections. It is a kind of synthesis of identity theory and dualism. According to functionalism, mental events are identified by the functional role that they play. The functional role is in turn understood in terms of three types of relations: input relations, the kind of conditions that cause the mental event (e.g., pain is caused by touching a hot stove); output relations, the kind of reactions the mental event causes (e.g., pain causes removing the hand from the heat source), and internal relations, the kind of interactions with other mental states the given mental state enters into (e.g., pain may cause the learning of not touching hot objects, it may lead to fear of heat, etc.). If pains are those events that play so understood a functional role, then they may be realized as C-fiber firing in human beings but they may be realized differently in other beings. Thus while functionalists do agree with identity theorists that to feel pain (for a human) is to have one's C-fibers firing, they disagree with an all-out identification of pain with C-fiber firing. For it may very well be that there are other kinds of beings for whom pain is realized by some other state of the nervous system, or indeed by some other state of the system. Functionalism is the view that grounds the program of AI: a machine may have a certain thought $T$ as long as it has a state whose functional role is identical to the functional role played by $T$ in us. Similarly, functionalism offers a way of understanding the possibility of prostheses as long as their introduction to the system does not change the functional role of states realized on them. Functionalism can be captured by the slogan "the mind is to the brain as software is to hardware."

Functionalism is often associated[1] with token identity theory (Davidson, 1980a). In the latter account, there might not exist type identities between mental states and brain states but only so-called token identities—especially for mental states such as beliefs or thoughts, which possess contents. It may be that the thought that green herrings grow on willows will be identical in each of us with some state of the brain (with what brain state will depend on the complex developmental history of the person and his or her brain), but it may very well be that in each of us the type of brain state with which the thought is identical will be different. So it may be that the only way to capture this strange thought is to identify it at the psychological level (at the neurophysiological level, it will be dispersed in different types of brain states). Many functionalists argue that type identities are more probable for such primitive mental states as pain sensations but are quite improbable for so-called higher mental states—especially those imbued with contents such as beliefs, desires, or intentions, for which only token identities are present.

Just as type identity theory leads to reductionism, so functionalism leads to antireductionism. If functionalism is correct, then psychological regularities are autonomous and should be formulated at the psychological level. It may be that for such states as pain, one could partly (but only partly) derive psychological laws from neuroscientific ones, but such a derivation will not constitute reduction: it will at best be a derivation of pain-related laws (e.g., for vertebrates). By definition, however, since pain is not identified as C-fiber firing but merely happens to be realized as C-fiber firing in vertebrates, there remains an "underived" portion of pain-related laws for invertebrates and perhaps other types of creatures whose makeup is completely unknown to us at this time (possibly artificial intel-

---

[1] While functionalism is certainly compatible with token identity theory, it is also compatible with other theories—even with nonmaterialistic theories such as dualism. There is a famous argument by David Lewis (1972) that functionalism is indeed compatible with type identity theory. See also Jackson, Pargetter, and Prior (1982).

ligence or extraterrestrial beings). Things are even worse for the reduction of eventual laws concerning beliefs, desires, intentions, thoughts, and so forth.[2]

Eliminative materialism (Churchland, 1979) is the most radical position in philosophy of mind, which rejects the belief that folk-psychological mental categories (such as beliefs, intentions, desires, sensations, etc.) are going to be explicated in science. According to eliminativism, folk psychology is a radically wrong theory and should be simply rejected just as the phlogiston theory of combustion, the caloric theory of heat, or the hexation theory of mental illness were rejected. There is no place for the notion of mind at all in science: minds do not exist just as phlogiston does not exist. The whole science of psychology will not be reduced but replaced by the neurosciences.

This brief overview of the three main materialist positions is not sufficient to enable one to decide which of the positions is correct. It is, however, sufficient to make one realize that the belief that the brain is significant for what we call mental functions does not lead to reductionism. Each of the positions assigns an important role to the brain but the views differ, among others, in how they envisage the future of psychology. According to the identity theory, future psychology is going to be reduced to the neurosciences (and those finally to physics). According to functionalism, future psychology will remain an autonomous scientific discipline whose laws will be irreducible to neuroscientific laws. According to eliminativism, psychology will be eliminated from the sciences altogether and replaced by the neurosciences. So it is an error to jump to the conclusion that reductionism is correct just because one believes that dualism is false and materialism is correct.

## The Argument from AI Paradigms

There is a long-standing philosophical debate between individualism and various forms of anti-individualism. Individualists believe that mental concepts can be defined by reference to an individual in abstraction from the environment (Fodor, 1975, 1994; Searle, 1983). Anti-individualists argue that mental concepts require reference to the reality beyond the individual (see Burge, 1979; Clark, 1997; Paprzycka, 2002; Putnam, 1975c; Wilson, 1995, 2004). The debate spans the fields of philosophy of language, philosophy of mind, philosophy of action, and epistemology. Anti-individualism is prima facie incompatible with reductionism.

Since the debate is quite complex and highly technical, I will look at just one way in which it is relevant to the debate about reductionism. I will focus on the three paradigms of artificial intelligence (classical, connectionist, embodied) and will argue that they differ—among other respects—in the projected relevance of neuroscientific research for psychology. If we accept the classical paradigm of thinking about the mind, then the projected role for neuroscientific research

---

[2] This so-called multiple-realizability argument against reductionism has been called into question by Kim (1992, 1998). For responses see, for example, Fodor (1997).

would be most significant. If we accept the embodied paradigm, then the projected role for neuroscientific research would be relatively minor.

Classic AI (see, e.g., Simon, 1969) systems were based on the assumption that minds are formal systems and that to think is to apply rules to representations. For a classic AI system to behave intelligently in the world (or its fragment), the relevant portions of the world must be represented in the system. This is the source of one of the most difficult problems for classic AI, the so-called frame problem (see, e.g., Dennett, 1987). It turns out that our common-sense knowledge about the world is extremely difficult to codify in the forms of explicit beliefs, for example. We all know that walls do not move spontaneously at the velocity of 1 millimeter per hour, but such a belief would never come to our mind.

The problem of representation is handled quite differently by the connectionist paradigm (Rumelhart & McClelland, 1986). Mind is thought of as a huge "neural" net with no place for classical representations to which logical rules could be applied, and to which the programmer could have access. Connectionist systems rely on the so-called distributed representations. Such representations are the result of the system learning various tasks. In the process of learning to recognize a face, for example, the system adjusts the strengths of the connections between the nodes of the net. Once the system has succeeded in learning the task, the stabilized connections between the nodes constitute a distributed representation of a face. Such representations, however, are in principle inaccessible to the programmer. Although there exist some statistical tools for uncovering such representations, access to them remains very difficult and depends on a number of conditions. To aggravate the difficulty, the form of a distributed representation depends on such conditions as the architecture of the net, its starting point, the shape of the learning sample, and so on. So it is not the case that a distributed representation of the face of Hillary Clinton, say, will look the same in any net. In fact, one might begin to doubt that connectionist representations are representations at all. However, connectionist systems have proven to be able to perform very well—especially on tasks with which the classical systems had problems (such as in learning nonalgorithmic tasks).

The so-called embodied mind paradigm is still further removed from classic AI. In a widely read paper with the remarkable title "Intelligence Without Representation" (1997), Rodney Brooks—one of the pioneers of the new paradigm—describes a robot, Herbert, whose single task was to collect soda cans in one of the MIT buildings. Though Herbert's task was simple, he had to operate in the real world where lots of things can happen. Moreover, Herbert was not equipped with any representation of the building at all. Brooks's working assumption was that the best representation of the world is the world itself: the system only needs to select the relevant information in acting on the world. Herbert's programming consisted of independent modules that were invoked by appropriate environmental cues. Remarkably, there was no central module to coordinate the other ones. The robot would spontaneously move forward. If his sensors detected some obstacle, the change-direction module would be activated, which in turn would trigger the move-forward module. If can-like shapes were perceived by the robot's camera, the extend-arm and grasp modules would be activated. And so on. It was quite remarkable that Herbert performed his simple task so well in a real-life, multiple-story building.

Brooks's research is a classic example of the embodied mind paradigm, which seeks to find the mind beyond the skin/shell of the organism/system. Clark and Chalmers (1998) argue that just as we will not hesitate in perhaps the not-so-distant future to treat some sort of memory chip as part of our mind, so we should not hesitate to treat a calculator, a computer, a piece of paper, a map, a book, and other tools as literally parts of our minds—as long as we can properly use them. Our mind extends beyond our skull and even beyond our skin.

When we treat the three different paradigms of thinking about artificial intelligence as approaches for thinking about human intelligence, it is remarkable how different is the role of the brain in each of the paradigms. The brain would play the greatest role according to the classical paradigm. If the classical paradigm were right, then neuroscientists would have to find the neural vehicles of representations of the world, our beliefs, and logical operations. If the connectionist paradigm were correct, then the brain would be thought of as a huge net allowing the adaptation of the organism to the environment. This time, however, neuroscientists would probably not even hope to find neural vehicles for the representations of the world—for the simple reason that distributed representations are largely inaccessible and too dependent on the particular individual system. Of course the more primitive the representations, the higher the chance of finding neural substrata for them. If the embodied mind paradigm were correct, then the role to be played by the brain is more modest still. This time the main function of the brain would be to appropriately hook up to the world to use the information contained in it without internalizing it.

The different role assigned to the brain in these three paradigms suggests an answer to the question of whether pure neuroscience can give us a complete theory of mind. There would be at least a chance for a positive answer to this question in the classical paradigm. However, if either the connectionist paradigm or the embodied world paradigm are correct, then the answer must be negative. If the embodied world paradigm is correct, then intelligence is simply invisible without reference to a more holistic picture of the system dealing with its environment. Even complete neuroscience cannot offer a complete understanding of the mind for the mind lies outside the brain to a large extent.

## Conclusion

This survey of various arguments for antireductionism is certainly not complete and is insufficient to help one make up one's mind. It should be sufficient, however, to push us out of a common rut into which we tend to fall—the view that a scientific approach to the study of mind dictates the acceptance of reductionism. The arguments presented show that antireductionism is at least a respectable alternative.

## ON THE DANGERS OF REDUCTIVISM

Both reductionism and antireductionism are speculative positions. Their quarrel is about the ultimate shape of science. One frequently encounters, especially among enthusiasts of the neurosciences, a different kind of position that is impatient. According to such reductivism, as we initially called the position, we should at this very moment (not in the distant, unachievable future) prefer neuroscientifc theories and research over purely psychological theories and research (see, e.g., Bickle, 2003). Reductivism can take various forms. In an extreme version, we should right now drop all psychological research that is unrelated to the brain. In a more moderate version of reductivism, if we have a choice between two comparable (systematized to the same degree, supported by evidence to the same degree, etc.) theories, we should prefer the theory that offers greater prospects for reduction to neuroscience.

Reductionism involves a vision about the ultimate state of science while reductivism tries to put this vision into practice right now. I believe that reductivism is wrong and even dangerous, for two reasons that do not depend on the debate between reductionism and antireductionism. I will argue that even a reductionist should deny reductivism.

First, reduction requires the existence of higher level theories to be reduced. If there are such higher level theories, then reduction leads to epistemic progress: we gain a deeper insight into how higher level regularities depend on lower level ones. So, paradoxically, a reductionist should be an antireductivist—that is, should promote the development of science at all its levels, because only when science is fully developed at the higher levels can one even think about carrying out a reduction.

Reductivism tries to find a shortcut for reduction. In such a case, however, it seeks not the reduction but elimination of higher level sciences. This in turn leads not to the enrichment but to the impoverishment of our knowledge. Let us illustrate this through a fictitious example based on an actual reduction of qualitative thermodynamics to statistical thermodynamics.

According to Charles's law, the increase in the temperature of a gas leads to the increase of pressure given constant volume. This regularity can be nicely explained in terms of statistical thermodynamics. The temperature of a gas can be thought of as the mean kinetic energy of the gas molecules. The pressure of a gas can be identified with the mean momentum of the molecules. From the laws of mechanics, we can derive a dependency between the increase of kinetic energy and the increase of momentum, which explains why the heating of a gas increases its pressure given constant volume.

Let us imagine for a moment that the science of physics developed differently than it did in fact. Imagine that once mechanics developed, the microworld of molecules was also discovered and mechanics was immediately applied on the microlevel as well. In fact, we may suppose that scientists accepted reductivism and decided to study mechanics exclusively at the microlevel. The point is that if physics developed in such a way, taking an immediate shortcut to the microlevel, the macrolevel regularities such as Boyle's, Charles's, and Mariotte's laws might never have been discovered—for the simple reason that if we looked at the world from the point of view of the mechanics of molecules, we might never have come across the idea of drawing a mean of the kinetic energy or momentum of a bunch of molecules (how would that bunch have been identified?) or of connecting them with macrophenomena. Such macrophenomena must be well identified and at least partially understood for them to be explained at the microlevel.

Second, reductivism stands in the way of a free development of science. As long as psychologists who are reductionists turn away from purely psychological research and engage in brain-related research, and as long as psychologists who favor antireductionism refrain from engaging in brain-related research and study pure psychology, everything is just as it should be. Science develops freely and the question of whose philosophical views were right will be settled later. We should worry, however, if either group of psychologists were to dominate the field. This would be detrimental to everybody.

There are many examples of this kind of conflict. Let me recall but one. In the 1950s two paradigms of AI research existed: classic AI (already mentioned) and the so-called perceptrons. Perceptrons were precursors of contemporary neural networks. They were systems composed of only two types of units (input and output) and involved linear activation functions. Classic AI systems as well as perceptrons developed in parallel. Each excelled in dealing with different tasks. In 1969 Minsky and Papert published their famous critique of perceptron research. They argued that despite considerable promise, perceptrons are in principle limited. They proved that there is a class of tasks (such as the task of learning the truth table for exclusive disjunction, the so-called XOR problem) that is beyond the reach of perceptrons. The effect of this legitimate critique was devastating. Perceptron research was virtually stopped for over a decade—or at any rate the grant money stopped flowing.

This case is all the more illuminating when we note that the grant money started flowing again in the 1980s, when it was showed that neural networks ("perceptrons" with an additional layer of hidden units and a nonlinear activation function) can handle the XOR problem. Moreover, neural networks did fare much better in areas where classical systems performed poorly.

Let me stress once again: even if reductionism is correct, reductivism can only be detrimental to the development of science. It is higher level theories that begin the initial carving of regularities (especially those that are significant from a practical point of view), develop methodologies of experimental research in a given area, and introduce methods of measurement and experimental intervention. It is a myth that if reductionism is correct, then higher level research is spurious. If that were the case, then every scientist should be studying physics right now.

What, then, is the source of reductivism? Its first source is the failure to distinguish between the two positions (speculative reductionism and practical reductivism) or the failure to realize the dangers involved in the extrapolation of the speculative position onto the practical plane. The second source of reductivism is the fact that we are in the middle of a scientific revolution due to the development of new technologies in brain research. Every scientific revolution generates great research dynamics and accompanying enthusiasm (Kuhn, 1970). This is understandable because each scientific revolution opens up apparently infinite research possibilities, which lead to an intense development of knowledge.

This otherwise understandable revolutionary excitement should not preclude a cool judgment. It would be wrong, of course, not to admire the discoveries already made and those that are within arm's reach. It would be just as wrong to promote only such discoveries. It is one thing to believe that one is right and to strive to demonstrate this; it is quite another thing to believe that one has a monopoly on truth. In science, just as in politics, scientific institutions should guard the free development of thought. Reductivism thwarts such a development, reminding us of the old adage: the road to hell is paved with good intentions.

## SUMMARY

One sometimes hears the opinion that our beliefs must somehow be coded in our brains, so brain research will eventually tells us how. This opinion can be treated in at least three ways:

- As a motivation for engaging in neuroscientific research.
- As an argument for reductionism.
- As an argument for reductivism.

As long as this opinion motivates researchers to engage in neuroscience, they should be applauded for the fruits of their endeavors will only enrich our knowledge. But if the opinion were taken as an argument for reductionism (i.e., for the view that all knowledge about the mind can be derived from the knowledge about the brain), then it would be a poor argument which ignores the possibility that functionalism is right in philosophy of mind or that the paradigm of the embodied mind is correct in artificial intelligence. And if the opinion were taken as a call for reductivism (i.e., for abandoning pure psychology in favor of neuroscience), then it would be decidedly wrong since—as we have seen—even a reductionist should be an antireductivist.

## REFERENCES

Bickle, J. (2003). *Philosophy and neuroscience: A ruthlessly reductive account.* Dordrecht, The Netherlands: Kluwer Academic.

Brooks, R. A. (1997). Intelligence without representation. In J. Haugeland (Ed.), *Mind design II: Philosophy, psychology, artificial intelligence* (pp. 395–420). Cambridge, MA: MIT Press.

Burge, T. (1979). Individualism and the mental. In P. A. French, T. E. Uehling, Jr., & H. K. Wettstein (Eds.), *Studies in metaphysics: Midwest studies in philosophy* (Vol. 4, pp. 73–122). Minneapolis: University of Minnesota Press.

Cartwright, N. (1983). *How the laws of physics lie.* Oxford, UK: Clarendon Press.

Churchland, P. M. (1979). *Scientific realism and the plasticity of mind.* Cambridge, UK: Cambridge University Press.

Clark, A. (1997). *Being there: Putting brain, body, and world together again.* Cambridge, MA: MIT Press.

Clark, A., & Chalmers, D. (1998). The extended mind. *Analysis, 58,* 7–19.

Davidson, D. (1980a). Mental events. Reprinted in D. Davidson, *Essays on actions and events* (pp. 207–228). Oxford, UK: Clarendon Press.

Davidson, D. (1980b). The material mind. Reprinted in D. Davidson, *Essays on actions and events* (pp. 245–261). Oxford, UK: Clarendon Press.

Dennett, D. C. (1987). Cognitive wheels: The frame problem of AI. In M. A. Boden (Ed.), *The philosophy of artificial intelligence* (pp. 147–170). Oxford, UK: Oxford University Press.

Dupré, J. (1993). *The disorder of things: Metaphysical foundations of the disunity of science.* Cambridge, MA: Harvard University Press.

Fodor, J. A. (1974). Special sciences (or: the disunity of science as a working hypothesis). *Synthese, 28,* 97–115.

Fodor, J. A. (1975). *The language of thought.* New York: Crowell.

Fodor, J. A. (1994). *The elm and the expert: Mentalese and its semantics.* Cambridge, MA: MIT Press.

Fodor, J. A. (1997). Special sciences: Still autonomous after all these years. *Philosophical Perspectives, 11,* 149–163.

Jackson, F., Pargetter, R., & Prior, E. (1982). Functionalism and type-type identity theories. *Philosophical Studies, 42,* 209–225.

Kim, J. (1992). Multiple realization and the metaphysics of reduction. *Philosophy and Phenomenological Research, 52,* 1–26.

Kim, J. (1998). *Mind in a physical world: An essay on the mind-body problem and mental causation.* Cambridge, MA: MIT Press.

Kuhn, T. (1970). *The structure of scientific revolutions* (2nd ed.). Chicago: University of Chicago Press.

Lewis, D. (1972). Psychophysical and theoretical identifications. *Australasian Journal of Philosophy, 50,* 249–258.

Minsky, M., & Pappert, S. (1969). *Perceptrons.* Cambridge, MA: MIT Press.

Nagel, E. (1961). *The structure of science: Problems in the logic of scientific discovery.* London: Routledge and Kegan Paul.

Nowak, L. (1971). *U podstaw marksowskiej metodologii nauk* [The foundations of Marxian methodology of science]. Warsaw: Państwowe Wydawnictwo Naukowe.

Nowak, L. (1980). *The structure of idealization.* Dordrecht, The Netherlands: Reidel.

Paprzycka, K. (2002). False consciousness of intentional psychology. *Philosophical Psychology, 15,* 271–295.

Paprzycka, K. (2004). How a type-type identity theorist can be a non-reductionist: An answer from the idealizational conception of science. In D. Gillies (Ed.), *Laws and models in science* (pp. 113–128). London: King's College Publications.

Putnam, H. (1975a). Philosophy and our mental life. Reprinted in H. Putnam, *Philosophical papers: Vol. 2. Mind, language, and reality* (pp. 291–303). Cambridge, UK: Cambridge University Press.

Putnam, H. (1975b). The nature of mental states. Reprinted in H. Putnam, *Philosophical papers: Vol. 2. Mind, language, and reality* (pp. 429–440). Cambridge, UK: Cambridge University Press.

Putnam, H. (1975c). The meaning of meaning. Reprinted in H. Putnam, *Philosophical papers: Vol. 2. Mind, language, and reality* (pp. 215–271). Cambridge, UK: Cambridge University Press.

Rumelhart, D. E., McClelland, J. L., & PDP Research Group. (Eds.) (1986). *Parallel distributed processing: Explorations in the microstructure of cognition.* Cambridge, MA: MIT Press.

Searle, J. R. (1983). *Intentionality: An essay in the philosophy of mind.* Cambridge, UK: Cambridge University Press.

Simon, H. A. (1969). *The sciences of the artificial.* Cambridge, MA: MIT Press.

Smart, J. J. C. (1959). Sensations and brain processes. *Philosophical Review, 68,* 141–156.

Wilson, R. A. (1995). *Cartesian psychology and physical minds: Individualism and the sciences of the mind.* Cambridge, UK: Cambridge University Press.

Wilson, R. A. (2004). *Boundaries of the mind: The individual in the fragile sciences.* Cambridge, UK: Cambridge University Press.

CHAPTER 2

# How Far Are We in Searching for the Biological Background of Personality?

## Jan Strelau

### INTRODUCTION

The term "personality," as understood in this chapter, needs some explanation before entering the domain of biology. Going back to the founders of personality psychology, such as Allport (1937), Cattell (1965), Diamond (1957), and Guilford (1959), personality may be regarded as a composition of traits, the latter understood as a set of more or less stable dispositions in which individuals differ and which have a genetic background. Under the critique of cognitive- and social-oriented researchers, among whom Mischel (1968) played the dominant role, for many years the concept of trait in personality psychology lost popularity or was even rejected for several reasons. As emphasized by this author, a trait—when referring to differences in behavior among individuals—is nothing less than an "etiquette" for given individual differences (ID). Although claimed by trait-oriented personality psychologists, cross-situational consistency in traits does not exist; this is expressed in the fact that when we compare a psychometric measure of a trait with any external criterion of the same trait, the coefficient of correlation between them does not exceed the score of 0.20–0.30 (Mischel, 1968). In their critique of the status of traits, Bem and Funder (1978) concluded that a trait is a fiction created by scientists.

Influenced by data collected in many studies illustrating cross-situational and cross-temporal consistency of traits and their role in explaining ID in behavior

*Personality from Biological, Cognitive, and Social Perspectives* edited by Tomasz Maruszewski, Małgorzata Fajkowska, and Michael W. Eysenck. Eliot Werner Publications, Clinton Corners, New York, 2010.

(see Epstein, 1979, 1984; Stagner, 1984; Strelau, 2001a), even the most radical opponent of traits changed his mind. In a paper entitled "Personality Dispositions Revisited and Revised: A View After Three Decades" (1990), published many years after his influential critique, Mischel wrote:

> It should be clear that the basic challenge was not and is not to the existence of dispositions, but to the assumptions about their nature. The challenge, then, has been focused on the limited utility of inferring broad context-free dispositions from behavioral signs as the basis for trying to explain the phenomena of personality and for predicting an individual's specific behavior in specific situations. (p. 131)

## THE BIOLOGICAL BASIS OF PERSONALITY TRAITS

In contrast to social- or cognitive-oriented personality psychologists, most contemporary trait-oriented personality researchers concentrate on the biological roots of this phenomenon. The purpose of such an approach is to demonstrate that traits to which these scientists refer are not just a generalized representation of behavior, or a perceptual phenomenon only, but that they really exist and their molding depends primarily on the genetic background and inborn neurochemical mechanisms in which individuals differ.

By tradition, going back to the ancient Greek typology (in which the notion of temperament was ascribed to biologically based personalities), many biologically oriented personality psychologists use the terms "personality" and "temperament" as synonyms, with a preference for the concept personality. For example, see the conceptualizations of Eysenck and Eysenck (1985), Gray (1991), Zuckerman (1985), and even Costa and McCrae (2001), who in their five-factor personality theory take this position. In contrast to those authors, in this chapter temperament is regarded as one of the composites of personality and distinguished from other personality traits by such inseparable features as being present since birth, not only in human beings but also in other animals; primarily based on inborn physiological and neurochemical mechanisms; and constituting the bases for the development of other personality structures (Strelau, 1983, 1998).

The very fact that individual differences in the biological mechanisms underlying temperament are mainly expressed not in the anatomical structure and pathways of neurotransmitters, but in their susceptibility or reactivity to be activated under various conditions, has prompted researchers on temperament to concentrate on (among others) the physiological phenomenon of arousal and relatively stable ID in arousal expressed in arousability (see Gray, 1964; Strelau, 1994). As seen in Figure 1, these constructs refer to different levels of biological functioning.

To return to the construct of trait, of which temperament and other personality structures are composed, the status of trait as applied in this chapter has to be

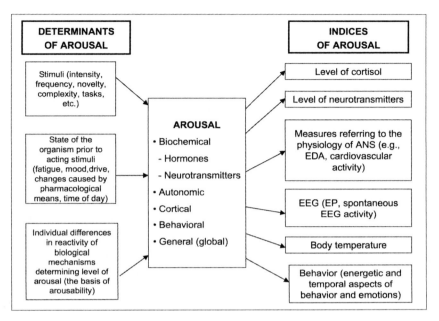

**Figure 1.** Arousal: Its indicators and determinants. ANS = autonomic nervous system; EDA = electrodermal activity; EP = evoked potential. From "The Place of the Construct of Arousal in Temperament Research" by J. Strelau, 2001b. In R. Riemann, F. M. Spinath, and F. Ostendorf (Eds.), *Personality and Temperament: Genetics, Evolution, and Structure* (p. 118). Copyright 2001 by Pabst Science Publishers. Reprinted with permission.

described in order to comprehend the role of biology as a codeterminant of a given trait. A trait, understood as a generalized tendency toward specific behaviors manifested in various tendency-consistent situations or settings, is determined by internal mechanisms. They are inborn or acquired, but a trait cannot be reduced to these mechanisms alone. It is the outcome of specific connections and interactions between many internal mechanisms and has a specific status, expressed in the tendency to behave (react) in a specific way. This tendency, which has a genetic background, can be modified by ontogenetically developing physiological mechanisms and external contingencies—such as learning and other environmental factors—that affect the individual from the moment of conception. Since we still have a long way to go before we gain a full understanding of the biological bases of traits, we must give them the status of a hypothetical construct (see Strelau, 2001a, 2008). Figure 2 illustrates the complexity of links and interactions between many environmental and biological factors and the individual's own activity contributing to the molding of a trait.

It seems obvious that behavior, psychological processes, and learning (broadly understood) are influenced by biological factors such as genes, the brain,

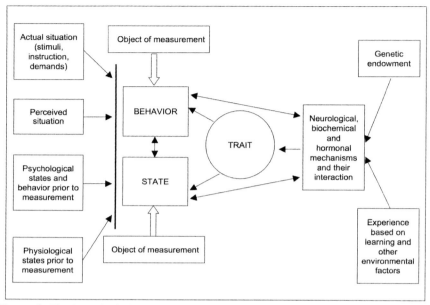

**Figure 2.** The hypothetical status of traits. From "The Concept and Status of Trait in Research on Temperament" by J. Strelau, 2001a, *European Journal of Personality, 15*, p. 319. Copyright 2001 by John Wiley & Sons. Reprinted with permission

the autonomic nervous system (ANS), and neurochemical substrates. At the same time, however, these behaviors and processes induce changes in the biological backgrounds that consist (among others) of changes in the structure, function, and organization of the brain as well as in the expression of genes. Under individual-specific, repetitive, and long-lasting psychological and social experience, neuronal networks and synaptic connections of the brain undergo changes, thus leading—together with the individually molded expression of genes—to a unique biological foundation of psychological traits. As postulated by Curtis and Cicchetti (2003):

> Neuronal and synaptic modifications not only exert a prominent role in initiating and maintaining the behavioral changes that are provoked by experience but also contribute to the biological bases of *individuality* [emphasis added], as well as to individuals being differentially affected by similar experiences. (p. 777)

Changes in the brain occur on at least two levels:

• Cellular level comprising (among others) synaptic formation and efficiency, development of dendrites, and sensitivity of neuron postsynaptic receptors and their sensitivity in synaptic transmission. This level of neural functioning, although of interest to cognitive-oriented scientists, has rarely been related to personality studies.

• Global level consisting of neuronal networks and biochemical pathways (neurotransmitters located in different structures and interacting with each other).

The neuronal networks have a hierarchical structure representing different levels of complexity. One may expect that tendencies expressed in personality traits are the result of interactions between the neural networks and biochemical pathways representing different structures. These hierarchically organized structures can be localized in the brain, whereas the tendencies—having a status of emergent properties resulting from interactions between these structures—are unlocalizable (see, e.g., Willingham & Dunn, 2003). Psychological phenomena are immaterial entities but their bases are located in the brain, which means that they cannot be disembodied. As such they have a status of emergent properties resulting from neurobiochemical processes taking part on different levels of brain structures interacting with each other. One has to agree with Albert Bandura who writes that "emergent properties differ qualitatively from their constituent elements and therefore are not reducible to them" (Bandura, 2001, p. 4). To use a car metaphor, to which I often refer when explaining the status of a trait (Strelau, 1998), the "accelerability" of a car is a result of many of its aggregates interacting with each other and easily localized in the engine. Meanwhile accelerability, although existing in reality (see records about acceleration in the car manual) and being an emergent property resulting from these interacting aggregates, is unlocalizable, as the human tendencies (traits) are. This is one of the reasons why personality traits (dimensions or factors) have a status of hypothetical constructs.

In neuroscience the notion of neuronal plasticity, understood as an inherent property of the central nervous system (CNS), has gained popularity. The term refers to the inherited ability of the neural substrates to change or be modified under external and internal events, thus resulting in adaptive behavior and assuring optimal functioning (Bavelier & Neville, 2002). As pointed out by Huttenlocher (2002), manifestation of neuronal plasticity should be regarded as a normative process occurring in the nervous system of all mammalian species. "Plasticity should be viewed as a continuous, dynamic relationship between environmental experience and change in the underlying neural substrate, which can occur across the life span" (Curtis & Cicchetti, 2003, p. 777).

Due to neuronal plasticity, the biological background of personality traits undergoes changes that may result in both (a) changes in personality tendencies (in traits) as well as (b) changes expressed in the behavioral repertoire of a given tendency, a process that occurs during the life span. The latter explains, among other things, why personality inventories aimed at measuring the same constructs (traits) contain different items for infants, children, and adults (see Strelau, 1998).

Traits understood as psychic phenomena are not inherited. Inherited are neurological structures and reactivity (broadly understood) of the neurochemical substrates that enhance or reduce the probability that given behavioral tendencies expressed in traits develop. On the behavioral level, they are expressed in all kinds of behavior and reactions for which the level or duration of arousal—or the property known as arousability—are factors contributing to the development of given tendencies. They refer mainly to the formal characteristics of behavior and reactions, such as (for example) intensity, endurance, persistence, speed, and mobility, but not to the content. The latter is expressed in the relationship of the individual with others, the world, and himself or herself. Among personality traits such as conscientiousness, agreeableness from the Big Five repertoire may be mentioned, as well as all nontrait personality constructs such as the self, attitudes, interests, and values.

Genetic studies show that almost all (if not all) psychic phenomena have a genetic background, and that the extent of genetic factors contributing to ID in personality (including temperament) does not differ from non-trait-oriented personality phenomena—such as, for example, attitudes, values, interests, and ego development (see Arvey, McCall, Bouchard, Taubman, & Cavanaugh, 1994; Newman, Tellegen, & Bouchard, 1998; Waller, Kojetin, Bouchard, Lykken, & Tellegen, 1990).

The most significant role in the identification of neural structures and biochemical substrates underlying temperament traits should be ascribed to Hans Eysenck and Jeffrey Gray, who are representatives of an emotion-centered theory of personality (temperament). Eysenck put forward the hypothesis that the activity of the corticoreticular loop (cortical arousal) is responsible for the individual's position on the extraversion-introversion dimension, and that the activity of the physiological center located in the visceral brain (hippocampus, amygdale, cingulum, septum, hypothalamus) determines the position of the individual on the neuroticism-emotional stability dimension. Strictly speaking, it is the responsitivity of the anatomo-physiological mechanisms that is responsible for ID in these traits (for details see Eysenck, 1967; Eysenck & Eysenck, 1985; see also Strelau, 1998; Zuckerman, 1991). In turn, Jeffrey Gray postulated that anxiety and impulsivity are two basic dimensions of temperament. When the two main axes are rotated through approximately 45 degrees, they result in extraversion-introversion and neuroticism-emotional stability.

Gray's temperament dimensions have their biological background in the susceptibility in two basic systems—anxiety in the Behavioral Inhibition System (BIS) and impulsivity in the Behavioral Activation System (BAS). The core structure of the BIS, which is sensitive to signals of punishment, mediates anxiety expressed in behavioral inhibition, increment in arousal, and increased attention. The BIS comprises three basic neural structures: the hippocampal formation, the septal area, and the Papez circuit. Ascending monoaminergic pathways (both noradrenergic and serotonergic) originating in the brain stem have a boosting effect on the activity of the septohipocampal system. Reactivity of the operating parameters of the BIS (e.g., thresholds, ease of excitation, speed of operation) determines ID in anxiety. The neurological structure of the BAS, which is sensitive to signals of rewards, mediates impulsivity expressed in behavior motivated by positive reinforcement, thus related to positive emotionality. The BAS is composed of such structures as basal ganglia, dopaminergic fibers ascending from the mesencephalon, thalamic nuclei, and neocortical areas. Release of dopamine from the terminals of neurons whose cell bodies are in the nucleus accumbens activates the BAS. As a consequence, dopamine release elicits approach behavior (for details see Gray, 1982, 1991; Gray, Owen, Davis, & Tsaltas, 1983; see also Fowles, 2006; Strelau, 1998; Zuckerman, 1991).

The hypotheses put forward by Eysenck and Gray regarding the biological bases of personality (temperament) and studies aimed at proving their validity may be considered as a point of departure for most temperament theories referring to biological backgrounds, such as the ones developed by Zuckerman (1979, 1994), Cloninger (Cloninger, Svrakic, & Przybeck, 1993; Švrakić, Švrakić, & Cloninger, 1996), Buss and Plomin (1975, 1984), Rothbart (Rothbart, Derryberry, & Posner, 1994), Kagan (1994), and Strelau (1998, 2006). As shown in Table 1, the neurochemical mechanisms underlying the specific temperament dimensions postulated by these authors are different. However, in one way or another they are similar in that they explain ID in these traits by referring to reactivity or susceptibility of those mechanisms.

## STUDIES AIMED AT SEARCHING FOR BIOLOGICAL BACKGROUNDS OF PERSONALITY TRAITS

In general, there are several approaches that can be used to prove the validity of the hypothesis that a given trait has a biological background. These include records from the ANS, behavior genetic studies, electroencephalographic (EEG) records, functional magnetic resonance imaging (fMRI), positron emission tomography (PET), and molecular genetics. Each of these approaches adds different information regarding the biological background of personality. For example, when using fMRI it is possible to locate brain activity in given neural structures during information processing or performing specific tasks by individuals differing in personality traits. In turn, EEG recording does not allow us to locate brain activity but gives information about the course of this activity in mostly unlimited time sequences, which is not possible in respect to fMRI. In this section I will refer very selectively to these studies, instead paying attention to the discrepancies and inconsistencies in the data obtained—assuming it is they that stimulate further investigations and the search for new solutions.

### Records from the Autonomic Nervous System

Records from the ANS refer (among others) to such measures as heart rate, electrodermal activity, respiration rate, and pupil response. These physiological markers were the first to be studied in respect to personality traits, especially to

TABLE 1. Arousability and Selected Temperament Traits

| Author | Arousability | | Biological mechanisms |
| --- | --- | --- | --- |
| | Low | High | |
| H. J. Eysenck | Extraversion | Introversion | Cortico-reticular loop |
| H. J. Eysenck | Emotional stability | Neuroticism | Visceral brain (limbic system) |
| A. H. Buss & R. Plomin | Low emotionality | High emotionality | Autonomous nervous system |
| J. Strelau | Low emotional reactivity | High emotional reactivity | Limbic system and autonomous nervous system |
| J. Strelau | High activity | Low activity | Cortical structures and brain-stem reticular formation |
| M. Zuckerman | Sensation seeking | Sensation avoidance | Catecholamine system |
| I. P. Pavlov | High strength of excitation | Low strength of excitation | Cortical and subcortical centers |
| J. A. Gray | Low anxiety | High anxiety | Behavioral inhibition system |
| J. A. Gray | High impulsivity | Low impulsivity | Behavioral activation system |
| J. Kagan | Uninhibited temperament | Inhibited temperament | Limbic system (amygdala and hypothalamus) |
| C. R. Cloninger | Harm avoidance | No harm avoidance | Serotonin activity in the limbic system |
| C. R. Cloninger | Novelty seeking | Novelty avoidance | Activity of dopaminergic paths in the *locus cinereus* |
| C. R. Cloninger | Reward dependence | Reward independence | Basal noradrenegic activity |

*Note.* From *Psychologia różnic indywidualnych* [Psychology of individual differences] by J. Strelau, 2006, p. 265. Copyright 2006 by Wydawnictwo Naukowe Scholar. Reprinted with permission.

the ones that refer to emotionality characteristics. Individual differences in the functioning of the ANS, especially in the balance between the sympathetic and parasympathetic systems, have been linked by Wenger (1943) to differences in the intensity and expressiveness of human reaction, mainly in respect to emotional states. The view of Eysenck (1967), that neuroticism has its biological background in the visceral brain, stimulated many scientists to test this hypothesis. The most advanced studies in this domain were conducted by Fahrenberg and coworkers (Fahrenberg, 1987; Fahrenberg, Walschburger, Foerster, Myrtek, & Müller, 1983). After over a decade of studies in which neuroticism was related to about a dozen measures of ANS activity, this author arrived at the conclusion that there is no basis for assuming that physiological measures of visceral arousal can be regarded as markers of psychometrically measured neuroticism (Fahrenberg, 1987).

Results from one of the many studies conducted in Fahrenberg's laboratory support this statement. Physiological measures of autonomic arousal—such as heart rate, pulse volume amplitude, electrodermal activity, respiratory irregularity, eyeblink activity, and electromyography recorded during rest states—and active states in normal and stressful situations have shown no relationship with psychometrically measured neuroticism. Among the 21 coefficients of correlation recorded in this study, not one was statistically significant (Fahrenberg, 1992). Lack of consistency between physiological measures of visceral activity and other temperament characteristics was also found in other laboratories—for example, in relation to trait-anxiety (van Heck, 1988), inhibited temperament (Kagan, 1994), or psychometrically measured behavior characteristics (referring to the Pavlovian traits of higher nervous activity; Strelau, 1983).

## Behavior Genetic Studies

During the first half of the twentieth century, substantial evidence had been collected to show the genetic determination of temperament traits in animals. Selective breeding (mainly applied to rats and mice) allowed researchers to conclude that this method results after several generations have been bred in strains that are evidently different in such traits as emotionality, aggression, and motor activity (see Hall, 1941; Hunt & Schlosberg, 1939; Rundquist, 1933). Analogical data were obtained by using comparisons of genetically different strains (see, e.g., Fuller & Thomson, 1978).

These and other data collected in animal research stimulated investigators to search for genetic determinants of ID in personality traits in humans. In the first studies, mainly limited to comparisons between monozygotic (MZ) and dizygotic (DZ) twins reared together, extraversion and neuroticism were the focus of interest. Using the twin study method, Eysenck and Prell (1951, 1956), who should be regarded as among the pioneers in genetic studies on personality, stated that heritability of neuroticism and extraversion varies between 60% and 80%. In many subsequent studies, in which—besides the twin method—such methods as the adoption design, adoption/twin design, and comparisons of family members have been applied, the heritability score of personality traits has undergone considerable revision. Meta-analysis of data collected from several studies and based on different behavior genetic methods allowed Loehlin (1992) to arrive at the following conclusion:

> The genes accounted for 35% to 39% of the individual variation in Extraversion, depending on the particular model, with shared environment from 0% to 19%—values above 4% being found only for MZ twins. Remaining factors,

including environmental influences not shared by family members, possible gene-environment interactions, and errors of measurement, account collectively for 46% to 63%. (p. 46)

Among others, studies conducted by Zuckerman (1994) and Heath, Cloninger, and Martin (1994) suggest that genes contribute up to 60% to individual differences in temperament traits postulated by them. But the data were obtained by means of the MZ and DZ twins-reared-together method only and need further replications by using other genetic paradigms.

In order to document the extent to which both the genetic factor and the environment factor contribute to ID in temperament traits, we conducted a study based on MZ and DZ twins reared together (Oniszczenko et al., 2003). Self-report records were collected in two samples of pairs of twins, a German sample ($N = 1,009, 732$ MZ and 277 DZ) and a Polish sample ($N = 546, 317$ MZ and 229 DZ). Statistical analysis of the data collected in both samples by means of four temperament inventories (Revised Dimensions of Temperament Survey: Windle & Lerner, 1986; Pavlovian Temperament Survey: Strelau, Angleitner, & Newberry, 1999; Formal Characteristics of Behavior–Temperament Inventory: Strelau & Zawadzki, 1993; Emotionality–Activity–Sociability Temperament Survey: Buss & Plomin, 1984) allowed us to conclude that the average contribution of genes to individual differences in 24 temperament traits is around 0.35%, whereas the environment (limited to nonshared environment) contributed 65% (including measurement error). Meta-analysis of data comprising all possible behavior genetic methods show higher heritability scores—about 50%—in respect to intelligence measured by means of psychometric tests (see, e.g., Bouchard & McGue, 1981; Plomin, DeFries, McClearn, & McGuffin, 2001).

## Electroencephalographic Studies

Both tonic cortical arousal expressed in spontaneous EEG activity when no stimuli are exposed, and phasic cortical arousal expressed in evoked potentials (EP, average evoked potentials) when stimuli are exposed (causing changes in bioelectrical activity), have been applied to studies on personality.

The first studies in which personality traits were related to spontaneous EEG activity were conducted in the late 1930s and early 1940s (Gottlober, 1938; Henry & Knott, 1941) and concentrated primarily on extraversion as understood by Jung (1923), but the results of these experiments were not unequivocal. Since tonic (chronic) arousal of the corticoreticular loop was assumed to be the physiological background of extraversion as postulated by Eysenck, it was obvious that many personality researchers were searching for the biological substrate of this trait concentrated on spontaneous EEG activity. Gale (1986), taking into account more than thirty studies devoted to searching for links between this activity and extraversion-introversion, undertook a series of meta-analyses and concluded that there are contradictions or lack of differences in EEG measures between extraverts and introverts that are caused mainly by differences in experimental settings. Only when moderate arousal was warranted by experimental settings have most experiments shown a relationship between EEG characteristics and extraversion, as predicted by Eysenck. Meta-analyses conducted by others (Bartussek, 1984; O'Gorman, 1984) did not add very much to the conclusion stated by Gale. However, O'Gorman was able to show that it is the impulsivity component of extraversion—but not the sociability one—that shows some relationship with EEG activity, whereas Bartussek arrived at the conclusion that some links between extraversion and EEG occur when this trait is considered in interaction with neuroticism.

A more sophisticated study conducted by Stenberg (1992), in which the whole EEG spectrum and measures from all scalp positions were taken into account together with personality measures based on the Eysenck Personality Inventory (EPI) and the Karolinska Scales of Personality (KSP), allowed for more unequivocal conclusions. The three EPI scales (Extraversion, Neuroticism, and Psychotocism) and fifteen scales from the KSP were factor analyzed, resulting in two factors: impulsivity and anxiety interpreted in terms of Gray's theory. It came out that high-impulsive individuals compared with low-impulsive ones have EEG characteristics typical for a lower level of arousal, and anxious individuals exhibit higher tonic arousal compared with subjects low in trait anxiety. This study shows, as do many others, that the same physiological markers may be related to many personality characteristics and are not trait-specific.

Studies in which evoked potentials are related to personality traits offer a different perspective on the relationship between these traits and EEG activity. In this case personality is considered as a variable mediating the relationship between exposed stimuli and evoked potentials registered during phasic arousal.

Probably the first study in which evoked potentials were related to personality was conducted by Buchsbaum and Silverman (1968), but rather from a diagnostic perspective. Taking into account the amplitude of EP, the authors concluded that the increase of EP amplitude is not only a function of intensity of stimuli, but also of individual differences in the subjects' level of arousal. The authors characterized individuals showing higher EP amplitudes as augmenters, whereas the ones with lower EP amplitudes were characterized as reducers. A similar procedure, but in the context of assessing strength of the CNS, was applied by Bazylevich (1974).

In studies in which the amplitude of EP was related to temperament traits, numerous inconsistencies occurred due mainly to the fact that the range of intensity of stimuli, their modality (visual, auditory, somatosensory), the peaks at which the amplitude of EP is measured, and the position from which the EP is recorded (e.g., vertex versus occipital) differed across studies (see Andrès Pueyo & Tous Ral, 1992; Strelau, 1998). When stimuli of high intensity are administered to individuals characterized by high arousability, so-called protective inhibition may occur that causes a decrease in EP amplitude in spite of growing intensity of stimuli (a phenomenon described previously by Pavlov, 1938). Protective inhibition may not occur in individuals with a low level of arousability. Thus, depending on whether the exposed stimuli are in the range of low, moderate, or high intensity, both phenomena—augmenting and reducing—may occur in individuals with both chronically high and chronically low levels of arousal. Let me give a few examples illustrating that we are still in a blind alley when searching for relationships between temperament traits and the amplitude of EP.

Stelmack and Michaud-Achorn (1985) have taken Eysenck's theory—that introverts, when chronically highly aroused, are expected to respond to stimuli of weak and moderate intensity with higher EP amplitudes compared with extraverts—as a point of departure of their study. Using in the experiment auditory stimuli of two different frequencies (500 Hz and 1000 Hz) and of intensities not higher than 80 dB, the authors were able to confirm Eysenck's postulate but only in respect to the 500-Hz tone. Does this mean that extraversion is expressed in reactions to frequency specific stimuli? Andrès Pueyo and Tous Ral (1992) compared thirteen studies in which EP amplitudes were related to extraversion. Six studies confirmed the predicted relationship, while in four of them this relationship was partially confirmed and in three contradictory results were obtained. In turn, Stenberg, Rosen, and Risberg (1988) demonstrated that when amplitudes are measured for different modalities of stimuli, the relationship between extraversion as well as disinhibition (measured by Zuckerman's Sensation Seeking Scale) does not generalize across modalities. The EP amplitude-temperament relationship was in accordance with Eysenck's expectations in respect to visual stimuli, but did not emerge when auditory stimuli were administered. Also, in the analysis of data from sixteen studies cited by Zuckerman (1990), it was revealed that there is a clear-cut inconsistency when data based on auditory and visual stimuli are compared.

The number of studies in which other personality traits—such as, for example, neuroticism (Lolas, Campsano, & Etcheberrigaray, 1989), impulsivity (Barratt, Pritchard, Faulk, & Brandt, 1987), or psychoticism (Lolas et al., 1989)—were related to EP amplitude has been increasing, however, for the most part also with confusing results. A lesson to be learned from inconsistencies regarding the relationships between EP and selected personality/temperament traits is that conclusions deriving from these studies should be limited to experiment-specific situations.

Temperament traits have also been related to other aspects of evoked potentials such as contingent negative variation, which occurs during a state of expectancy (readiness for reaction), and P300, presumed to be related to cognitive activity consisting of learning and memory performance. The number of studies in which these components of cerebral activity were related to temperament is rather scanty and conducted on a small number of subjects. Thus it is impossible to draw any unequivocal conclusions regarding the relationship of temperament traits with these EEG components (for details regarding these kinds of studies, see Strelau, 1998).

## Functional Magnetic Resonance Imaging and Positron Emission Tomography

The neuronal activity demands—in the brain regions to be activated—increased oxygen and glucose, which is ensured by an increase of blood pushed to these regions. It is functional magnetic resonance imaging and positron emission tomography that provide indirect measures of blood flow. These procedures (mainly fMRI, which has much better temporal resolution compared with PET), successfully applied in locating cognitive processes in the brain (see Deary, 2000), have been also used in some studies on personality (see, e.g., Canli, 2006; Reuter et al., 2004). Their application has provided new insight into the neuroanatomical and neurophysiological markers of psychological traits. Probably one of the first studies in which personality traits were related to functional brain imaging was conducted by Hair, Sokolski, Katz, and Buchsbaum (1987) by means of the PET[1] method. The results of this study were predictive in that extraverts and neurotics—as measured by the Eysenck Personality Questionnaire—only partially showed neural activity in the regions predicted by Eysenck's theory.

Regarding the research aimed at measuring neuronal activity in the brain regions, I will limit myself to functional magnetic resonance imaging. Compared with positron emission tomography, fMRI (which is also valid for studies of intelligence) has gained greater popularity among personality researchers. The reason is that PET scanning, regarded as an invasive method, involves ionizing radiation exposure to the subject and is mainly applied to patients rather than research subjects.

The best candidates for searching for the neuronal structures of given personality traits are emotional stimuli, since the temperament traits postulated by Eysenck and Gray (see Eysenck & Eysenck, 1985; Gray, 1991; Gray et al., 1983) refer to emotions—extraversion and impulsivity to positive emotions, neuroticism and anxiety to negative ones (see Costa & McCrae, 1980; Eysenck, 1990; Meyer & Shack, 1989). Canli et al. (2001) have undertaken a pioneering fMRI study on fourteen females in order to test whether individual differences in brain reactivity to emotional stimuli are correlated with extraversion and neuroticism, both traits measured by means of the NEO Five Factor Inventory (NEO-FFI). Twenty positive and twenty negative pictures were shown to the subjects. The study was based on a hypothesis that extraversion, introversion and the valence of emotion corresponding with these temperament traits have a common neural substrate, where these traits moderate the processing of emotional stimuli exposed during the experiment. The results have shown that activation in the frontal cortex located in the left middle gyrus correlates with both extraversion

---

[1] According to the authors' information, the cost of PET research conducted on one subject was about $2,500; however, that was twenty years ago. Together with the rather complicated procedure, this explains why the number of subjects exposed to functional brain imaging rarely exceeds one to two dozen.

and introversion but to stimuli of opposite valence: in the case of extraversion, with the response to emotionally positive pictures compared with negative ones; and in the case of introversion, with the response to emotionally negative pictures compared with positive ones. Additionally, it came out that there was a correlation between extraversion and high brain activity in response to positive stimuli in the temporal lobe in the right hemisphere, whereas neuroticism correlated with higher brain activity in response to negative stimuli in the same brain region but located in the left hemisphere. This outcome indirectly contradicts Davidson, Ekman, Saron, Senulis, and Friesen's (1990) EEG findings, which show that approach reactions as expressed in positive emotions are associated with cortical left-sided anterior activation, whereas withdrawal reactions expressed in negative emotions are accompanied rather by cortical right-sided anterior activation.

A study in which the fRMI was also applied, but in order to test Gray's BAS and BIS theory, was conducted by Reuter et al. (2004). The aim of the study was (among other things) to test whether there is an association between the subjects' BAS temperament and their brain reactivity to emotionally positive stimuli compared with neutral ones, and whether the BIS temperament correlates with the postulated brain reactivity to negative stimuli compared with positive stimuli. According to Gray's theory, it was expected that the BAS system is not sensitive to negative stimuli, whereas BIS does not respond to emotionally positive stimuli. In this study Gray's temperament constructs were measured in 24 healthy subjects by means of the BIS-BAS inventory developed by Carver & White (1994). Emotional pictures were selected from the International Affective Picture System (Lang, Bradley, & Cuthbert, 1995). Without going into the details regarding the anatomical structures being activated during exposure of emotional stimuli, it came out that the BIS traits influenced neural activity in the brain to emotional stimuli higher than the BAS traits, irrespective of the valence of exposed stimuli. However, a positive correlation between BAS and neural activity to negative stimuli was not expected by the authors. Although many of the anatomical structures of the brain postulated by Gray as referring to the BIS and BAS have been activated in response to emotional stimuli, the links between the BIS-BAS temperament dimensions and activated brain regions were not in line with Gray's theory. As the authors stated, "The hippocampus-parahippocampus system was associated with the BAS instead of with the BIS. . . . Activity in the amygdala and the brainstem were correlated with the BIS, although these structures should belong to the FFS [Fight or Flight System]" (Reuter et al., 2004, p. 468).

These rather convincing results contradicted the postulates proposed by Gray's theory and underscore the importance of brain imaging—especially fMRI—as the best method for verifying the extent to which neuronal activity associated with a given personality/temperament trait, hypothetically located in given anatomical brain structures, confirms the researcher's theory. One has to add, however, that such contradictory results also encourages researchers to revise the view regarding the postulated trait itself. By the way, Gray (1982) developed his BAS and BIS theory based on results from studies on rats. The question arises to what exent animal data can be directly transferred to humans.

## Molecular Genetics

Molecular genetics, which gained popularity in studies aimed at identifying genes for several diseases and disorders, entered the domain of normal human behavior during the 1990s, mainly in studies on intelligence and personality. Since normal behavior and traits have a polygenic determination in order to identify the genes of psychological traits, the quantitative trait loci (QTL) approach has been applied in most molecular genetic studies; this refers to cognitive abilities as well as to the personality domain (see Plomin et al., 2001). The best candidate for QTL is allelic association expressed in correlation between phenotype and particular allele. Since psychological traits (as already mentioned) are not inherited, genetic transmission refers to physiological and biochemical mechanisms that are supposed to underlie specific traits. Therefore it seems reasonable to apply methods of molecular genetics to traits to which genes contribute essentially to individual differences, and for which some specific physiological and biochemical mechanisms have been discovered—or at least postulated. The tendency to identify genes in the personality domain is nowadays widespread and refers to many traits postulated by most popular temperament theories (see Benjamin, Ebstein, & Belmaker, 2002; Canli, 2006; Dragan & Oniszczenko, 2005). The review of studies aimed at identifying genes for the separate traits does not allow, however, for unequivocal conclusions: the number of confirmatory and contradictory results is almost equal. To illustrate this state of affairs, I will refer to few examples.

The finding that neuroticism, as expected, is mediated by serotonin transmission prompted Lesch et al. (1996) to conduct a study aimed at answering the question whether there exists an allelic association between functional polymorphism in the serotonin (5-HTT) and neuroticism as measured by the Revised NEO Personality Inventory. Data were collected on over five hundred subjects. It came out that this functional polymorphism accounts for 3% to 4% of the total variance of this temperament trait. We (Ball et al., 1997) replicated the study conducted by Lesch et al. in two different versions regarding the assessment of neuroticism diagnosed by means of NEO-FFI. Self-report data and peer-report data (two peers for each target) were taken into account. Subjects were selected from a sample of over two thousand adults and sorted into a high-N group and a low-N group (fifty subjects each). The result of this study is negative: no association was found between peer-rated neuroticism and the serotonin transporter gene and the same result emerged when self-report data were taken into account. Of course one may argue that these studies differ essentially in the way neuroticism was assessed and subjects were recruited. Nevertheless, if we assume that in both studies subjects were selected for neuroticisms measured by means of the Costa and McCrae (1992) inventories, one should expect at least some consistencies between them.

Probably the largest number of studies aimed at searching for allelic associations between temperament traits and functional polymorphism in neurotransmitters receptor or transporter genes was conducted in the domain of Cloninger's temperament theory (see Cloninger 1986, 1997; Cloninger et al., 1993). Taking as a starting point for his theory conceptualizations regarding the biological bases of temperament as proposed by Eysenck and Gray, Cloninger developed a psychobiology model of temperament. According to this model, the four temperament traits that make up the structure of temperament—reward dependence, novelty seeking, harm avoidance, and persistence—are mediated by a specific neurotransmitter system: reward dependence and persistence by noradrenaline, novelty seeking by dopamine, and harm avoidance by serotonin. These rather definite statements encouraged researchers to undertake studies aimed at verifying the existence of allelic associations between functional polymorphisms in these neurotransmitters and Cloninger's temperament traits.

Several dozen studies concentrated on novelty seeking and harm avoidance measured by means of the Tridimentional Personality Questionnaire (TPQ; Cloninger, Przybeck, & Svrakic, 1991) or Temperament and Character Inventory (TCI; Cloninger et al., 1993). The reports are almost equally divided in supporting or not supporting—and even contradicting—the allelic associations between the neurotransmitters proposed by Cloninger for the separate temperament traits (see Persson et al., 2000). Most important, however, in verifying Cloninger's postulates are meta-analyses devoted to this issue.

Let me very briefly refer to two of the studies based on such methodology. Kluger, Siegfried, and Ebstein (2002) reviewed twenty studies, including altogether almost four thousand subjects, aimed at searching for associations between DRD4 polymorphisms and novelty seeking. Based on their analysis, they arrived at the following conclusion: "[O]n average, there is no association between DRD4 polymorphism and novelty seeking (average $d^2 = 0.06$ with 95% CI of $\pm 0.09$),[2] where thirteen reports suggest that the presence of longer alleles is associated with higher novelty seeking scores and seven reports suggest the opposite" (p. 712). Additionally, the association between DRD4 polymorphism and novelty seeking does not differ from an analogical association with the two remaining traits: the d score for reward dependence is 0.10 and for harm avoidance –0.14.

Probably the most comprehensive meta-analysis regarding polymorphisms and personality in healthy adults was undertaken by Munafo et al. (2003). A total of 79 studies from 18 countries conducted between 1995 and 2002 were analyzed, taking into account (among other things) such criteria as author, year of publication, country of origin, method of recruitment, personality measure, candidate gene, and polymorphism. Forty-six of these studies were included in the analyses: 17 studies reported data on approach traits (mainly novelty seeking), 22 reported on avoidance traits (mainly harm avoidance), and 12 reported on aggres-

---

[2] d = standardized difference in mean continuous variable between people who have and people who do not have the long allele.

sion traits (according to Gray, the fight-or-flight behavior).[3] In almost all these studies, personality was measured by means of Cloninger's TCI or TPQ inventories. The most investigated candidate genes were 5HTT, DRD4, DRD2, and DRD3. A multivariate analysis—including age, sex, and ethnicity as covariates when applied in respect to 5HTT and DRD4 length polymorphism data—has shown that only the association between the 5HTT polymorphism and avoidance traits was statistically significant. Among other conclusions, the authors found that of the 79 studies included prior to the selection procedure, "fifty reported evidence of a significant association between genotype and personality. The results of the meta-analysis do not support the conclusion that might be drawn by simply counting the number of studies reporting significant results" (Munafo et al., 2003, p. 481).

## FINAL REMARKS

This very selective review of studies aimed at searching for the biological background of biologically oriented personality traits, mainly referring to temperament, allows for several conclusions. First, it seems obvious that independent of the kind of biological mechanisms postulated as constituting the basis for a given trait, whether referring to the ANS, EEG data, neuronal activity imaging, or the genetic domain (both behavior and molecular genetics), contradictory results have been obtained. One may argue that this conclusion is due to the biased selection of studies reported in this chapter. To some extent this is true because my aim has been to underscore, in contrast to the biological postulates presented in many temperament theories (specifically the ones developed by Eysenck, Gray, and Cloninger), the lack of consistency in data cited to support these theories.

Second, there is still a long way to go before unequivocal conclusions can be drawn regarding the biological background of temperament traits. One reason is that many variables often not taken into account—such as number of subjects (mostly very low), age, gender, ethnicity, and environmental factors—influence the "biological basis/personality trait" relationship. One should also mention that under different personality labels, an essential part of behavior and the reactions to which they refer share common variance, which is expressed in the fact that among item pools referring to different inventories, a crucial part of items is common for scales measuring different traits. This takes place if we compare, for example, such scales as Neuroticism and Harm Avoidance or Extraversion and Novelty Seeking.

Third, more meta-analytic studies have to be conducted in order to bring us closer to discovering given relationships between biology and traits. The Munafo et al. (2003) study is an excellent example showing that different conclusions are drawn depending on whether we count the number of studies supporting or contradicting given findings, or whether the data from these studies are analyzed

---

[3] Five of the studies reported data on more than one trait.

from a perspective that takes into account the many variables influencing the "biology-personality" relationship.

Fourth, the confusing results regarding the search for biological backgrounds should stimulate further investigations that go beyond psychometric measures of personality traits loaded with considerable measurement errors ($\geq 0.20$).

Finally, it is my strong belief that the biological basis of personality traits is very complex and that the final outcome is a result of many interactions and transactions among the separate mechanisms, including the influence of environment (broadly understood). Each of these mechanisms, when studied separately, results in findings that are hardly comparable with findings resulting from the same mechanism being analyzed in interaction (mostly uncontrolled) with other ones. Therefore, when speaking about the biological basis of temperament traits, I prefer to use the concept neurobiochemical individuality (Strelau, 1998), which underscores individual specific interactions between the biological mechanisms underlying personality traits.

And in closing, one more remark has to be made. I have to agree with Wiesel (1994), who wrote that "[t]he operations of the brain result from a balance between inputs from heredity and environment—nature and nurture—and this balance should also be reflected in research into the biological basis of behavior" (p. 1647).

## REFERENCES

Allport, G. W. (1937). *Personality: A psychological interpretation*. New York: Holt.

Andrès Pueyo, A., & Tous Ral, J. M. (1992). *Potenciales evocados cerebrales y dimensiones de personalidad* [Cerebral evoked potentials and dimensions of personality]. *Psicothema, 4*, 209–220.

Arvey, R. D., McCall, B. P., Bouchard, T. J., Jr., Taubman, P., & Cavanaugh. M. A. (1994). Genetic influences on job satisfaction and work values. *Personality and Individual Differences, 17*, 877–889.

Ball, D., Hill, L., Freeman, B., Eley, T. C., Strelau, J., Riemann, R., et al. (1997). The serotonin transporter gene and peer-rated neuroticism. *NeuroReport, 8*, 1301–1304.

Bandura, A. (2001). Social cognitive theory: An agentic perspective. *Annual Review of Psychology, 52*, 1–26.

Barratt, E. S., Pritchard, W. S., Faulk, D. M., & Brandt, M. E. (1987). The relationship between impulsiveness subtraits, trait anxiety, and visual N100-augmenting-reducing: A topographic analysis. *Personality and Individual Differences, 8*, 43–51.

Bartussek, D. (1984). Extraversion und EEG: Ein Forschungsparadigma in der Sackgasse? [Extraversion and EEG: A research paradigm in a blind alley?]. In M. Amelang & H. J. Ahrens (Eds.), *Brennpunkte der Personlichkeitsforschung* (pp. 157–189). Göttingen, Germany: Hogrefe & Huber.

Bavelier, D., & Neville, H. J. (2002). Cross-modal plasticity: Where and how? *Nature Reviews: Neuroscience, 3*, 443–452.

Bazylevich, T. F. (1974). The expression of strength of the regulative brain system in the dynamics of the somatosensory evoked potential. In V. D. Nebylitsyn (Ed.), *Problems of differential psychophysiology: Electrophysiological studies on the fundamental properties of the nervous system* (pp. 77–92). Moscow: Nauka (in Russian).

Bem, D. J., & Funder, D. C. (1978). Predicting more of the people more of the time. Assessing the personality of situations. *Psychological Review, 85*, 485–501.

Benjamin, J., Ebstein, R. P., & Belmaker, R. H. (Eds.). (2002). *Molecular genetics and the human personality.* Washington, DC: American Psychiatric Publishing.

Bouchard, T. J., Jr., & McGue, M. (1981). Familial studies of intelligence: A review. *Science, 212*, 1055–1059.

Buchsbaum, M. S., & Silverman, J. (1968). Stimulus intensity control and the cortical evoked response. *Psychosomatic Medicine, 30*, 12–22.

Buss, A. H., & Plomin, R. (1975). *A temperament theory of personality development.* New York: Wiley.

Buss, A. H., & Plomin, R. (1984). *Temperament: Early developing personality traits.* Hillsdale, NJ: Erlbaum.

Canli, T. (2006). Genomic imaging of extraversion. In T. Canli (Ed.), *Biology of personality and individual differences* (pp. 93–115). New York: Guilford Press.

Canli, T., Zhao, Z., Desmond, J. E., Kang, E., Gross, J., & Gabrieli, J. D. E. (2001). An fMRI study of personality influences on brain reactivity to emotional stimuli. *Behavioral Neuroscience, 115*, 33–42.

Carver, C. S., & White, T. L. (1994). Behavioral inhibition, behavioral activation, and affective responses to impending reward and punishment: The BIS/BAS scales. *Journal of Personality and Social Psychology, 67*, 319–333.

Cattell, R. B. (1965). *The scientific analysis of personality.* Baltimore, MD: Penguin Books.

Cloninger, C. R. (1986). A unified biosocial theory of personality and its role in the development of anxiety states. *Psychiatric Developments, 3*, 167–226.

Cloninger, C. R. (1997). A psychobiological model of personality and psychopathology. *Journal of Psychosomatic Medicine, 37*, 91–102.

Cloninger, C. R., Przybeck, T. R., & Svrakic, D. M. (1991). The Tridimensional Personality Questionnaire: U.S. normative data. *Psychological Reports, 69*, 1047–1057.

Cloninger, C. R., Svrakic, D.M., & Przybeck, T. R. (1993). A psychobiological model of temperament and character. *Archives of General Psychiatry, 50*, 975–990.

Costa, P. T., Jr., & McCrae, R. R. (1980). Influence of extraversion and neuroticism on subjective well-being: Happy and unhappy people. *Journal of Personality and Social Psychology, 38*, 668–678.

Costa, P. T., Jr., & McCrae, R. R. (1992). *Revised NEO Personality Inventory (NEO-PI-R) and NEO Five Factor Inventory* (NEO-FFI): Professional manual. Odessa FL: Psychological Assessment Recources.

Costa, P. T., Jr., & McCrae, R. R. (2001). A theoretical context for adult temperament. In T. D. Wachs & G. A. Kohnstamm (Eds.), *Temperament in context* (pp. 1–21). Mahwah, NJ: Erlbaum.

Curtis, W. J., & Cicchetti, D. (2003). Moving research on resilience into the 21st century: Theoretical and methodological considerations in examining the biological contributors to resilience. *Development and Psychopathology, 15*, 773–810.

Davidson, R. J., Ekman, P., Saron, C., Senulis, J. A., & Friesen, W. V. (1990). Approach-withdrawal and cerebral asymmetry: Emotional expression and brain physiology I. *Journal of Personality and Social Psychology, 58*, 330–341.

Deary, I. J. (2000). *Looking down on human intelligence: From psychometrics to the brain.* Oxford, UK: Oxford University Press.

Diamond, S. (1957). *Personality and temperament.* New York: Harper & Brothers.

Dragan, W. Ł., & Oniszczenko, W. (2005). Polymorphisms in the serotonin tranporter gene and their relationship to temperamental traits measured by the Formal Characteristics of Behaviour–Temperament Inventory: Activity and emotional reactivity. *Neuropsychobiology, 51*, 269–274.

Epstein, S. (1979). The stability of behavior: On predicting most of the people much of the time. *Journal of Personality and Social Psychology, 37*, 1097–1126.

Epstein, S. (1984). The stability of behavior across time and situations. In R. Zucker, J. Aronoff, & A. I. Rabin (Eds.), *Personality and the prediction of behavior* (pp. 209–268). San Diego, CA: Academic Press.

Eysenck, H. J. (1967). *The biological basis of personality.* Springfield, IL: Charles C. Thomas.

Eysenck, H. J. (1990). Biological dimensions of personality. In L. A. Pervin (Ed.), *Handbook of personality: Theory and research* (pp. 244–276). New York: Guilford Press.

Eysenck, H. J., & Eysenck, M. W. (1985). *Personality and individual differences: A natural science approach.* New York: Plenum Press.

Eysenck, H. J., & Prell, D. B. (1951). The inheritance of neuroticism: An experimental study. *Journal of Mental Science, 97*, 441–465.

Eysenck, H. J., & Prell, D. B. (1956). The inheritance of introversion-extraversion. *Acta Psychologica, 12*, 95–110.

Fahrenberg, J. (1987). Concepts of activation and arousal in the theory of emotionality (neuroticism): A multivariate conceptualization. In J. Strelau & H. J. Eysenck (Eds.), *Personality dimensions and arousal* (pp. 99–120). New York: Plenum Press.

Fahrenberg, J. (1992). Psychophysiology of neuroticism and anxiety. In A. Gale & M. W. Eysenck (Eds.), *Handbook of individual differences: Biological perspectives* (pp. 179–226). Chichester, UK: Wiley.

Fahrenberg, J., Walschburger, P, Foerster, F., Myrtek, M., & Müller, W. (1983). An evaluation of trait, state, and reaction aspects of activation processes. *Psychophysiology, 20*, 188–195.

Fowles, D. C. (2006). Jeffrey Gray's contributions to theories of anxiety, personality, and psychopathology. In T. Canli (Ed.), *Biology of personality and individual differences* (pp. 7–34). New York: Guilford Press.

Fuller, J. L., & Thompson, W. R. (1978). *Foundations of behavior genetics.* St. Louis, MO: Mosby.

Gale, A. (1986). Extraversion-introversion and spontaneous rhythms of the brain: Retrospect and prospect. In J. Strelau, F. H. Farley, & A. Gale (Eds.), *The biological bases of personality and behavior: Vol. 2. Psychophysiology, performance, and applications* (pp. 25–42). Washington, DC: Hemisphere.

Gottlober, A. B. (1938). The relationship between brain potentials and personality. *Journal of Experimental Psychology, 22*, 67–74.

Gray, J. A. (Ed.). (1964). *Pavlov's typology: Recent theoretical and experimental developments from the laboratory of B. M. Teplov.* Oxford, UK: Pergamon Press.

Gray, J. A. (1982). *The neuropsychology of anxiety: An inquiry into the functions of the septo-hippocampal system.* Oxford, UK: Oxford University Press.

Gray, J. A. (1991). The neuropsychology of temperament. In J. Strelau & A. Angleitner (Eds.), *Explorations in temperament: International perspectives on theory and measurement* (pp. 105–128). New York: Plenum Press.

Gray, J. A., Owen, S., Davis, N., & Tsaltas, E. (1983). Psychological and physiological relations between anxiety and impulsivity. In M. Zuckerman (Ed.), *The biological bases of sensation seeking, impulsivity, and anxiety* (pp. 181–217). Hillsdale, NJ: Erlbaum.

Guilford, J. P. (1959). *Personality.* New York: McGraw-Hill.

Hair, R. J., Sokolski, K., Katz, M., & Buchsbaum, M. S. (1987). The study of personality with positron emission tomography. In J. Strelau & H. J. Eysenck (Eds.), *Personality dimensions and arousal* (pp. 251–267). New York: Plenum Press.

Hall, C. S. (1941). Temperament: A survey of animal studies. *Psychological Bulletin, 38,* 909–943.

Heath, A. C., Cloninger, C. R., & Martin, N. G. (1994). Testing a model for the genetic structure of personality: A comparison of the personality systems of Cloninger and Eysenck. *Journal of Personality and Social Psychology, 66,* 762–775.

Henry, C. T., & Knott, J. R. (1941). A note on the relationship between "personality" and the alpha rhythm of the electroencephalogram. *Journal of Experimental Psychology, 28,* 362–366.

Hunt, J. McV., & Schlosberg, H. (1939). General activity in the male white rat. *Journal of Comperative Psychology, 28,* 23–38.

Huttenlocher, P. R. (2002). *Neural plasticity: The effects of experience on the development of the cerebral cortex.* Cambridge, MA: Harvard University Press.

Jung, C. G. (1923). *Psychological types.* London: Routledge & Kegan Paul.

Kagan, J. (1994). *Galen's prophecy: Temperament in human nature.* New York: Basic Books.

Kluger, A. N., Siegfried, Z., & Ebstein, R. P. (2002). A meta-analysis of the association between DRD4 polymorphism and novelty seeking. *Molecular Psychiatry, 7,* 712–717.

Lang, P. J., Bradley, M. M., & Cuthbert, B. (1995). *International affective picture system.* Gainesville, FL: University Press of Florida.

Lesch, K. P., Bengel, D., Heils, A., Sabol, S. Z., Greenberg, B. D., Petri, S., et al. (1996). Association of anxiety-related traits with a polymorphism in serotonin transporter gene regulatory region. *Science, 274,* 1527–1531.

Loehlin, J. C. (1992). *Genes and environment in personality development.* Newbury Park, CA: Sage.

Lolas, R., Camposano, S., & Etcheberrigaray, R. (1989). Augmenting/reducing and personality: A psychometric and evoked potential study in a Chilean sample. *Personality and Individual Differences, 10,* 1173–1176.

Meyer, G. J., & Shack, J. R. (1989). Structural convergence of mood and personality: Evidence for old and new directions. *Journal of Personality and Social Psychology, 57,* 691–706.

Mischel, W. (1968). *Personality and assessment.* New York: Wiley.

Mischel, W. (1990). Personality dispositions revisited and revised: A view after three decades. In L. A. Pervin (Ed.), *Handbook of personality: Theory and research* (pp. 111–134). New York: Guilford Press.

Munafo, M. R., Clark, T. G., Moore, L. R., Payne, E., Walton, R., & Flint, J. (2003). Genetic polymorphisms and personality in healthy adults: A systematic review and meta-analysis. *Molecular Psychiatry, 8,* 471–484.

Newman, D. L., Tellegen, A., & Bouchard, T. J., Jr. (1998). Individual differences in adult ego development: Sources of influence in twins reared apart. *Journal of Personality and Social Psychology, 74,* 985–995.

O'Gorman, J. G. (1984). Extraversion and the EEG. I: An evaluation of Gale's hypothesis. *Biological Psychology, 19*, 95–112.

Oniszczenko, W., Zawadzki, B., Strelau, J., Riemann, R., Angleitner, A., & Spinath, F. M. (2003). Genetic and environmental determinants of temperament: A comparative study based on Polish and German samples. *European Journal of Personality, 17*, 207–220.

Pavlov, I. P. (1938). *Twenty-five years of objective study of the higher nervous activity (behaviour) of animals*. Moscow-Leningrad: Narkomzdraw SSSR (in Russian).

Persson, M-L., Wasserman, D., Geijer, T., Frisch, A., Rockah, R., Michaelovsky, E., et al. (2000). Dopamine D4 receptor gene polymorphism and personality traits in healthy volunteers. *European Archives of Psychiatry and Clinical Neuroscience, 250*, 203–206.

Plomin, R., DeFries, J. C., McClearn, G. E., & McGuffin, P. (2001). *Behavioral genetics* (4th ed.). New York: Worth Publishers.

Reuter, M., Stark, R., Hennig, J., Walter, B., Kirsch, P., Schienle, A., et al. (2004). Personality and emotion: Test of Gray's personality theory by means of an fMRI study. *Behavioral Neuroscience, 118*, 462–469.

Rothbart, M. K., Derryberry, D., & Posner, M. I. (1994). A psychobiological approach to the development of temperament. In J. E. Bates & T. D. Wachs (Eds.), *Temperament: Individual differences at the interface of biology and behavior* (pp. 83–116). Washington, DC: American Psychological Association.

Rundquist, E. A. (1933). Inheritance of spontaneous activity in rats. *Journal of Comparative Psychology, 16*, 415–438.

Stagner, R. (1984). Trait psychology. In N. E. Endler & J. McV. Hunt (Eds.), *Personality and the behavioral disorders* (pp. 3–38). New York: Wiley.

Stelmack, R. M., & Michaud-Achorn, A. (1985). Extraversion, attention, and habituation of the auditory evoked response. *Journal of Research in Personality, 19*, 416–428.

Stenberg, G. (1992). Personality and the EEG: Arousal and emotional arousability. *Personality and Individual Differences, 13*, 1097–1113.

Stenberg, G., Rosen, I., & Risberg, J. (1988). Personality and augmenting/reducing in visual and auditory evoked potentials. *Personality and Individual Differences, 9*, 571–579.

Strelau, J. (1983). *Temperament, personality, activity*. London: Academic Press.

Strelau, J. (1994). The concepts of arousal and arousability as used in temperament studies. In J. E. Bates & T. D. Wachs (Eds.), *Temperament: Individual differences at the interface of biology and behavior* (pp. 117–141). Washington, DC: American Psychological Association.

Strelau, J. (1998). *Temperament: A psychological perspective*. New York: Plenum Press.

Strelau, J. (2001a). The concept and status of trait in research on temperament. *European Journal of Personality, 15*, 311–325.

Strelau, J. (2001b). The place of the construct of arousal in temperament research. In R. Riemann, F. M. Spinath, & F. Ostendorf (Eds.), *Personality and temperament: Genetics, evolution, and structure* (pp. 105–128). Lengerich, Germany: Pabst Science Publishers.

Strelau, J. (2006). *Psychologia różnic indywidualnych* [Psychology of individual differences]. Warsaw: Wydawnictwo Naukowe Scholar.

Strelau, J. (2008). *Temperament as a regulator of behavior: After fifty years of research*. Clinton Corners, NY: Eliot Werner Publications.

Strelau, J., Angleitner, A., & Newberry, B. H. (1999). *Pavlovian Temperament Survey (PTS): An international handbook.* Göttingen, Germany: Hogrefe & Huber.

Strelau, J., & Zawadzki, B. (1993). The Formal Characteristics of Behaviour–Temperament Inventory (FCB-TI): Theoretical assumptions and scale construction. *European Journal of Personality, 7*, 313–336.

Švrakić, N. M., Švrakić, D. M., & Cloninger, C. R. (1996). A general quantitative theory of personality development: Fundamentals of self-organizing psychobiological complex. *Development and Psychopathology, 8*, 247–272.

van Heck, G. L. (1988). Modes and models in anxiety. *Anxiety Research, 1*, 199–214.

Waller, N. G., Kojetin, B. A., Bouchard, T. J., Jr., Lykken, D. T., & Tellegen, A. (1990). Genetic and environmental influences on religious interests, attitudes, and values: A study of twins reared apart and together. *Psychological Science, 1*, 138–142.

Wenger, M. A. (1943). An attempt to appraise individual differences in level of muscular tension. *Journal of Experimental Psychology, 32*, 213–225.

Wiesel, T. N. (1994). Genetics and behavior. *Science, 264*, 1647.

Willingham, D. T., & Dunn, E. W. (2003). What neuroimaging and brain localization can do, cannot do, and should not do for social psychology. *Journal of Personality and Social Psychology, 85*, 662–671.

Windle, M., & Lerner, R. M. (1986). Reassessing the dimensions of temperamental individuality across the life-span: The Revised Dimensions of Temperament Survey (DOTS-R). *Journal of Adolescent Research, 1*, 213–230.

Zuckerman, M. (1979). *Sensation seeking: Beyond the optimal level of arousal.* Hillsdale, NJ: Erlbaum.

Zuckerman, M. (1985). Biological foundations of sensation-seeking temperament. In J. Strelau, F. H. Farley, & A. Gale (Eds.), *The biological bases of personality and behavior: Vol. 1. Theories, measurement techniques, and development* (pp. 97–112). Washington, DC: Hemisphere.

Zuckerman, M. (1990). The psychophysiology of sensation seeking. *Journal of Personality, 58*, 313–345.

Zuckerman, M. (1991). *Psychobiology of personality.* New York: Cambridge University Press.

Zuckerman, M. (1994). *Behavioral expressions and biosocial bases of sensation seeking.* New York: Cambridge University Press.

# CHAPTER 3

# A Neurocognitive Model of the Self

## Marek Cielecki

### ORGANIZATION OF THE SELF

Interestingly enough, the cognitive approach that dominated personality and social psychology for the last decades of the twentieth century brought about theoretical solutions reviving the basic thesis of psychoanalytic doctrine that personality is an internally differentiated, potentially conflictual structure. Most of these solutions juxtapose an internally and externally oriented facet of the self (subjective vs. objective self-awareness: Duval & Wicklund, 1972; private vs. public self: Fenigstein, Scheier, & Buss, 1975; personal vs. social identity: Tajfel, 1978; cf. Figure 1 below; low vs. high self-monitoring: Snyder, 1979; individualism vs. collectivism: Hofstede, 1980; Triandis, 1989; nonverbal vs. verbal self: Greenwald, 1982; independent vs. interdependent self: Markus & Kitayama, 1991). Conceptual opposition does not necessarily mean negative correlation; contrary to Tajfel, Deschamps (1979) proposed that the differentiation between self and others covariates with that between ingroup and outgroup.

Similar to most concepts in psychology, the opposition between internal and external aspects of the self has undergone transformation from a bipolar, $-1 - +1$ type dimension to a pair of unipolar, $0-1$ type dimensions, giving rise to a kind of 2 x 2 conceptual table and thereby surmounting the opposition between the individual and the social. Greenwald and Pratkanis (1984; see Figure 2 below) distinguish four developmentally ordered facets of the self: a diffuse self characterized by freedom from both personal demands and social constraints, a public self conforming to social demands, a private self keeping with internal standards,

*Personality from Biological, Cognitive, and Social Perspectives* edited by Tomasz Maruszewski, Małgorzata Fajkowska, and Michael W. Eysenck. Eliot Werner Publications, Clinton Corners, New York, 2010.

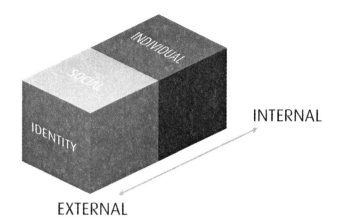

**Figure 1.** A simple dichotomous model of the self: individual versus social identity. Graphical illustration of Tajfel's (1978) approach.

and a collective self that internalizes the goals of a reference group. Jarymowicz (1986) defines social identity as a differentiation of we against the background of others and personal identity as a differentiation of the self from we. Although structurally this may best be depicted as shown in Figure 3, Jarymowicz (1986, 1994) also argues that concurrent differentiation of personal and social identity gives rise to the most mature form of the self.

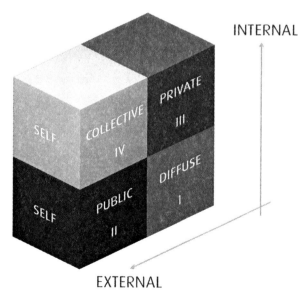

**Figure 2.** A 2 x 2 model of the self: from diffuse, through public and private, to collective self. Graphical illustration of Greenwald & Pratkanis's (1984) approach.

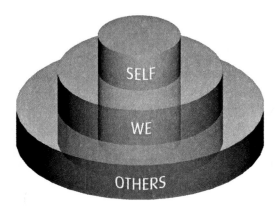

**Figure 3.** The self as a result of schematic differentiation self-we-others. Graphical illustration of Jarymowicz's (1986) approach.

As in the area of self-structure, many ambiguities exist with respect to motivation of the self. Is self-differentiation just another way of providing positive information about oneself (Snyder & Fromkin, 1980)? Why are locus of control and self-esteem so closely related (Hersh & Scheibe, 1967)? To what extent are the perceptual and psychological differentiation related to social independence, as suggested by field independence research (Witkin, Goodenough, & Oltman, 1979)? Despite theoretical and empirical overlaps, the notions of identity, esteem, and control have been functioning for decades as describing separate standards of behavior regulation, providing thereby another example of a trichotomizing approach to the self.

It should be remembered, however, that the prototype of a trichotomizing approach to the self/personality structure and function is embedded in psychoanalytic doctrine (Freud, 1923/1937). It describes Id as a socially inaccessible, internal, nonevaluative generator of tension using primary (imagery) processes; Superego as an external, socially originated evaluator; and Ego as an integrator ensuring balance of power between internal and external sources of behavior.

The aim of this chapter is to show that the above trichotomies do have a (common) structural basis in the functional specialization of the right (RH) and left (LH) hemispheres of the human brain and the integrative function of the corpus callosum.

## HEMISPHERIC ORGANIZATION

The integrative power of research on hemispheric asymmetry stems from two related sources. The first is its pertinence to all levels of psychological analysis, beginning with sensory processes and ending with sociocultural aspects of human behavior. The second is the variety and convergence—but not identity—of hypotheses about the core difference between the functions served by LH and RH.

## Extant Hypotheses

According to the extant hypotheses, LH and RH functions may differ with respect to:

- Content or format of the information processed: verbal, linguistic, or discrete versus visuospatial, imaginal, or diffuse (Kimura, 1961; Semmes, 1968).

- Mode of information processing: analytic, serial, or propositional versus synthetic/holistic, parallel, or appositional (Bever, 1975; Bogen, 1969; Cohen, 1973).

- Level of behavior regulation: cognitive/rational versus emotional (Gainotti, 1972; Tucker, 1981).

- Dominant affective and/or behavioral tendency: positive or approach versus negative or avoidance/withdrawal (Davidson, 1983, 1995).

- Direction of energetic and informational trade-off with environment: expressive, operating, or executive versus perceptive, storing, or holding. Perhaps the terms "active/output" versus "passive/input" best summarize these views (Anderson, Bruner, and Hughlings-Jackson, cited in Bogen, 1969; Corballis, 1991).

- Main focus of attention, related to the above: external versus internal (e.g., Bakan, 1969; Day, 1967).

## Propositions

The following set of propositions is offered to account in a noncontradictory way for the above hypotheses. Propositions 1–4 are represented graphically in Figure 4.

*Proposition 1*
Differentiation of function in the central nervous system (CNS) has proceeded directionally, along the three following functional dimensions: from reaction to action, from emotion to cognition, and from inward to outward orientation. In *Homo erectus* these functions rely on structures ordered along back-front, bottom-up, and right-left dimensions, respectively.

*Proposition 2*
Development of function in the CNS is subject to the acceleration principle: of two structures that underlay an older and a more recent function ordered along dimension A, the latter gives rise to faster development of a new function ordered along dimension B. It follows that cognition develops more rapidly within structures responsible for action than in those responsible for reaction, that outward orientation develops more rapidly in structures responsible for cognition than in those responsible for emotion, and so forth.

*Proposition 3*
It follows from Propositions 1 and 2 that RH, being oriented inward, has remained reactive and emotional relative to LH, which in turn has become relatively active and cognitive.

*Proposition 4*
The line of development of the CNS described in Propositions 1–3 results in (a) breaking the immediacy of and complicating the stimulus-response link, thereby providing the organism with increasing autonomy with respect to its environment (e.g., Bogen, 1969; Lewis, 1986; Witkin et al., 1979); and (b) articulation of a new dimension defined by clusters of inward orientation, emotionality, and reactivity at one pole, and outward orientation, cognitivity, and activity at the other.

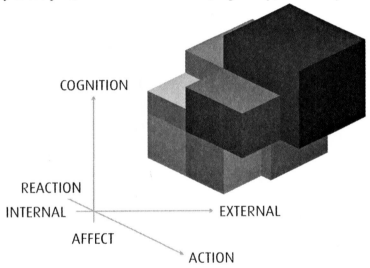

**Figure 4.** Development of functions in the CNS along back-front, bottom-up, and right-left dimensions with reference to the acceleration principle. Graphical illustration of Propositions 1–4.

*Proposition 5*
The functional and evolutionary gain from the development of the CNS as described in Proposition 4 lies in the emergence of two systems of behavior regulation, of which one (related to RH) serves a basic, primary function of preserving or defending the organism as an individual, while the other (related to LH) serves a derived, secondary function of improving its adjustment through communication and cooperation with conspecifics.

Development along each dimension enumerated in Proposition 1 has contributed to the articulation of these two adaptive systems, the specific contribution of the right-left split based on allocation of communicative functions to LH (Walker, 1980).

*Proposition 6*
The primary and secondary adaptive functions can be served due to hemisphere-specific organization of function on cognitive, emotional, and behavioral levels.

*Proposition 7*
Given the defensive function of RH, its basic task is to detect physically present threats. Immediate differentiation of the whole (potentially threatening) object from the perceptual field (Kinsbourne & Bemporad, 1984; Milner, 1971) is the cognitive ability that best serves this task. The basic task of LH is to analyze an object in sufficient detail to communicate its properties to others and to manipulate it. In humans, location of the object on descriptive and evaluative dimensions that are generated socially and transmitted verbally best serves this task. In short, the questions of "What is it?" and "How is it?" are relevant to the cognitive tasks of RH and LH, respectively.

The distinction made between the figural and dimensional representations in RH versus LH (respectively) parallels a number of dichotomies proposed by cognitive psychologists—for example, stimulus features versus dimensions (Garner, 1978), item-specific versus relational memory processes (Hunt & Einstein, 1981), and conceptualization of prototypes as still imaginable, all-or-none activable concepts versus matrix concepts, based on dichotomous classifications (Rosch, 1978).

*Proposition 8*
Activation of RH representation of an object produces a startle or freezing reaction. These reactions are satiated with negative affect since, genetically, they signal a threat (Vallortigara & Rogers, 2005; Zajonc, 1980). Activation of LH representation of an object produces an evaluative reaction that may be communicated to others and used to change the object's attributes so that they fit better the subject's needs. The resulting positive affect signals the possibility of improvement of the subject's prospects for survival through communication and cooperation with others in changing environment (cf. the notion of LH as a generative assembling device; Corballis, 1991).

It is also possible that RH identification of threat amplifies LH-specific positive affect, blending it with tension and giving rise to feelings of interest or excitement, provided that the organism is capable of coping with the threat (see Kinsbourne and Bemporad's [1984] characterization of LH frontal areas as exerting action control, in contrast to RH frontal areas as exerting emotional control). This triggering of LH activity may underlay the positive relationship between right parietal and left frontal activation revealed by Schaffer, Davidson, and Saron (cited in Davidson, 1983), and relative LH overactivation under stress—for example, with very difficult tasks (Newlin, 1981) and in high trait anxiety (Tyler & Tucker, 1982) and coronary-prone (Ketterer, 1982) subjects. Davidson's (1983, 1995) analysis of anger (which is negative but implies approach) as an LH emotion points in the same direction, and it is possible that sexual behavior (related to RH overactivation but certainly implying approach) is subject to a similar hypothesis (Cohen, Rosen, & Goldstein, 1976; Cohen, Rosen, & Goldstein, 1985; Tremblay, 1980).

Davidson's (1983, 1995) position and specifically his laboratory's finding that implication of the self may be necessary in eliciting RH- and LH-specific affective responses, as well as his view on anger as an approach-related emotion, was recently confirmed by Harmon-Jones, Lueck, Fearn, and Harmon-Jones (2006). These authors found significant relative left-to-right hemisphere overactivation when the participant faced an issue that evoked feeling of anger and the instruction prepared him or her for action. However, using a dot-discrimination task as a dependent variable, Robinson and Compton (2006) returned to the juxtaposition between the arousal and valence hypotheses. They found that reaction time for low versus high arousing stimuli differed more with RH than LH presentation. The authors discarded the valence hypothesis despite the fact that in two out of three analyses presented, the three-way interactions were marginally significant and the effect was stronger for negative than positive stimuli. In light of the present approach, such a final cross-test solution is unnecessary. The arousal and valence hypotheses are aspects of the same mechanism that alerts the organism in a case of threat and leads it through strong negative emotions to flight, mimicry, or stagnancy; whereas in a case of favorable conditions, the organism is instigated through moderately positive or negative emotions to communication, cooperation, or fight.

*Proposition 9*
With the development of distinct cognitive, affective, and behavioral functions in RH and LH, the organism faces the problem of integration of possible divergent outputs from the two systems of behavior regulation. The process of separation and—at the same time—integration of RH and LH functions depends on maturation of the corpus callosum (Blakemore & Choudhury, 2006; Lewandowski, 1982).

## HEMISPHERIC ORGANIZATION AND REPRESENTATION OF THE SELF

As with the representation of any other object, representation of the self may be located in RH and LH. The former consists of a set of visual, auditory, and proprioceptive traces corresponding to the subject's physical experience of himself or herself; the latter corresponds to a set of locations on abstract, verbally anchored, socially generated, mostly evaluative dimensions. It appears, then, that conceptualization of the self in hemisphere-specific terms provides a structural basis for the distinction between its two forms. These not only correspond to its internal and external aspects as identified in the introductory part of this chapter. They also share important definitional features—as well as affective and behavioral consequences—with the concepts of self-identity versus self-esteem and Id versus Superego, respectively.

To elaborate more on this notion, we conceive of the internal self as an RH representation encompassing physical experiences from within the organism (including those related to contacts with other people and personal standards encoded as physical action). These contents are difficult to communicate, socially monitor, evaluate, and modify, and hence they may be highly idiosyncratic. Their figure-like organization ensures a subjective feeling of differentiation from others and personal importance, irrespective of relationships with others. Activation of this structure gives rise to either self-differentiating or self-hiding (freezing and mimicry) behavior, depending on whether parietal RH processing is subsumed by frontal left (approach, action control) or right (withdrawal, emotion control) centers. In any case the behavior is regulated along the dimension of self-differentiation, and it is accompanied by amplification of affect with negative affect predominance.

On the other hand, the external self is meant as an LH representation consisting of a set of locations along socially generated dimensions anchored at verbal labels that assign descriptive and evaluative meaning to the dimensions. These locations are thus comparable with those occupied by other people, subject to social monitoring and social and personal redefinition. Locating oneself close to valued others ensures a feeling of belongingess, social acceptance, and self-esteem, as posited by social categorization theories (Tajfel, 1978) and the sociometer hypothesis (Leary, Tambor, Terdal, & Downs, 1999). Activation of this structure produces movement toward highly valued and/or from low-valued others along a dimension of social comparison.

Further, we conceive of the (potentially) integrated self as a specific organization of self-structure based on well-developed and equally strong RH and LH representations of the self. Given their simultaneous activation, an individual faces the problem of choosing between behaviors satisfying the needs of internal and external selves. A successful integration of these tendencies gives rise to a feeling of control (ego-strength, autonomy), which encompasses freedom from both necessary separation from others in service of the internal self, and necessary movements toward or from others in service of the external self. On the contrary, an individual is able to choose, justify, and pursue his or her own goals. Given lack of integration, a conflict is experienced: demands from external and internal selves are experienced as loss of control over oneself and others.

Finally, we conceive of the undifferentiated self as an organization of information about the self with unspecialized hemispheric functions. In these cases information from within the organism is not structurally separated from social information. Since no distinct instances exist for internal and external control over behavior, an individual reconciles possible divergent tendencies as smoothly as possible, unable nevertheless to develop the characteristic autonomy of the integrated self. Consequently, the standards of esteem, identity, and control are weakly differentiated, rendering striving for pleasure and avoiding displeasure the most parsimonious standards of behavior regulation.

A resemblance of the classification obtained to those referred to above—for example, private, public, collective, and diffuse selves by Greenwald and Pratkanis (1984) in particular—should not be overlooked. It has been built on the distinction between figural versus dimensional representation of the self characteristic of RH versus LH that, in turn, provides a common denominator for such dichotomies as self-images versus self-schemas (Lord, 1980) and behavioral/autobiographical versus abstract/trait (Klein & Loftus, 1993) or experiential versus cognitive (Epstein, 1990) selves.

## AVAILABLE EVIDENCE

Empirical evidence supporting the above proposals, although expanding, is still scarce. Given the tendency to conceive of the self as a social product of interaction and language, it has usually been assigned to LH; and even when some self-representational faculty was admitted to RH, it was believed to be developed less than, subject to, or suppressed by LH function (Eccles, 1981; LeDoux, 1985; Oakley & Eames, 1985). Therefore we will first point to data indicating that (a) RH is at least as good a candidate to represent the self as LH and (b) relationships between different aspects of the self exist that can be inferred from the hypothesis formulated in the preceding section.

### The Internal versus the External Self

The data supporting the idea that RH and LH are hosts for the internal and external selves, respectively, come from five areas of research.

#### Clinical and Personality Correlates
The earliest premises to locate the self—or at least its internal aspects that are less accessible to consciousness in the right rather than left hemisphere—came from research on lateralization of conversion symptoms, use of hemisphere-specific defense mechanisms, and more general personality traits. For example, Gur and Gur (1975) found that people who responded to reflexive questions by moving their eyes predominantly to the left (RH-dominant) disclosed mainly inner-directed symptoms, such as repression and denial, whereas right-movers (LH-dominant) displayed turning against others and projection. It was also found in this study that left movers had generally more somatic symptoms.

Bakan (1969) found that predominance of left eye-movements is associated with greater hypnotizability as well as humanistic interest, poorer mathematical performance, and clearer imagery. The relationship between left-movements and hypnotizability was confirmed by Morgan, McDonald, and Macdonald (1971). Using the same measure of hemisphericity, Smokler and Shevrin (1979) found that people of hysterical personality style (affective, anxious, concrete, labile, naive, repressive) were RH-dominant, whereas those of obsessive-compulsive style (analytical, intellectual, isolating, negative, restrained) were LH-dominant. In another study Otteson (1980) ascertained that women (but not men) who moved their eyes predominantly to the left were more internally focused (e.g., scored lower on social desirability and extraversion) and less dogmatic than those who moved their eyes to the right. Also, Meskin and Singer (1974) described typical left-movers as inner-attentive. Stern (1977) found that in all categories of conversion reactions distinguished (weakness, paralysis, sensory loss/numbness), the left side of the body was affected more than the right side. Accordingly, Galin, Diamond, and Braff (1977) found that in 63% of the cases investigated (71% of females), the conversion symptoms were lateralized to the left side of the body. The lateralization of conversion symptoms findings were not confirmed by Roelofs, Näring, Moene, and Hoogduin (2000), either in their review of the extant data or by their own results.

Apart from the latter source, early research on individual differences in hemispheric dominance converges in describing RH as soft, subjective, and inner oriented and LH as hard, objective, and outer oriented. Data obtained by Fisher and confirmed by Tremblay (1980), in turn, direct our attention to a relationship between RH predominance, self-focus, and sexual adaptation. Male high school students and juvenile delinquents treated residentially who focus on the left side of their bodies are more narcissistic and have fewer problems in their relationships with girls and women than those who focus on the right body side.

*Self-Recognition*
A series of research studies on self-recognition of a photograph via right or left hemisphere more directly supports the claim that physical (i.e., internal) aspects of the self are mainly represented in RH. Preilowski (1977) found in two split-brain patients of the so-called initial West Coast series markedly stronger galvanic skin responses when pictures of their own faces were presented to RH compared with LH, and in contrast to a number of other stimuli. Further evidence of RH representation of the self was provided by Keenan, Nelson, O'Connor, and Pascual-Leone (2001), who anesthetized the right versus left hemisphere of their patients for clinical test purposes. During this time the participants were presented with photographs of a face generated by morphing the patient's face with that of a celebrity. Following anesthesia the patient was asked which of the two faces had been presented. With RH inactivated the famous face was chosen; with LH inactivated the self-face was selected. Kircher et al. (2001), in turn, investigated activation of various brain regions by means of a functional magnetic resonance imaging (fMRI) technique in people viewing either their own or partner's morphed faces. In both cases right limbic areas were activated; however, left-sided associative and executive regions were also activated with the own face presentation. The problem with Kircher et al.'s study is that the participants were asked to press a right button with the right index finger if they saw their own face, and a left button with the left index finger if they saw the partner's face. This could

shift activation contralaterally to what one would expect on the basis of the present hypothesis and the rest of the results.

Physical self-representation is not limited to the face. Indeed, Weinstein (1978) presented evidence that the feeling of one's own body as determined by the tactual sensitivity threshold is better on the left than right body side. Data obtained by Davidson, Horowitz, Schwartz, and Goodman (cited in Davidson, 1980) suggest, in turn, a better "insight" of RH in autonomic processes since synchronization of heartbeat and finger tapping is better with the left than right finger. The fact that chimpanzees and orangutans (but not gorillas who are less lateralized than the other two species of the great apes), whose cognitive abilities seem to model RH rather than LH processing in humans, recognize themselves in the mirror points in the same direction (Anderson, 1999; Gallup & Suarez, 1986).

The data reviewed so far seem to be questioned by Uddin, Rayman, and Zaidel (2005), who found equally good recognition of the self and a familiar other in RH, but only the self-recognition in LH of a split-brain patient. It appears, however, that the patient was the same N.G.—now 70 years old—who had been tested by Preilowski (1977) in the early 1970s and had shown the most consistent RH specialization for self-recognition. Most likely the present results are due to plasticity of the human brain(s), and specifically N.G.'s LH faculty to subsume typical RH function that evolved during a forty-year-long split-brain condition.

Assuming RH versus LH specialization for processing concrete, imagery versus abstract, and verbal information, we can use data obtained from research on the format of self-representation to support neuropsychological considerations. Brown, Keenan, and Potts (1986) found that imaging external objects in relation to oneself gives rise to better memory for the nouns denoting these objects than imaging them in relation with nonself objects. This effect was found in a series of six studies that outweighed its reversal reported initially by Lord (1980). In addition, Yarmey and Johnson (1982) found that the false alarm effect—consisting of erroneous recognition of new items showing some degree of similarity to the prototype of self as items presented previously—holds for photographs of the subject equally well as for words describing him or her. These results support the claim that important aspects of the self are represented in the imagery format and RH. Drawing upon the distinction between imagery and verbal processing, Winczo-Kostecka and Cielecki (1985) found that excessive similarity to others resulted in a decrease in both mood and self-acceptance in people relying on the verbal code, whereas in those relying on the imagery code, a decrease in mood was unrelated to changes in self-acceptance. The authors concluded that (a) different aspects of the self were threatened in subjects relying on the verbal versus imagery code, and (b) self-identity as a construct separable from self-esteem is only characteristic of people able to form imagery representations of themselves.

Taken together, data from research on self-recognition and perception of one's own body, complemented by comparative research and research on imagery-verbal representation, support the claim that internal versus external aspects of the self are represented in the right versus left hemisphere of the human brain.

## Theory of Mind

Another line of research on hemispheric representation of internal versus external aspects of the self elaborates on the notions of "perspective taking" and "theory of mind" as psychological states, allowing an individual to take the perspective of another person and read his or her mind—that is, understanding beliefs, intentions, and other internal states versus seeing the world from the internal point of view. Vogeley et al. (2001) took functional magnetic resonance images of eight volunteers who were processing information concerning the self, the other, both, and neither of the two (as well as baseline). The results showed right anterior cingulate cortical activation with processing of any social information, right temporoparietal junction activation with taking self-perspective, and left temporal activation as specific to reading the other's mind. The authors noticed that the right self-specific areas of activation found in this study are the best candidates for a more general visuospatial representation of oneself. Basing their work on the same notion of theory of mind but using event-related potential (ERP) rather than fMRI methodology, Sabbagh and Taylor (2002) presented participants with short stories describing a person looking at versus taking a picture of two objects and then asked them about the location of each object as seen by a character versus seen in the photograph. ERP analysis revealed significant RH relative to LH increases in positivity for the frontal sites in the 300–400 and 600–800 ms time windows. These results indicate that perspective-taking or mind-reading evoke more LH than RH processing.

Another study conceptually close to the mind-reading problem and of most direct relevance to the hypothesis that internal versus external aspects of the self are related to its RH versus LH representations, respectively, deals with externalization versus internalization. Baumann, Kuhl, and Kazén (2005) found that activation of LH facilitates attribution to the self of actions and preferences that in fact had been done or expressed by other people. This self-infiltration (internalization) was prevented by activation of RH, which in turn facilitates attribution of one's own preferences to other people (externalization).

Although theory of mind studies yield support for the LH as an external self hypothesis, it should be noted that Griffin et al. (2006) found LH rather than RH specialization for reading the minds of humorous cartoon characters.

## Self-Reference

Two unpublished studies conducted within the self-reference paradigm produced more data in favor of the RH as a self-embodiment hypothesis. Cielecki and Karwańska (1990) showed that with right ear (LH) presentation, the adjectives classified as describing external aspects of the self were referred more often to the self than those classified as describing internal aspects of the self, whereas the reverse was true with left ear (RH) presentation. This interaction, however, was limited to the condition in which the participant and the experimenter were of the same sex. Mueller, Thompson, and Grove (1991), in turn, found that previously self-referenced trait words were responded to faster and recalled better when presented to the left (RH) than right (LH) visual field. This was only true for positive—as opposed to neutral or negative—trait words, and for the self in contrast to others or synonymity judgments.

In another pair of experiments, Kircher et al. (2002) presented participants with a series of words that had previously been judged as self-descriptive or not. Data combined for both studies showed that the common areas of activation for intentional (Experiment 1) and incidental (Experiment 2) processing of information about the self were the left fusiform gyrus and the left superior parietal lobe. However, this time the experimenters asked the participants to respond with their right thumb, and additionally they did not match the words with respect to likeability and meaningfulness. The very use of trait words could also activate more LH than RH. In these conditions the seemingly left-shifted activation for the self is questionable. Another study with the use of words was performed by Craik et al. (2002). Their participants had to refer a series of adjectives to the self or another person to judge the desirability of each adjective as a trait, or to count the number of syllables in each. All tasks demanding semantic processing evoked more LH (mainly prefrontal) activation than processing physical information. However, the authors noticed some right prefrontal activation specific to self-reference and otherwise typical of episodic processing. This effect could possibly be stronger, but Craik et al. required participants to perform relatively complex, quantitatively differentiated responses assigned to the four fingers of the right hand.

The data gathered within the self-reference paradigm, although not contradictory, speak less persuasively in favor of the right versus left hemisphere as a host for the self hypothesis (see Lieberman and Pfeifer, 2005, for a similar conclusion). Irregular findings and repetitious methodological shortcomings—such as use of material unmatched with respect to concreteness, affect intensity, and valence, as well as unbalanced use of the right response hand—decrease the validity of these studies. However, a more important source of relative ineffectiveness of this portion of research may be inherent in the paradigm: evaluatively loaded adjectives are ideal candidates for LH processing independent of how they are referred to by the subject.

### Affective Correlates

The data reviewed so far suggest that the dimension underlying RH- and LH-specific representation of the self may be that of nonverbal versus verbal format of representation. As far as affective specialization is concerned, studies by Davidson, Moss, Saron, and Schaffer and Schaffer, Davidson, and Saron (cited in Davidson, 1983) suggest that involvement of the self may be necessary to elicit RH- and LH-specific affective responses. It was found that the intensity of positive and negative facial expressions presented to the right and left visual fields differed significantly when subjects were asked to rate emotions elicited by a series of photographs, but did not when they were simply asked to rate the photographs themselves.

Other evidence pertinent to the affective specialization hypothesis comes from outside hemispheric research and shows correspondence between internal versus external orientation of the self on the one hand, and negative/intense versus positive/moderate affective response on the other. Contrary to a well-established positivity bias in the perception of the external world (Czapiński, 1985), self-focus by means of mirror presence produces either negative feelings about oneself or intensification of the dominant evaluative response, be it positive or negative (Wicklund, 1979). This suggests that an orientation toward others or focus on the external aspect of the self give rise to the affective response characteristic of LH, whereas a focus on the internal aspect of the self produces affective response ascribed to RH. In line with this reasoning, Greenberg and Pyszczynski (1985) found differential affective responses to the self depending on the public versus private context of failure: increased favorability of self-image following public and decreased favorability following private failure. These same authors (Pyszczynski & Greenberg, 1985) presented data of special significance in light of evidence on relative RH overactivation in depression (Tucker, 1981). Depressive individuals, contrary to normals, do not avoid self-focus in the mirror following failure. Accordingly, it is possible to prevent depressive individuals from pessimistic thinking and negative memory bias through focusing them externally (Pyszczynski, Hamilton, Herring, & Greenberg, 1989; Pyszczynski, Holt, & Greenberg, 1987). Negative thinking about oneself as a result of self-focus in depressive people is automatic (Bargh & Tota, 1988) and culture-independent (it also appears in Japan; Sakamoto, 1988).

The evidence reviewed so far treats self-focus as an independent and negativity as a dependent variable. If, however, this relationship has to be systemic or structural, the reverse should also be true. In fact, Wood, Saltzberg, and Goldsamt (1990) showed that experimental induction of sadness led to increased self-focus. This evidence is even more compelling if we take into account that one's own face is more important than the faces of (presumably most) other people: it interferes more with recognition of a classmate's name than this classmate's face interferes with recognition of one's own name, and the effect is not attributable to a particular resistance of one's own name (Brédart, Delchambre, & Laureys, 2006). Interestingly, the same pattern of results appears if one replaces the face versus name pair by the negative face versus positive face pair: the negative one interferes more with the positive than vice-versa (Horstmann, Borgstedt, & Heumann, 2006). These results converge with those obtained in the self-focus paradigm in showing that the strength of affinity between the internal, the negative, and the intense on the one hand, and the external, the positive, and the moderate on the other, supports the philosophical statement that a man is his own worst enemy. This may be rooted in early development: Lewis (1986) notes that the self as a schema separating stimulus from reaction originates with stranger wariness and that self-recognition in the mirror is speeded up by insecure attachment. The positive relationship between self-recognition and intensity of reaction to stress appears as early as between six and eighteen months of age (Lewis & Ramsey, 1997).

Basing their research on a tripartite model of the private, collective, and relational selves, Bromgard, Trafimow, and Bromgard (2006) found that priming the collective and relational selves leads to the generation of more positive self-statements than priming the private self. The authors interpreted this finding post hoc, claiming that self-enhancement is strengthened when representations of other people are involved. In light of the present approach, this kind of reasoning is unnecessary: orientation outward is positive because it stems from the same regulating instance (LH). This view is also justified in light of a positive correlation between extraversion and positive mood (Costa & McCrae, 1980). Lischetzke and Eid (2006) proposed a more specific model of how introversion-extraversion regulates mood. In their view extraverts' positive mood is something they maintain or savor, whereas introverts' bad mood is something with which they cope. The positive part of this thesis received stronger empirical support than the negative one. Of interest is a parallel between this line of reasoning and Davidson's (1983) approach-avoidance formulation regarding the core difference between LH and RH function, as well as our view of self-esteem as a standard to be attained versus self-identity as a standard to be defended.

We find, then, a sufficient body of evidence that there is a relationship between the internal orientation of a person and an increase in his or her affective responsiveness with negative affect predominance on the one hand, and external orientation and positive affect predominance on the other. This relationship exactly fits the characteristics of RH and LH described above.

## The Integrated Self

As far as the integrated self is concerned, empirical evidence is scarcer and our argument must be confined to the following premises: (a) a general notion of psychological and neuropsychological differentiation as a factor enhancing autonomy of the organism (e.g. Bogen & Bogen, 1969; Witkin et al., 1979); (b) the fact that the corpus callosum, the main interhemispheric commisure, completes its maturation only in a person's twenties—that is, in the period of an active break in one's social life in which a person-specific way of balancing individual needs and social necessities develops in the form of personality (Blakemore & Choudhury, 2006; Lewandowski, 1982); and (c) the role of the corpus callosum in creative thinking (Bogen & Bogen, 1969; Martindale, Hines, Mitchell, & Covello, 1984), which also may be regarded as an ability to put idiosyncratic images of the world (RH) in a socially communicable and useful form (LH).

More recent research introduced a variable that may appear crucial for understanding integration of the self against the background of hemispheric differentiation and cooperation. The notion of intra- and interhemispheric coherence describes the magnitude of cross-correlation between the power of electroencephalography (EEG) within a specified frequency band in different brain areas. It was found, for example, that women exhibit stronger interhemispheric coherence than men, specifically in lowest spontaneous EEG bands (from delta to alpha; Johnson, Petsche, Richter, von Stein, & Filz, 1996). Similarly, trained musicians show more interhemispheric coherence than nonmusicians. Volf and Razumnikova (1999) also found more pronounced interhemispheric coherence in females than males in task-dependent EEG theta band. It is interesting to note that similar to Johnson's et al.'s musicians, Volf and Razumnikova's women exhibited most evident coherence between right posterior and left frontal regions.

Findings of an increased temporal-parietal intrahemispheric coherence in the beta1 range with presentation of common objects independent of the modality of presentation (von Stein, Rappelsberger, Sarnthein, & Petsche, 1999), and an increased synchrony in the gamma band with presentation of a meaningful or regular—as contrasted to a meaningless or irregular—pattern (Rodriguez et al., 1999; von Stein & Sarnthein, 2000), led von Stein and Sarnthein to an interesting generalization. Perception of single (visual) patterns manifests itself in local (less than 10 mm, most probably monosynaptic) gamma (35–70 Hz) coherence, and perception of supramodal objects manifests itself in beta1 (12–18 Hz) coherence between adjacent cortex areas (mainly temporal-parietal), whereas working memory retention (or response preparation) results in a long-range (up to parietal-prefrontal and interhemispheric) coherence in the slow theta (4–8 Hz) frequency. Worded in more theoretical terms, this means that cortical coherence changes from local, high frequency for simple bottom-up (e.g., perceptual, associative) processes to long range, low frequency for complex top-down (e.g., planning and control) processes, including psychological integration of a person.

In line with this reasoning, it was found that complex tasks demand more interhemispheric cooperation than simple ones (Hochman & Eviatar, 2006). In the same vein, people with less hemispheric specialization or more hemispheric interaction (mixed-handed as opposed to right-handed), as well as an experimental induction of interhemispheric cooperation (through bilateral saccadic eye movements), yield earlier offset of childhood amnesia (Christman, Propper, & Brown, 2006). In addition, autobiographical memories following lateral eye movements prove less vivid and less emotional, be they on the positive or negative side of the scale (van den Haut, Muris, Salemink, & Kindt, 2001). Both studies show that concomitant activation of both hemispheres leads to a more mature, integrated psychological functioning. We perceive people who look directly into others' eyes as sincere and strong, in agreement with Meskin and Singer's (1974) observation that this is what field-independent people do during interaction with the interviewer.

The stronger right posterior-left anterior low-frequency coherence characteristic of women (Volf & Razumnikova, 1999) and musicians (Johnson et al., 1996) referred to above can be conceived of in the same terms. Women are characterized as either less hemispherically differentiated than men (Hiscock, Israelian, Inch, Jacek, & Hiscock-Halil, 1995; McGlone, 1980) or as more effective in applying left-hemisphere strategies to right-hemisphere tasks (O'Boyle, Benbow, & Alexander, 1995; Safer, 1981; but see Burton & Levy, 1989, for contradictory data)—that is, using more hemispheric interaction. Accordingly, musicians were shown to be more bilaterally attentive than nonmusicians (Patston, Hogg, & Tippett, 2007) and musical training in childhood was shown to increase cognitive abilities and educational attainments of children and youth, with a number of potential confounding variables held constant (Schellenberg, 2005). Also, and in concordance with what has been said about the importance of hemispheric interaction for creative thinking, more interhemispheric coherence is needed for the resolution of complex than simple mental problems (Jaušovec & Jaušovec, 2000).

One finding, coming from a study by Sarntheim, Rappelsberger, Shaw, and von Stein and cited in von Stein and Sarnthein (2000, p. 309, Figure 3), seems to be at odds with the data presented hitherto. It shows a posterior-anterior coherence in the theta range in a working memory condition, but this time the coherence is between the left posterior and right anterior areas. Although not discussed by the authors, this result remains in agreement with a more general rule of contralateral posterior-anterior transfer of activity, and with Schaffer, Davidson, and Saron's (cited in Davidson, 1983) finding of negative correlation between the parietal and frontal asymmetry in desynchronization from the alpha to beta range. It may be that the differences in the results reported by Sarntheim et al. (cited in von Stein & Sarnthein, 2000), Johnson et al. (1996), and Volf and Razumnikova (1999) are due to the different difficulty of the tasks, imposing different coordination demands and therefore arousal, or to a difference in their contents (modality).

## CONCLUDING COMMENTS

The goal of this chapter has been to provide a structural basis for a tripartite model of the self. Despite theoretical and empirical overlaps, the triads of private, public, and "complete" selves; identity, esteem, and control as self-standards; and the Id, Superego, and Ego as personality substructures have been functioning in personality and social psychology for years. I proposed that the common denominator for these triads is an internal versus external orientation of two basic regulating instances and a faculty to balance them as a third one. Then I suggested that RH, LH, and the integrative function of the corpus callosum are the best candidates to serve as a substrate for the tripartite self. A review of extant empirical findings encompassing personality differences between RH- and LH-dominant people, hemispheric mediation of self-recognition, self-reference (less compelling), and mind reading—as well as the affective consequences of focusing on internal versus external aspects of the self—has provided support for the hypothesis that RH and LH represent the internal and external selves, respectively. In addition, research on interhemispheric EEG coherence and the consequences of concurrent activation of both hemispheres provides support for the claim that the integrated brain renders psychological functioning more effective, mature, and independent.

The approach taken may appear excessively reductionist and localizational. It is not. I do not believe in a "red button" theory of the self: we will never see a specified point or spot on an MRI or positron emission tomography scan that would correspond to the self and its internal or external aspects. Rather, the tripartite self is fueled by clusters of functions that have philogenetically evolved thanks to the structural duplication, then specialization, and finally reintegration of the brain. This structure is sufficiently abundant and flexible to preclude one-to-one correspondence between a cell and a function, both intra- and interindividually.

Despite this reservation, the approach taken attempts to impose some order on theorizing in personality and social psychology. It contradicts tabula rasa-type theories of the self—for example, those rendering self-structure entirely dependent on cultural, historical, or economic circumstances. Although it does propose some universals, however, it does not say that all selves are alike, but that there is room for internal and external facets of the self in everyone.

The major weakness of research on the role of hemispheric specialization in understanding personality and social psychology phenomena is insufficient theorizing. What model of the self are we attempting to confirm, bipartite or tripartite? Are internal and external aspects of the self positively or negatively correlated? How are other people related to the self? Included or in different distances? These kinds of questions can be asked in every area of interest common to a social or personality psychologist and a neuropsychologist.

Unfortunately a disregard for theory, which leaves too much space for technology, can also be noticed on the hemispheric specialization side of research. Excessive use of verbal material, lack of affective match between different classes of stimuli, and unbalanced use of one response hand suggest that the format of representation theory, cognition/emotion theory, affect intensity theory, valence theory, approach/withdrawal theory, reafferent contralateral activation possibility, and so forth have been sacrificed for pursuit of a self.

## REFERENCES

Anderson, J. R. (1999). Primates and representations of self. *Current Psychology of Cognition, 18*, 1005–1029.

Bakan, P. (1969). Hypnotizability, laterality of eye-movements and functional brain asymmetry. *Perceptual and Motor Skills, 28*, 927–932.

Bargh, J. A., & Tota, M. E. (1988). Context-dependent automatic processing in depression: Accessibility of negative constructs with regard to self but not others. *Journal of Personality and Social Psychology, 54*, 925–939.

Baumann, N., Kuhl, J., & Kazén, M. (2005). Left-hemispheric activation and self-inflitration: Testing a neuropsychological model of internalization. *Motivation and Emotion, 29*, 135–163.

Bever, T. G. (1975). Cerebral asymmetries in humans are due to the differentiation of two incompatible processes: Holistic and analytic. *Annals of the New York Academy of Sciences, 263*, 251–262.

Blakemore, S.-J., & Choudhury, S. (2006). Development of the adolescent brain: Implications for executive function and social cognition. *Journal of Child Psychology and Psychiatry, 47*, 296–312.

Bogen, J. E. (1969). The other side of the brain II: An appositional mind. *Bulletin of the Los Angeles Neurological Societies, 34*, 135–162.

Bogen, J. E., & Bogen, G. M. (1969). The other side of the brain III: The corpus callosum and creativity. *Bulletin of the Los Angeles Neurological Societies, 34*, 191–200.

Brédart, S., Delchambre, M., & Laureys, S. (2006). One's own face is hard to ignore. *Quarterly Journal of Experimental Psychology, 59*, 46–52.

Bromgard, G. D., Trafimow, D., & Bromgard, I. K. (2006). Valence of self-cognitions: The positivity of individual self-statements. *Journal of Social Psychology, 146*, 85–94.

Brown, P., Keenan, J. M., & Potts, G. R. (1986). The self-reference effect with imagery encoding. *Journal of Personality and Social Psychology, 51*, 897–906.

Burton, L. A., & Levy, J. (1989). Sex differences in the lateralized processing of facial emotion. *Brain and Cognition, 11*, 210–228.

Christman, S. D., Propper, R. E., & Brown, T. J. (2006). Increased hemispheric interaction is associated with earlier offset of childhood amnesia. *Neuropsychology, 20*, 336–345.

Cielecki, M., & Karwańska, K. (1990, April). Right and left hemisphere of the brain as a structural basis for internal and external self. Paper presented at the annual meeting of the Midwestern Psychological Association, Chicago.

Cohen, A. S., Rosen, R. C., & Goldstein, L. (1985). EEG hemispheric asymmetry during sexual arousal: Psychophysiological patterns in responsive, unresponsive, and dysfunctional men. *Journal of Abnormal Psychology, 94*, 580–590.

Cohen, G. (1973). Hemispheric differences in serial versus parallel processing. *Journal of Experimental Psychology, 97*, 349–356.

Cohen, H. D., Rosen, R. C., & Goldstein, L. (1976). Electroencephalographic laterality changes during human sexual orgasm. *Archives of Sexual Behavior, 5*, 189–199.      .

Corballis, M. C. (1991). *The lopsided ape: Evolution of the generative mind.* New York: Oxford University Press.

Costa, P. T., Jr., & McCrae, R. R. (1980). Influence of extraversion and neuroticism on subjective well-being: Happy and unhappy people. *Journal of Personality and Social Psychology, 38*, 668–678.

Craik, F. I. M., Moroz, T. M., Moscovitch, M., Stuss, D. T., Winocur, G., Tulving, E., et al. (2002). In search of the self: A positron emission tomography study. In J. T. Cacioppo et al. (Eds.), *Foundations in social neuroscience* (pp. 189–202). Cambridge, MA: MIT Press.

Czapiński, J. (1985). *Wartościowanie—zjawisko inklinacji pozytywnej* [Valuation: The phenomenon of positivity bias]. Wrocław, Poland: Ossolineum.

Davidson, R. J. (1980). Consciousness and information processing: A biocognitive perspective. In J. M. Davidson & R. J. Davidson (Eds.), *The psychobiology of consciousness* (pp. 11–46). New York: Plenum Press.

Davidson, R. J. (1983). Affect, cognition, and hemispheric specialization. In C. E. Izard, J. Kagan, & R. B. Zajonc (Eds.), *Emotions, cognition, and behavior* (pp. 320–365). New York: Cambridge University Press.

Davidson, R. J. (1995). Cerebral asymmetry, emotion, and affective style. In R. J. Davidson & K. Hugdahl (Eds.), *Brain asymmetry* (pp. 361–387). Cambridge, MA: MIT Press.

Day, M. E. (1967). An eye-movement indicator of type and level of anxiety: Some clinical observations. *Journal of Clinical Psychology, 23*, 438–441.

Deschamps, J. C. (1979). Différenciations inter-individuelles et inter-groupes [Interindividual and intergroup differentiations]. In P. Tap (Ed.), *Identité individuelle et personnalisation* (pp. 187–190). Toulouse, France: Privat.

Duval, S., & Wicklund, R. A. (1972). *A theory of objective self-awareness.* New York: Academic Press.

Eccles, J. C. (1981). Mental dualism and commisurotomy [Response to Pucetti]. *Behavioral and Brain Sciences, 4*, 105.

Epstein, S. (1990). Cognitive-experiential self-theory. In L. A. Pervin (Ed.), *Handbook of personality: Theory and research* (pp. 165–192). New York: Guilford Press.

Fenigstein, A., Scheier, M. F., & Buss, A. H. (1975). Public and private self-consciousness: Assessment and theory. *Journal of Consulting and Clinical Psychology, 43*, 522–557.

Freud, S. (1937). The Ego and the Id (J. Riviere, Trans.). In J. Rickman (Ed.), *A general selection from the works of Sigmund Freud* (pp. 245–274). London: Hogarth Press. (Original work published in 1923)

Gainotti, G. (1972). Emotional behavior and hemispheric side of the lesion. *Cortex, 8*, 41–55.

Galin, D., Diamond, R., & Braff, D. (1977). Lateralization of conversion symptoms: More frequent on the left. *American Journal of Psychiatry, 134*, 578–580.

Gallup, G. G., & Suarez, S. D. (1986). Self-awareness and the emergence of mind in humans and other primates. In J. Suls & A. G. Greenwald (Eds.), *Psychological perspectives on the self* (Vol. 3, pp. 3–26). Hillsdale, NJ: Erlbaum.

Garner, W. R. (1978). Aspects of a stimulus: Features, dimensions, and configurations. In E. Rosch & B. B. Lloyd (Eds.), *Cognition and categorization* (pp. 99–133). Hillsdale, NJ: Erlbaum.

Greenberg, J., & Pyszczynski, T. (1985). Compensatory self-inflation: A response to the threat to self-regard of public failure. *Journal of Personality and Social Psychology, 49*, 273–280.

Greenwald, A. G. (1982). Is any*one* in charge? Personalysis versus the principle of personal unity. In J. Suls (Ed.), *Psychological perspectives on the self* (Vol. 1, pp. 151–181). Hillsdale, NJ: Erlbaum.

Greenwald, A G., & Pratkanis, A. R. (1984). The self. In R. S. Wyer & T. K. Srull (Eds.), *Handbook of social cognition* (Vol. 3, pp. 129–178). Hillsdale, NJ: Erlbaum.

Griffin, R., Friedman, O., Ween, J., Winner, E., Happé, F., & Brownell, H. (2006). Theory of mind and the right cerebral hemisphere: Refining the scope of impairment. *Laterality, 11*, 195–225.

Gur, R. E., & Gur, R. C. (1975). Defense mechanisms, psychosomatic symptomatology, and conjugate lateral eye-movements. *Journal of Consulting and Clinical Psychology, 43*, 416–420.

Harmon-Jones, E., Lueck, L., Fearn, M., & Harmon-Jones, C. (2006). The effect of personal relevance and approach-related action expectation on relative left frontal cortical activity. *Psychological Science, 17*, 434–440.

Hersch, P. D., & Scheibe, K. E. (1967). Reliability and validity of internal-external control as a personality dimension. *Journal of Consulting Psychology, 31*, 609–613.

Hiscock, M., Israelian, M., Inch, R., Jacek, C., & Hiscock-Kalil, C. (1995). Is there a sex difference in human laterality? II. An exhaustive survey of visual laterality studies from six neuropsychology journals. *Journal of Clinical and Experimental Neuropsychology, 17*, 590–610.

Hochman, E. Y., & Eviatar, Z. (2006). Do the hemispheres watch each other? Evidence for a between-hemispheres performance monitoring. *Neuropsychology, 20*, 666–674.

Hofstede, G. (1980). *Culture's consequences*. Beverly Hills, CA: Sage.

Horstmann, G., Borgstedt, K., & Heumann, M. (2006). Flanker effects with faces may depend on perceptual as well as emotional differences. *Emotion, 6*, 28–39.

Hunt, R. R., & Einstein, G. O. (1981). Relational and item-specific information in memory. *Journal of Verbal Learning and Verbal Behavior, 20*, 497–514.

Jarymowicz, M. (1986, April). Self-distinctness and social identifications. Paper presented at the Polish-American Conference on Self and Social Involvement, Princeton, NJ.

Jarymowicz, M. (Ed.). (1994). *Poza egocentryczną perspektywą widzenia siebie i świata* [Beyond an egocentric perspective on the self and world]. Warsaw: Wydawnictwo Instytutu Psychologii PAN.

Jaušovec, N., & Jaušovec, K. (2000). EEG activity during the performance of complex mental problems. *International Journal of Psychophysiology, 36*, 73–88.

Johnson, J. K., Petsche, H., Richter, P., von Stein, A., & Filz, O. (1996). The dependence of coherence estimates of spontaneous EEG on gender and music training. *Music Perception, 13*, 563–582.

Keenan, J. P., Nelson, A., O'Connor, M., & Pascual-Leone, A. (2001). Self-recognition and the right hemisphere. *Nature, 409*, 305.

Ketterer, M. (1982). Lateralized representation of affect, affect cognizance, and the coronary-prone personality. *Biological Psychology, 15*, 171–189.

Kimura, D. (1961). Cerebral dominance and the perception of verbal stimuli. *Canadian Journal of Psychology, 15*, 166–177.

Kinsbourne, M., & Bemporad, B. (1984). Lateralization of emotion: A model and the evidence. In A. Fox & R. J. Davidson (Eds.), *The psychobiology of affective development* (pp. 250–291). Hillsdale, NJ: Erlbaum.

Kircher, T. T. J., Brammer, M., Bullmore, E., Simmons, A., Bartels, M., & David, A. S. (2002). The neural correlates of intentional and incidental self processing. *Neuropsychologia, 40*, 683–692.

Kircher, T. T. J., Senior, C., Philips, M. L., Rabe-Hesketh, S., Benson, P. J., Bullmore, E. T., et al. (2001). Recognizing one's own face. *Cognition, 78*, B1–B15.

Klein, S. B., & Loftus, J. (1993). The mental representation of trait and autobiographical knowledge about the self. In T. K. Srull & R. S. Wyer, Jr. (Eds.), *Advances in social cognition* (Vol. 5, pp. 1–50). Hillsdale, NJ: Erlbaum.

LeDoux, J. E. (1985). Brain, mind and language. In D. A. Oakley (Ed.), *Brain and mind* (pp. 197–216). London: Methuen.

Leary, M. R, Tambor, E. S., Terdal, S. K., & Downs, D. L. (1999). Self-esteem as an interpersonal monitor: The sociometer hypothesis. In R. F. Baumeister (Ed.), *The self in social psychology* (pp. 87–104). New York: Psychology Press.

Lewandowski, L. (1982). Hemispheric differences in children. *Perceptual and Motor Skills, 54*, 1011–1019.

Lewis, M. (1986). Origins of self-knowledge and individual differences in early self-recognition. In J. Suls & A. G. Greenwald (Eds.), *Psychological perspectives on the self* (Vol. 3, pp. 55–78). Hillsdale, NJ: Erlbaum.

Lewis, M., & Ramsey, D. (1997). Stress reactivity and self-recognition. *Child Development, 68*, 621–629.

Lieberman, M. D., & Pfeifer, J. H. (2005). Three kinds of questions in social cognitive neuroscience. In A. Easton & N. J. Emery (Eds.), *The cognitive neuroscience of social behaviour* (pp. 195–235). Hove, UK: Psychology Press.

Lischetzke, T., & Eid, M. (2006). Why extraverts are happier than introverts: The role of mood regulation. *Journal of Personality, 74*, 1127–1161.

Lord, C. G. (1980). Schemas and images as memory aids: Two modes of processing social information. *Journal of Personality and Social Psychology, 38*, 257–269.

Markus, H., & Kitayama, S. (1991). Culture and the self: Implications for cognition, emotion, and motivation. *Psychological Review, 98*, 224–253.

Martindale, C., Hines, D., Mitchell, L., & Covello, E. (1984). EEG alpha asymmetry and creativity. *Personality and Individual Differences, 5*, 77–86.

McGlone, J. (1980). Sex differences in functional brain asymmetry: A critical survey. *Behavioral and Brain Sciences, 3*, 215–264.

Meskin, B. B., & Singer, J. L. (1974). Daydreaming, reflective thought, and laterality of eye movements. *Journal of Personality and Social Psychology, 30*, 64–71.

Milner, B. (1971). Interhemispheric differences in the localization of psychological processes in man. *British Medical Bulletin, 27*, 272–277.

Morgan, A. H., McDonald, P. J., & Macdonald, H. (1971). Differences in bilateral alpha activity as a function of experimental task, with a note on lateral eye movements and hypnotizability. *Neuropsychologia, 9*, 459-469.

Mueller, J. H., Thompson, W. B., & Grove, T. R. (1991, May). Self-referent processing and hemisphericity. Paper presented at the annual meeting of the Midwestern Psychological Association, Chicago.

Newlin, D. B. (1981). Hemisphericity, expressivity, and autonomic arousal. *Biological Psychology, 12*, 13–23.

Oakley, D. A., & Eames, L. C. (1985). The plurality of consciousness. In D. A. Oakley (Ed.), *Brain and mind* (pp. 217–257). London: Methuen.

O'Boyle, M. W., Benbow, C. P., & Alexander, J. E. (1995). Sex differences, hemispheric laterality, and associated brain activity in the intellectually gifted. *Developmental Neuropsychology, 11*, 415–443.

Otteson, J. P. (1980). Stylistic and personality correlates of lateral eye movements: A factor analytic study. *Perceptual and Motor Skills, 50*, 995–1010.

Patston, L. L. M., Hogg, S. L., & Tippett, L. J. (2007). Attention in musicians is more bilateral than in non-musicians. *Laterality, 12*, 262–272.

Preilowski, B. (1977). Self-recognition as a test of consciousness in left and right hemisphere of "split-brain" patients. *Activitas Nervosa Superior (Praha), 19* (Suppl. 2), 343–344.

Pyszczynski, T., & Greenberg, J. (1985). Depression and self-focusing stimuli after success and failure. *Journal of Personality and Social Psychology, 44*, 1066–1075.

Pyszczynski, T., Hamilton, J. C., Herring, F. H., & Greenberg, J. (1989). Depression, self-focused attention, and the negative memory bias. *Journal of Personality and Social Psychology, 57*, 351–357.

Pyszczynski, T., Holt, K., & Greenberg, J. (1987). Depression, self-focused attention, and expectancies for positive and negative future life events for self and others. *Journal of Personality and Social Psychology, 52*, 994–1001.

Robinson, M. D., & Compton, R. J. (2006). The automaticity of affective reactions: Stimulus valence, arousal, and lateral spatial attention. *Social Cognition, 24*, 469–495.

Rodriguez, E., George, N., Lachaux, J. P., Martinerie, J., Renault, B., & Varela, F. J. (1999). Perception's shadow: Long-distance synchronization of human brain activity. *Nature, 397*, 430–433.

Roelofs, K., Näring, G. W., B., Moene, F. C., & Hoogduin, C. A. L. (2000). The question of symptom lateralization in conversion disorder. *Journal of Psychosomatic . Research, 49*, 21–25.

Rosch, E. (1978). Principles of categorization. In E. Rosch & B. B. Lloyd (Eds.), *Cognition and categorization* (pp. 28–49). Hillsdale, NJ: Erlbaum.

Sabbagh, M. A., & Taylor, M. (2002). Neural correlates of theory-of-mind reasoning: An event-related potential study. In J. T. Cacioppo et al. (Eds.), *Foundations in social neuroscience* (pp. 235–243). Cambridge, MA: MIT Press.

Safer, M. A. (1981). Sex and hemisphere differences in access to codes for processing emotional expressions and faces. *Journal of Experimental Psychology: General, 110*, 86–100.

Sakamoto, S. (1998). The effects of self-focus on negative mood among depressed and nondepressed Japanese students. *Journal of Social Psychology, 138*, 514–523.

Schellenberg, E. G. (2005). Music and cognitive abilities. *Current Directions in Psychological Science, 14*, 317–320.

Semmes, J. (1968). Hemispheric specialization: A possible clue to mechanism. *Neuropsychologia, 6*, 11–26.

Smokler, I. A., & Shevrin, H. (1979). Cerebral lateralization and personality style. *Archives of General Psychiatry, 36*, 949–954.

Snyder, C. R., & Fromkin, H. L. (1980). *Uniqueness: The human pursuit of difference.* New York: Plenum Press.

Snyder, M. (1979). Self-monitoring processes. In L. Berkowitz (Ed.), *Advances in experimental social psychology* (Vol. 12, pp. 85–128). New York: Academic Press.

Stern, D. B. (1977). Handedness and the lateral distribution of conversion reactions. *Journal of Nervous and Mental Disease, 164*, 122–128.

Tajfel, H. (1978). Interindividual behaviour and intergroup behaviour. In H. Tajfel (Ed.), *Differentiation between social groups: Studies in the social psychology of intergroup relations* (pp. 27–60). London: Academic Press.

Tremblay, R. E. (1980). L'image du corps, les difficultés de relations avec les femmes et le narcissisme chez des adolescents délinquents (en internat de rééducation) [Body image, difficulties in relations with women and narcissism in juvenile delinquents (under residential treatment)]. *Revue de Psychologie Appliquée, 30*, 149–155.

Triandis, H. C. (1989). The self and social behavior in differing cultural contexts. *Psychological Review, 96*, 506–520.

Tucker, D. M. (1981). Lateral brain function, emotion, and conceptualization. *Psychological Bulletin, 89*, 19–46.

Tyler, S. K., & Tucker, D. M. (1982). Anxiety and perceptual structure: Individual differences in neuropsychological function. *Journal of Abnormal Psychology, 9*, 210–220.

Uddin, L. Q., Rayman, J., & Zaidel, E. (2005). Split-brain reveals separate but equal self-recognition in the two cerebral hemispheres. *Consciousness and Cognition, 14*, 633–640.

Vallortigara, G., & Rogers, L. J. (2005). Survival with an asymmetrical brain: Advantages and disadvantages of cerebral lateralization. *Behavioral and Brain Sciences, 28*, 575–633.

van den Haut, M., Muris, P., Salemink, E., & Kindt, M. (2001). Autobiographical memories become less vivid and emotional after eye movements. *British Journal of Clinical Psychology, 40*, 121–130.

Vogeley, K., Bussfeld, P., Newen, A., Hermann, S., Happé, F., Falkai, P., et al. (2001). Mind reading: Neural mechanisms of theory of mind and self-perspective. *NeuroImage, 14*, 170–181.

Volf, N. V., & Razumnikova, O. M. (1999). Sex differences in EEG coherence during a verbal memory task in normal adults. *International Journal of Psychophysiology, 34*, 113–122.

von Stein, A., Rappelsberger, P., Sarnthein, J., & Petsche, H. (1999). Synchronization between temporal and parietal cortex during multimodal object processing in man. *Cerebral Cortex, 9*, 137–150.

von Stein, A., & Sarnthein, J. (2000). Different frequencies for different scales of cortical integration: From local gamma to long range alpha/theta synchronization. *International Journal of Psychophysiology, 38*, 301–313.

Walker, S. (1980). Lateralization of function in the vertebrate brain: A review. *British Journal of Psychology, 71*, 329–367.

Weinstein, S. (1978). Functional cerebral hemispheric asymmetry. In M. Kinsbourne (Ed.), *Asymmetrical function of the brain* (pp. 17–48). Cambridge, UK: Cambridge University Press.

Wicklund, R. A. (1979). The influence of self-awareness on human behavior. *American Scientist, 67*, 187–193.

Winczo-Kostecka, M., & Cielecki, M. (1985). Self-identity or self-esteem? Vivid and non-vivid imagers' responses to threat to self-differentiation. *Cahiers de Psychologie Cognitive, 5*, 171–186.

Witkin, H. A., Goodenough, D. R., & Oltman, P. K. (1979). Psychological differentiation: Current status. *Journal of Personality and Social Psychology, 37*, 1127–1145.

Wood, J. V., Saltzberg, J. A., & Goldsamt, L. A. (1990). Does affect influence self-focused attention? *Journal of Personality and Social Psychology, 58*, 899–908.

Yarmey, A. D., & Johnson, J. (1982). Evidence for the self as an imaginal prototype. *Journal of Research in Personality, 16*, 238–246.

Zajonc, R. B. (1980). Compresence. In P. B. Paulus (Ed.), *Psychology of group influence* (pp. 35–60). Hillsdale, NJ: Erlbaum.

CHAPTER 4

# Perceptual Identity and Personal Self
## Neurobiological Reflections

## Ernst Pöppel

### WHAT IS THE PROBLEM TO CREATE "IDENTITY"?

How is it possible that I can see something as something for some time and that this "something" does not change its identity? This may sound like a strange question, but from a neurobiological point of view, perceptual identity is a great enigma. What is the problem? Activities of single neurons change their activities within milliseconds, whereas perceptual identity is maintained over a much longer time. We tend to take identity for granted, but it is not only a challenge for perception: it is also a central question for our emotions, our memories, our intentions, our thoughts, and also for our personal self. Where does the knowledge of myself come from? How can I refer to myself as myself throughout time without ever questioning the self-evidence of my personal identity (which in some pathological cases, however, may happen)?

This last question of personal identity is not at all a difficult question if from an epistemological point of view one favors a dualistic perspective. If mind and body are separate substances, it is (usually implicitly) assumed that personal identity or knowledge of oneself is a given: it is self-evident. The only question of interest under such an assumption is how a mind in its unity and lasting identity is linked to the physical properties of the brain. If one favors a monistic view, however, or if one carries the conviction of empirical realism—and this is my epistemological position (Pöppel, 1985/1988a, 2006)—then one is confronted with the fundamental problem of the creation of personal identity and with the question how experiential identity in perception, memory, emotion, or thought is made possible.

*Personality from Biological, Cognitive, and Social Perspectives* edited by Tomasz Maruszewski, Małgorzata Fajkowska, and Michael W. Eysenck. Eliot Werner Publications, Clinton Corners, New York, 2010.

From a pragmatic point of view, a monistic or realistic attitude toward such problems is well founded because it has been demonstrated again and again in the history of neurology and neuropsychology that every subjective phenomenon that can possibly be defined may be lost or substantially altered due to disturbances in the brain (e.g., Pöppel, 1989). The selective loss or qualitative change of a specific function can be taken as a proof of existence of this function, and this indeed favors a monistic view to explain any subjective phenomenon on the basis of neuronal activities.

The real challenges of the brain for the creation of identity become clearer if one looks at the neuronal machinery that is necessary for perceptual processes (e.g., Nauta & Feirtag, 1986; Szentágothai & Arbib, 1974). If one focuses on visual and auditory perception, one has to deal with the problem that the time required for the transduction of optic and acoustic information within the different modalities is different, being much shorter in the auditory modality (Pöppel, Schill, & von Steinbüchel, 1990). Furthermore, transduction in the retina is dependent on flux such that the necessary information to define a visual object being characterized by surfaces of different brightness arrives at different times in the visual cortex. In addition, there is nothing like a point-to-point projection within the sensory modalities but a large degree of divergence of projection. Thus, for instance, to create the perceptual identity of another person whom I see and to whom I talk, my brain has to overcome temporal uncertainty and spatial distributions of the neuronal information within the neuronal network, which is necessary to create the percept of this person.

## NEURONAL OSCILLATIONS CREATING THE LOGISTICAL BASIS FOR COMPLEXITY REDUCTION

Thus the brain is confronted with a logistical problem: how to extract the necessary information. It is my hypothesis that this logistical problem can be overcome by the use of neuronal oscillations (Pöppel 1971, 1978, 1994, 1997, 2004). It has been demonstrated that stimulus-triggered oscillations with a period in the temporal range of approximately 30–50 milliseconds can be used to integrate the neuronal information, which is distributed in space and time. Experimental evidence shows that temporal intervals of this duration are of an "atemporal" nature: the relationship of before and after is not defined within such intervals. All information is treated as "cotemporal."

Direct evidence comes from the measurement of order-thresholds in the visual, auditory, and tactile modality; only if some tens of milliseconds have passed is it possible to indicate their correct order (Hirsh & Sherrick, 1961; Kanabus, Szelag, Rojek, & Pöppel, 2002; Lewandowska, Bekisz, Szymaszek, Wrobel, & Szelag, 2008; Szymaszek, Szelag, & Slikowska, 2006; Wada, Moizumi, & Kitazawa, 2005; Wittmann, Burtscher, Fries, & von Steinbüchel, 2004). It can be assumed that this integrative function at the same time represents the neuronal machinery to create the basic material of conscious activities—that is, "primordial events." This hypothesis has an interesting sideline: it indicates that the continuity of time, as it is defined in classical physics, has to be disrupted by the neuronal machinery by creating atemporal zones of 30–50 milliseconds. Only on the basis of such atemporal zones can order for mental activities be established. This mechanism to create the building blocks of conscious activities can be conceived of as the first step of creating perceptual identity, and this is done by complexity reduction in the temporal domain.

Additional evidence for such a temporal mechanism comes from measurements of choice reaction or eye movements (Harter & White, 1968; Ilmberger, 1986; Jokeit, 1990; Pöppel, 1968, 1970; Pöppel & Logothetis, 1986); histograms of responses show significant multimodalities with modal distances of 30–40 ms, which can only be explained by an underlying process of discrete time sampling, and suggests stimulus-triggered neuronal oscillations (Pöppel, 1971, 1997). Such oscillations have been made visible in studies on auditory evoked potentials (Galambos, Makeig, & Talmachoff, 1981; Madler & Pöppel, 1987; Schwender, Madler, Klasing, Peter, & Pöppel, 1994) and they can also be seen in single cell recordings in different modalities (e.g., Gardner & Costanzo, 1980; Podvigin et al., 2004).

If one looks at the different mechanisms that characterize our mental processes in general and thinking in particular, it is obvious that such a first step of creating perceptual categories is necessary. Only on the basis of the availability of categories (the building blocks of consciousness) are further mental operations possible. These operations are to relate different categories to each other to allow a comparison. Such comparisons can be made with respect to the quantity or quality of different stimuli. On the basis of a comparison, a choice can be made that implies the allocation of a chosen category to a specific set. Only if this operation has been done can a decision be made that is characterized by anticipation of the consequences of such a decision. The next step in this hierarchy of mental operation is an action, which itself is characterized by the reafference principle; in parallel to the action program, an efference-copy is stored that allows a continuous monitoring of the action by comparing the achievements of the action program with the stored copy of the efference (Tanida & Pöppel, 2006; von Holst & Mittelstaedt, 1950). All these operations require the identity of the basic material of the mental machinery—that is, the perceptions, the results of the comparisons, the content of the decisions, or the anticipated goal to be reached. If identity is lost, as can be observed in certain brain diseases, the consistency and coherence of our mental life breaks down.

## PRESEMANTIC TEMPORAL INTEGRATION CREATING "WINDOWS OF PRESENCE"

To create perceptual identity in the visual domain, constancy mechanisms serve an important function. Brightness constancy, color constancy, or size constancy allow the maintenance of the identity of a perceptual object (Pöppel, 2006).

Experimental evidence has indicated that a specific temporal mechanism creates a "window of presence" with the duration of approximately 2–3 seconds. An automatic temporal integration mechanism provides a temporal stage on which conscious activity is represented. For every time window of up to three seconds, the identity of a percept or a memory is maintained. The internal dynamics of the brain can be interpreted on a subjective level with a statement like this: "What is new in the world?" The cognitive machinery controls in steps of just a few seconds whether the maintenance of identity is necessary or whether a new representation is necessary or desirable.

Examples for such a temporal integration within a few seconds and perceptual identity of what is represented come from speech (Kien & Kemp, 1994; Kowal, O'Connell, & Sabin, 1975; Vollrath, Kazenwadel, & Krüger, 1992), movement control (Gerstner & Fazio, 1995; Mates, Müller, Radil, & Pöppel, 1994; Miyake, Onishi, & Pöppel, 2004; Schleidt, Eibl-Eibesfeldt, & Pöppel, 1987; Takano & Miyake, 2007), the temporal control of short-term memory (Peterson & Peterson, 1959), the temporal range of "inhibition of return" as an indicator of attentional modulation (Bao, Zhou, & Fu, 2004; Zhou, 2008), research on mismatch negativity (Sams, Hari, Rif, & Knuutila, 1993), the spontaneous fluctuations of ambiguous figures (Gomez, Argandona, Solier, Angulo, & Vazquez, 1995), studies on subjective accentuation of sequential stimuli (Szelag, Kowalska, Rymarczyk, & Pöppel, 1998; Szelag, von Steinbüchel, & Pöppel, 1997), or even music (Pöppel, 1988b). It has been demonstrated that musical motifs that are experienced as a unity are implemented in a temporal window of approximately three seconds. Another example from the arts comes from poetry; it has been shown that a verse is represented in a time window of only a few seconds (Turner & Pöppel, 1988). Thus cultural artifacts, which also necessarily require the identity of cognitive content, use this temporal machinery.

A simple example that demonstrates the validity of such a presemantic temporal integration window of just a few seconds comes from experiments on temporal reproduction (Pöppel, 1971; Szelag, Kowalska, Rymarczyk, & Pöppel, 2002). If a subject has to reproduce different durations, he or she can do so up to approximately three seconds almost veridically and with small variance; stimuli with longer durations are reproduced shorter and with much larger variance. Information within this time window can be kept in mind as a unit. Interestingly, studies with autistic children have demonstrated that they have a tendency to reproduce all stimuli within approximately three seconds (Szelag, Kowalska, Galkowski, & Pöppel, 2004), suggesting that the experimental task initiates an internal temporal integration process that no longer can be modulated by external events. Such systematic alterations in specific pathologies support the notion of an underlying neuronal principle being operative under normal circumstances.

## PERSONAL IDENTITY AS SUBSTANTIATED BY BEING ONE'S OWN "DOPPELGÄNGER" IN EPISODIC MEMORY

With these temporal functions (i.e., a 30–50 millisecond integration interval and an approximate 3-second temporal stage), a neuronal basis may be given for the experience of identity. In my view this is a necessary neuronal machinery for the creation of subjective identity with respect to perceptions, emotions, memories, or thoughts, but it is certainly not the sufficient cause. For the creation of personal knowledge of identity, an external point of view toward mental activities is essential that has to go beyond the logistical basis of neuronal operations (Pöppel, 2006); but without such a logistical basis, the operations on the higher and more abstract level would be impossible (Pöppel, 1989). This basic neuronal machinery in the time domain is presumably also necessary to allow the creation of personal identity. But other neuronal and mental operations are necessary and here new experimental evidence gives some insight into this fundamental question: how can we refer to our self with the effortless assumption that we are always the same as we believe ourselves to be?

Before turning to some results from studies on episodic memory, I would like to refer to a specific challenge with respect to the creation of the personal self—the diurnal fluctuations of all somatic and psychological functions. Research in chronobiology, in particular on circadian rhythms, has indicated that every function shows a specific diurnal cycle (e.g., Pöppel 1985/1988a). Different functions, however, do not fluctuate in parallel but show different maxima and minima at different times of day. The so-called phase-map of functions changes continuously, and only in 24 hours do we observe again a similar constellation of the phase map. Thus we change our biological and also psychological identity continuously throughout the day, and we return to the same position in the phase-map only every 24 hours; we are always "self-identical" in steps of 24 hours. The great enigma is why do we not experience this? How is it possible that we are convinced to be the same person throughout a day, although this is objectively not the case? In fact, there are some cases with deep depression where the experience of self-identity is not maintained throughout a circadian cycle, which indicates that an active mechanism is responsible for the creation and maintenance of self-identity; otherwise it could not break down.

An answer may be given by some results from studies on episodic memory that indicate how we explicitly—and presumably also implicitly—can refer to our self and by doing so overcoming psychobiological fluctuations (Pöppel, 2006). This research began with a rather simple question: how many images in our mind can we actually activate when we time-travel to our personal past? In the meantime several hundred subjects have participated in this introspective exercise, men and women of different age groups, different professions, and members of different cultures. These time-traveling experiences to one's own past have indicated that everyone can activate only a few hundred images, although we may recognize many more images. This discrepancy indicates that very different neuronal mechanisms are involved in recognizing and remembering.

It is, however, another result that is of utmost importance for our question about how personal identity is established. Independently of each other, subjects report that in the images of their personal past they "see" themselves as an agent. This is of course physically impossible if images of the past are simply reflected in our memory system. Apparently the memory system changes the images that we have experienced such that we are projected as an agent into the image of the personal past. Thus we become our own "Doppelgänger": we double our self and by doing so—and this is the hypothesis—we can refer to our self. This observation suggests to me that the creation of personal identity is made possible by projecting our self into our own pictorial past. Only if such self-reference is possible can I refer to myself. This self-reference is an effortless process, and it is assumed that it happens continuously on an implicit level, but that it can be made explicit if under conscious control we make a time-travel to our own past. Thus the tragedy of a memory loss is not so much the loss of memory itself, but the loss of a potential and necessary self-reference. I know no longer who I am because I have lost myself in the personal mirror of my episodic memory. For the neuronal "construction" of self-identity, those mechanisms of temporal control that have been outlined above—that is, a process of complexity reduction providing the basic material (the "primordial events)" of mental activity and a process of temporal integration providing a temporal platform of subjective presence for our experiences and reflections—are essential.

## REFERENCES

Bao, Y., Zhou, J., & Fu, L. (2004). Aging and the time course of inhibition of return in a static environment. *Acta Neurobiologiae Experimentalis, 64*, 403–414.

Galambos, R., Makeig, S., & Talmachoff, P. J. (1981). A 40-Hz auditory potential recorded from the human scalp. *Proceedings of the National Academy of Sciences, 78*, 2643–2647.

Gardner, E. P., & Costanzo, R. M. (1980). Temporal integration of multiple-point stimuli in primary somatosensory cortical receptive fields in alert monkeys. *Journal of Neurophysiology, 43*, 444-468.

Gerstner, G. E., & Fazio, V. A. (1995). Evidence for a universal perceptual unit in mammals. *Ethology, 101*, 89–100.

Gomez, C., Argandona, E. D., Solier, R. G., Angulo, J. C. & Vazquez, M. (1995). Timing and competition in networks representing ambiguous figures. *Brain and Cognition, 29*, 103–114.

Harter, M. R., & White, C. T. (1968). Periodicity within reaction time distributions and electromyograms. *Quarterly Journal of Experimental Psychology, 20*, 157–166.

Hirsh, I. J., & Sherrick, C. E. (1961). Perceived order in different sense modalities. *Journal of Experimental Psychology, 62*, 423-432.

Ilmberger, J. (1986). Auditory excitability cycles in choice reaction time and order threshold. *Naturwissenschaften, 73*, 743–744.

Jokeit, H. (1990). Analysis of periodicities in human reaction times. *Naturwissenschaften, 77*, 288–291.

Kanabus, M., Szelag, E., Rojek, E., & Pöppel, E. (2002). Temporal order judgment for auditory and visual stimuli. *Acta Neurobiologiae Experimentalis, 62*, 263–270.

Kien, J., & Kemp, A. (1994). Is speech temporally segmented? Comparison with temporal segmentation in behavior. *Brain and Language, 46*, 662–682.

Kowal, S., O'Connell, D. C., & Sabin, E. J. (1975). Development of temporal patterning and vocal hesitations in spontaneous narratives. *Journal of Psycholinguistic Research, 4*, 195–207.

Lewandowska, M., Bekisz, A., Szymaszek, A., Wrobel, A., & Szelag E. (2008). Towards electrophysiological correlates of auditory perception of temporal order. *Neuroscience Letters, 437*, 139–143.

Madler, C., & Pöppel, E. (1987). Auditory evoked potentials indicate the loss of neuronal oscillations during general anaesthesia. *Naturwissenschaften, 74*, 42–43.

Mates, J., Müller, U., Radil, T., & Pöppel, E. (1994). Temporal integration in sensorimotor synchronization. *Journal of Cognitive Neuroscience, 6*, 332–340.

Miyake, Y., Onishi, Y., & Pöppel, E. (2004). Two types of anticipation in synchronization tapping. *Acta Neurobiologiae Experimentalis, 64*, 415–426.

Nauta, W. J. H., & Feirtag, M. (1986). *Fundamental neuroanatomy*. New York: Freeman.

Peterson, L. B., & Peterson, M. J. 1959 Short-term retention of individual items. *Journal of Experimental Psychology, 58*, 193–198.

Podvigin, N. F., Bagaeva, T. V., Boykova, E. V., Zargarov, A. A., Podvigina, D. N., & Pöppel, E. (2004). Three bands of oscillatory activity in the lateral geniculate nucleus of the cat visual system. *Neuroscience Letters, 361*, 83–85.

Pöppel, E. (1968). Oszillatorische Komponenten in Reaktionszeiten [Oscillatory components in reaction times]. *Naturwissenschaften, 55*, 449–450.

Pöppel, E. (1970). Excitability cycles in central intermittency. *Psychologische Forschung, 34*, 1–9.

Pöppel, E. (1971). Oscillations as possible basis for time perception. *Studium Generale, 24*, 85–107.

Pöppel, E. (1978). Time perception. In R. Held, H. W. Leibowitz, & H.-L. Teuber (Eds.), *Handbook of sensory physiology: Vol. 8. Perception* (pp. 713–729). Berlin: Springer-Verlag.

Pöppel, E. (1988a). *Mindworks: Time and conscious experience* (T. Artin, Trans.). Orlando, FL: Harcourt Brace Jovanovich. (Original work published in 1985)

Pöppel, E. (1988b). The measurement of music and the cerebral clock: A new theory. *Leonardo, 22*, 83–89.

Pöppel, E. (1989). Taxonomy of the subjective: An evolutionary perspective. In J. W. Brown (Ed.), *Neuropsychology of visual perception* (pp. 219–232). Hillsdale, NJ: Erlbaum.

Pöppel, E. (1994). Temporal mechanisms in perception. *International Review of Neurobiology, 37*, 185–202.

Pöppel, E. (1997). A hierarchical model of temporal perception. *Trends in Cognitive Sciences, 1*, 56–61.

Pöppel, E. (2004). Lost in time: A historical frame, elementary processing units and the 3-second-window. *Acta Neurobiologiae Experimentalis, 64*, 295–301.

Pöppel, E. (2006). *Der Rahmen: Ein Blick des Gehirns auf unser Ich* [The frame: A view of the brain toward our self]. Munich, Germany: Hanser-Verlag.

Pöppel, E., & Logothetis, N. (1986). Neuronal oscillations in the human brain: Discontinuous initiations of pursuit eye movements indicate a 30-Hz temporal framework for visual information processing. *Naturwissenschaften, 73*, 267–268.

Pöppel, E., Schill, K., & von Steinbüchel, N. (1990). Sensory integration within temporally neutral system states: A hypothesis. *Naturwissenschaften, 77*, 89–91.

Sams, M., Hari, R., Rif, J. & Knuutila, J. (1993). The human auditory sensory memory trace persists about 10 sec: Neuromagnetic evidence. *Journal of Cognitive Neuroscience, 5*, 363–370.

Schleidt, M., Eibl-Eibesfeldt, I., & Pöppel, E. (1987). A universal constant in temporal segmentation of human short-term behaviour. *Naturwissenschaften, 74*, 289–290.

Schwender, D., Madler, C., Klasing, S., Peter, K., & Pöppel, E. (1994). Anesthetic control of 40-Hz brain activity and implicit memory. *Consciousness and Cognition, 3*, 129–147.

Szelag, E., Kowalska, J., Galkowski, T., & Pöppel, E. (2004). Temporal processing deficits in high-functioning children with autism. *British Journal of Psychology, 95*, 269–282.

Szelag, E., Kowalska, J., Rymarczyk, K., & Pöppel, E. (1998). Temporal integration in a subjective accentuation task as a function of child cognitive development. *Neuroscience Letters, 257*, 69–72.

Szelag, E., Kowalska, J., Rymarczyk, K., & Pöppel, E. (2002). Duration processing in children as determined by time reproduction: Implications for a few seconds temporal window. *Acta Psychologica, 110*, 1–19.

Szelag, E., von Steinbüchel, N., & Pöppel, E. (1997). Temporal processing disorders in patients with Broca's aphasia. *Neuroscience Letters, 235*, 33-36.

Szentágothai, J., & Arbib, M. A. (1974). Conceptual models of neural organization. *Neurosciences Research Program Bulletin, 12*, 307–510.

Szymaszek, A., Szelag, E., & Sliwowska, M. (2006). Auditory perception of temporal order in humans: The effect of age, gender, listener practice and stimulus presentation mode. *Neuroscience Letters, 403*, 190–194.

Takano, K., & Miyake, Y. (2007). Two types of phase correction mechanism involved in synchronized tapping. *Neuroscience Letters, 417*, 196–200.

Tanida, K., & Pöppel, E. (2006). A hierarchical model of operational anticipation windows in driving an automobile. *Cognitive Processing, 7*, 275–287.

Turner, F., & Pöppel, E. (1988). Metered poetry, the brain, and time. In I. Rentschler, B. Herzberger, & D. Epstein (Eds.), *Beauty and the brain: Biological aspects of aesthetics* (pp. 71–90). Basel, Switzerland: Birkhäuser.

Vollrath, M., Kazenwadel, J., & Krüger, H.-P. (1992). A universal constant in temporal segmentation of human speech. *Naturwissenschaften, 79*, 479–480.

von Holst, E., & Mittelstaedt, H. (1950). Das Reafferenzprinzip [The reafference principle]. *Naturwissenschaften, 37*, 464–476.

Wada, M., Moizumi, S., & Kitazawa, S. (2005). Temporal order judgment in mice. *Behavioural Brain Research, 157*, 167–175.

Wittmann, M., Burtscher, A., Fries, W., & von Steinbüchel, N. (2004). Effects of brain lesion size and location on temporal-order judgment. *NeuroReport, 15*, 2401–2405.

Zhou, B. (2008). Disentangling perceptual and motor components in inhibition of return. *Cognitive Processing 9*, 175–187.

# PART II

# Nourishment of Personality
## *Information and External Conditions*

# CHAPTER 5

# Time and Cognition from the Aging Brain Perspective
## Individual Differences

Elzbieta Szelag
Joanna Dreszer
Monika Lewandowska
Justyna Medygral
Grzegorz Osinski
Aneta Szymaszek

## INTRODUCTION

Numerous publications and research projects in cognitive psychology are attempting to study the human mind in order to better understand the mental space and individual cognition that contribute significantly to our personal identity.

In recent decades the public interest in aging has grown with the huge population of people aged 60 and older in most European countries and the United States. Public interest in aging has risen along with the increased proportions of elderly people under these unique contemporary demographic conditions. According to the current demographic data (Park & Schwartz, 1999), instead of a typical population pyramid (i.e., more members of younger age groups and progressively few members of older groups), the age distribution is becoming "rectangularized" (i.e., equal proportions of people at each decade from birth through

*Personality from Biological, Cognitive, and Social Perspectives* edited by Tomasz Maruszewski, Małgorzata Fajkowska, and Michael W. Eysenck. Eliot Werner Publications, Clinton Corners, New York, 2010.

age 70). Because of the expanding population of seniors worldwide, the topic of cognitive functioning among the elderly has become increasingly important to individuals and scientists. Such interest has led to a profound development in research devoted to improving life expectancy, as well as to reducing limitations on the quality of life in old age. Much of the rationale for this research suggests that with the increasing number of the elderly in society, more individuals will probably exhibit cognitive deficits.

Although it is difficult to pinpoint the precise moment at which cognitive functioning begins to decline, a large body of experimental data and everyday observations have clearly demonstrated that cognitive deterioration occurs in memory, new learning ability, motor control, perception, attention, thinking, problem solving, decision making, or concept formation (see Park & Schwarz, 1999, for a review). Aging is therefore a complex subject in modern neuroscience, which can help explain neuronal processes and mechanisms associated with cognitive declines.

This chapter is designed to provide an overview of some aspects of age-related deterioration in cognition across the life span from 20 to 70 years of age. To that end we review cognitive declines reported in the existing literature as well as evidenced in experimental studies conducted in our laboratory using standardized batteries of neuropsychological tests. Next we discuss hypothetical neural processes and mechanisms underlying these cognitive changes. At that point we concentrate predominantly on slowed mental processing speed, deficits in working memory function, inhibitory processes, and deficient sensory function. The literature findings on the neural basis of cognitive aging are illustrated with our own findings on temporal information processing in different time domains (e.g., some tens or hundreds of milliseconds). Finally, we provide empirical evidence on individual differences in intellectual functioning that clearly shows that temporal processing may be considered a predictor of psychometric intelligence.

We explore the view that cognitive functioning across the adult life span is governed by temporal information processing and that such processing differs for younger and older adults. This chapter argues that specific timing mechanisms may be crucial for these age-related cognitive declines.

## AGE-RELATED DECLINES IN COGNITIVE FUNCTIONING

Both existing age-related stereotypes and scientific evidence have documented apparent limitations in processing capacity or resources, indicating that mental processes become less efficient in elderly people (Metcalfe, 1998; Salthouse, 1996, 1999).

Before presenting our data concerning the different aspects of cognitive changes, we provide a short overview of findings from the existing literature on cognitive aging, followed by a discussion of the neural mechanisms that may underlie this deterioration.

## Summary of the Existing Literature on Some Aspects of Age-Related Cognitive Declines

Research focusing on the aging brain has recently been addressed in many books and review articles (Birren & Schaie, 2001; Craik & Salthouse, 1992; Hasher & Zacks, 1988; Luo & Craik, 2008; Park & Schwarz, 1999). While a detailed discussion on the depth and breadth of these issues is beyond the scope of this chapter, our goal is to emphasize certain predominant changes in brain neuroanatomy and cognition typically associated with temporal mechanisms underlying cognitive aging. Empirical verification of common facts related to both neuroanatomical and neuropsychological studies devoted to normal aging constitutes a challenging topic in contemporary neuroscience. From a neuroanatomical point of view, aging may be defined as progressive changes in the brain tissue that underlie the behavioral and physiological impairments of many functions and eventually become fatal (Balcombe & Sinclair, 2001). The changes that occur without any serious neurological or systemic disorders are labeled in the literature as healthy aging or normal chronological aging.

In research on cognitive aging, it seems important to provide a definition of an "old" person. Some studies classify individuals as "old" at age 50, whereas others use age 60, 65, or even older. Traditionally many current demographic data, as well as experimental studies, have assumed 65 years as a boundary for old age. Thus the age typically associated with cognitive changes is above 65 years (Fitzgibbons & Gordon-Salant, 1998).

### Brain Changes

There is significant evidence on reduced size of the human brain with advancing age (see Lezak, Howieson, & Loring, 2004, for a review). The most pronounced changes occur in the area of the hippocampus, cerebellum, frontal (especially dorsolateral prefrontal cortex) and parietal lobes, thalamus, cerebellum, and corpus callosum (Lezak et al., 2004).

The brain achieves its maximum size at circa 20 years of age and then gradually shrinks. The more rapid rate of shrinkage process begins after age 55. Neuroimaging data show that this process results primarily from changes in the structure of neurons. It is generally agreed that the number of cells in the aging brain does not actually decrease; rather, it is their size that shrinks because of the subsiding of water. These processes can also be accompanied by a concomitant reduction in the number of synapses, which leads to reduced neurotransmission. On the other hand, more cerebrospinal fluid in the nervous system causes increased ventricular size as well as increasingly widened sulci, narrowed gyri, and thinning of the cortical mantle (Metcalfe, 1998). Recent studies suggest that the global number of neurons remains at a relatively stable level across the life span. Although we lose approximately 100,000 neurons per day, this constitutes only a small percentage of neurons in the human brain (Lezak, 1995).

*Cognitive Changes*

Cognitive aging (i.e., normal chronological aging) is defined as age-related changes in cognitive functioning—for example, lower fluid intelligence, poorer memory or attention function, and slower performance rate on many mental and motor tasks (e.g., Birren & Schaie, 2001; Engle, Sedek, von Hecker, & McIntosh, 2005; Park & Schwarz, 1999). The slowing of mental processes may be associated with damage to white matter structures (myelinated nerve fibers), which is often reported in elderly people (Birren & Fisher, 1995). However, both measures of general knowledge and crystallized intelligence seem to be stable across the life span (Park, 1999).

There is a significant body of evidence on age-related declines in memory function (Burke & MacKay, 1997; Park & Schwarz, 1999) that are likely related to changes in the volume of the hippocampus (Tisserand & Jolles, 2003). Since memory is not a single function, it may be described in terms of different systems that show differentiated age-related effects. It should be noted, however, that not all types of memory are disordered in advancing age (Burke & MacKay, 1997; Craik, 1999; Luo & Craik, 2008). For example, working memory, episodic memory, and prospective memory are often distinctively disturbed as a result of normal aging. Certain older adults exhibit major declines in episodic (context-dependent) memory, performing more poorly on various laboratory tests that involve episodic recall and recognition of exposed verbal or nonverbal material (Burke & MacKay, 1997). A consistent finding is that the search time per item and the duration of encoding or response phases are usually longer for elderly individuals than for younger ones (Madden, 2001). The age-related decline in episodic memory applies to new or recent events, but not to events experienced in the more distant past (i.e., at a younger age). Older adults typically demonstrate deficits in remembering the context for the specific events. For example, in laboratory experiments they are able to recognize presented stimuli, but may have difficulties identifying their modality (Lehman & Mellinger, 1984).

On the other hand, semantic (context-independent) or procedural memory are stable across the life span. These two types of memory probably require less mental effort and are relatively well preserved (Luo & Craik, 2008). In addition, memory performance involving well-trained skills or familiar information is relatively well preserved (Burke & MacKay, 1997; Park, 1999).

To summarize, older people often show deficits in memory tasks that require self-initiated, effortful processing, but not in tasks based on familiar, well-known material containing more automatic processing.

In addition to these declines, age-related deterioration in attention function has recently been reported (Hartley, 1992; McDowd & Shaw, 2000; Rogers & Fisk, 2001). Indeed, attention function is a fundamental processing component of every perceptual or memory task (McDowd & Shaw, 2000). It should be noted that attention is also not merely a single function, but rather comprises several aspects such as selectivity, alertness, and divided attention—which may be impaired in older people (Fozard, Vercryssen, Reynolds, Hancock, & Quilter,

1994; Klein, Fischer, Harnegg, Heiss, & Roth, 2000). It seems important to mention that experiments on attention often involve the speed of information processing. Several authors have reported that reaction time may be affected in elderly individuals, especially in tasks involving a number of irrelevant items (distractors) on display. By contrast, the use of spatial cues to improve reaction times seems age-invariant. Using reaction time measures, age-related declines in inhibitory functioning have been widely found. Longer response time associated with the application of distractors was interpreted as an indicator of less efficient inhibition of the distractors in older adults.

Additionally, several findings have suggested age-related deterioration in vision and hearing, motor control, or some aspects of language comprehension (Birren & Schaie, 2001; Park & Schwarz, 1999).

Although the majority of experimental data predominantly focused on declines associated with aging, some authors stressed not only losses, but also gains that may occur when we get older. These gains may involve an increase in wisdom, knowledge, and experience, which can be useful in solving complex moral and social problems as well as life dilemmas (Baltes & Staudinger, 1993). Thus when considering the mental status of older people, the interplay of "losses" and "gains" should always be taken into account.

## Examples of Age-Related Declines from Our Studies

During the last few years, we have undertaken a research project focusing on broad aspects of cognitive declines associated with advancing age. In these studies we compared the performance of young ($N = 20$, aged 20–29 years) and elderly ($N = 26$, aged 64–78 years) subjects. All the subjects were right-handed and had no history of any neurological deficits, psychiatric disorders, or systemic diseases. Both age groups comprised relatively healthy subjects.

*Procedures and Materials*
Cognitive functions were assessed using standardized batteries of tests. We used the Cambridge Neuropsychological Test Automated Battery (CANTABeclipse; Cambridge Cognition, 2005a, 2005b) to assess new learning abilities (Paired Associates Learning test, PAL) and memory function (Delayed Matching to Sample test, DMS). Attentional resources were assessed using the Test for Attentional Performance (TAP; Zimmermann & Fimm, 1997). Two aspects of attention were assessed: (a) alertness and (b) divided attention. All these research tools are briefly summarized below.

CANTABeclipse (Cambridge Cognition, 2005a, 2005b) is the renowned battery containing a number of language-independent tests. It comprises nineteen tests designed for the assessment of different aspects of human cognition: visual memory, new learning ability, executive functions, working memory, attention, and planning. It facilitates assessment of cognitive functions in healthy subjects, as well as in various clinical patient groups. Although the battery is fully computerized, elderly people find the touch-screen and press-pad technology comfortable in testing. A detailed description of this battery, as well as the administration of particular tests, appears in the CANTABeclipse test administration guide (Cambridge Cognition, 2005b). The worldwide use of these tests during the last few years enabled us to collect a normative database for particular cognitive functions that allows for comparison of a single case at a given age to normative data for this age group. However, to assess cognitive declines across the life span, group comparisons are necessary. In this chapter we concentrate on the Paired Associates Learning and Delayed Matching to Sample tests because they seem to be sensitive to neurodegenerative changes associated with cortical dementia. However, existing evidence on age-related deterioration in these measurements of normal aging is rather limited in the literature.

*Paired Associates Learning*
The PAL paradigm was originally developed to assess memory in monkeys and it required the animals to remember the spatial location of hidden objects (Mishkin & Pribram, 1956). This task was subsequently adapted for use in humans (Smith & Milner, 1981). A computerized analog of this test was developed as a part of the CANTAB (Morris, Evenden, Sahakian, & Robbins, 1987). It involves the ability to associate the stimulus ("what") with its spatial location ("where"; Fowler, Saling, Conway, Semple, & Louis, 2002). There is some evidence that the most important role in this association may be played by structures of the medial temporal lobes (Maguire, Frith, Burgess, Donnett, & O'Keefe, 1998). The CANTAB paired associate paradigm taps aspects of memory function, which represents the fundamental function of the hippocampal system (Burgess, Jeffrey, & O'Keefe, 1999).

In recent years the PAL has received increasing attention among scientists as a reliable neuropsychological tool for the early detection of Alzheimer's disease (AD; O'Connell et al., 2004). It may also be predictive in differential diagnosis between mild AD, depression, and normal controls (Swainson et al., 2001). Furthermore, the PAL may predict the degree of cognitive declines better than standard neuropsychological memory tests (Fowler et al., 2002; Swainson et al., 2001).

In the PAL test, the subject is required to remember a spatial location of different patterns (from 1 to 8) on a computer screen (Figure 1). Accordingly, six white boxes appear for three seconds on the screen and start to open in random order. First only one pattern in one box is shown. After opening all the boxes, this pattern is displayed in the center of the screen and the subject is required to indicate (by touching the screen) the box in which the pattern was located before. If the subject touches the correct box, the next trial with another single pattern is displayed. If the subject marks a wrong box, the trial is repeated until the correct choice is made (up to maximum of ten times). After two correct responses with one pattern, two patterns are presented and the proper boxes should be indicated again. If the subject cannot mark the correct localization of all presented patterns in ten consecutive trials, the test is terminated (Cambridge Cognition, 2005b; Fowler et al., 2002).

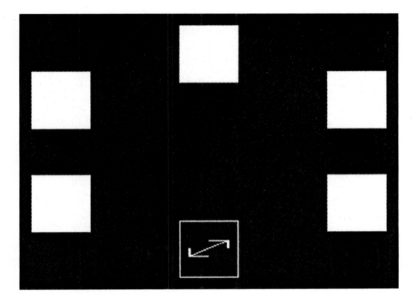

**Figure 1.** An example of an experimental situation in PAL.

### Delayed Matching to Sample

The DMS was designed to test simultaneous and delayed matching to sample. The test is sensitive to damage in the medial temporal lobes with some input from the frontal lobes (Cambridge Cognition, 2005b). The subject is presented with a visual pattern (a sample) and then four patterns are presented below on the screen (Figure 2). One of them is identical to the sample, whereas the other three are different (Fowler, Saling, Conway, Semple, & Louis, 1995). The subject's task is to match the identical pattern (by touching the screen). In some trials both the sample and four-choice patterns are presented simultaneously; in the other trials, the four-choice patterns are presented with a delay of 0 seconds (consecutively) or 4 seconds and 12 seconds. The number of correct responses at the longest 12-second delay condition is the most likely to be sensitive to hippocampal dysfunction (Fowler et al., 1995). If the first choice is incorrect, the subject is requested to match again until the correct choice is made (Cambridge Cognition, 2005b). Both the percent and number of correct responses are analyzed.

### Alertness of Attention

Alertness (Zimmermann & Fimm, 1997) is defined as the ability to raise and maintain a high level of attention in anticipation of a test stimulus. The subject is asked to press a key as quickly as possible when a visual stimulus (white cross) appears on the screen. This task is conducted two ways, with and without an auditory warning signal that cues the occurrence of visual stimulus.

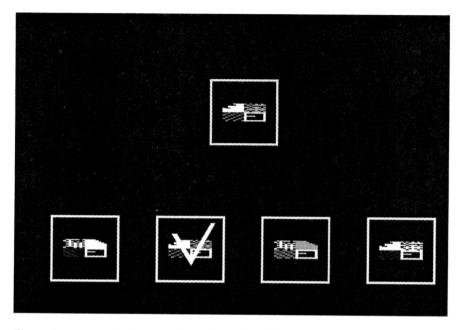

**Figure 2.** An example of an experimental situation in DMS.

The simple reaction time, as well as the difference in reaction time between cued (forty trial runs) and uncued (another forty trial runs), are analyzed. According to TAP guidelines, the simple reaction time has been shown to be a valid measure of general slowness (Zimmermann & Fimm, 1997). The difference in reaction time between cued and uncued runs constitutes an index of the phasic alertness response.

### Divided Attention

Divided attention (Zimmermann & Fimm, 1997) is defined as the ability to attend to more than one task at a given time. The divided attention performance is investigated by dual-tasks for both visual and acoustic modality. In the visual task, crosses appear in a random configuration on 4 x 4 matrix. The subject is asked to detect whether four crosses presented on the matrix form the corners of a square. The acoustic task includes a regular sequence of high and low tones presented in a sequence. The subject is required to press a button when the same tone occurs twice in a row. The mean reaction time, as well as the number of correct and incorrect responses (e.g., missed signals, false positives), are analyzed.

In our study all subjects followed the same procedure consisting of the PAL and then the DMS from the CANTABeclipse. Next two attention tests (i.e., Alertness and Divided Attention) from the Test for Attentional Performance were administered.

*Results*

The group comparison for performance of young versus elderly adults indicated significantly declining PAL results with advancing age (Figure 3). It should be noted that elderly people were still able to successfully complete the test, but their performance was poorer than that of young people. Elderly groups obtained poorer results at almost all PAL variables. They committed about 35 total errors, whereas young adults only committed approximately 12 errors. Furthermore, in comparison with the young subjects, elderly subjects needed more trials to complete the PAL; thus they performed fewer stages during measurement. Similarly, the performance on the DMS was significantly poorer in elderly than in young people (Figure 4). Elderly individuals correctly matched fewer patterns and committed more errors for the longest 12-second delay condition. To summarize, a deterioration in both new learning abilities and visual memory was evidenced in our studies.

★ $p < 0.05$

**Figure 3.** The mean number of errors and trials (with standard deviations) in PAL in young versus elderly adults.

Age-related deterioration was also found for some aspects of attention. For alertness, elderly subjects showed longer mean reaction time compared to young subjects, both in trials with and without the warning signal. Moreover, elderly subjects committed more omissions than younger ones and had higher differences in reaction time between cued and uncued conditions, as well as making more errors (false positives). For the Divided Attention Task, elderly participants showed increased mean reaction time compared with young individuals (Figure 5).

These results showed declining attentional resources in the elderly in terms of (a) general slowness, (b) lower competency to raise and maintain a high level of attention, and (c) difficulties in devoting attention to more than one task at the

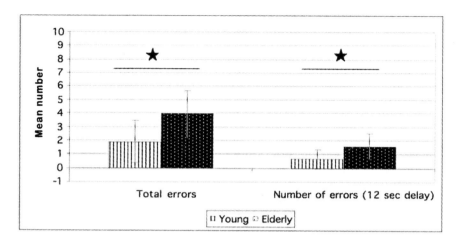

★ *p* < 0.05

**Figure 4.** The mean number of errors (with standard deviations) in DMS in young versus elderly adults.

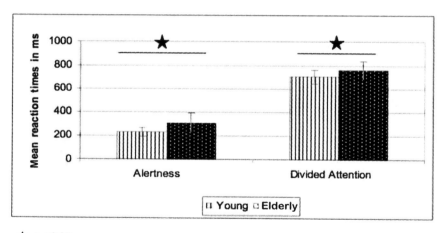

★ *p* < 0.05

**Figure 5.** The mean reaction times (with standard deviations) for Alertness and Divided Attention in young versus elderly adults.

same time. In general, our data are consistent with results reported by other authors and provides further evidence of significant declines in associative learning, visual memory, and attention resources in individuals above the age of 65.

Although age-related declines are already well documented in the existing literature and further supported by our results presented above, very little is actually known about the neural mechanisms underlying these now familiar losses.

The key question that should be answered at this point is whether human mental activity has a common element (or elements) that is crucial for processing resources.

## NEURAL MECHANISMS OF COGNITIVE AGING

One of the major challenges in cognitive aging research is to understand neural mechanisms underlying age-related declines. The existing literature indicates that there are some common conceptual premises. Several different mechanisms have been hypothesized to underlie cognitive aging—that is, slower speed at which incoming information is processed, poorer working memory, inhibitory processes, and poorer sensory function (Park, 1999). Each of these mechanisms may be conceptualized as a defined single measure of cognitive functioning; however, several authors have postulated that a combination of (or interplay between) these mechanisms may better reflect age-related deterioration than any single, separate mechanism (Salthouse, 1996). Additionally, a substantial quantity of data suggests that age-related deterioration is observed in broad aspects of cognitive functioning, including attention, memory, problem solving, and speed of information processing—all of which can be related to interplay between these mechanisms.

With respect to our consideration of age-related deterioration in temporal processing, in this chapter we concentrate on the first two mechanisms mentioned above (i.e., declines in the speed of information processing and working memory) because their association with timing is relatively well documented in the existing studies. We also provide a brief overview of the other mechanisms, both inhibitory processes and poorer sensory function.

### Slowed Mental Processing Speed

This theory was developed by Salthouse (1991, 1996), who postulated declines in a single fundamental measure underlying all subsequent mental functions. His theory was based on earlier work by Birren (1965) and others and concentrated on the decreased speed of information processing, resulting in reduction of the speed of mental operations executed. Such slowness is observed in nearly every kind of perceptual or motor task and has been identified as the earliest and most pronounced symptom of cognitive aging.

This slowing theory points to two different mechanisms that may underlie deteriorated speed of mental operations: (a) the limited time mechanism and (b) the simultaneity mechanism. The former assumes restricted time for processing of earlier information when the next new information is delivered. As a result, cognitive performance is degraded because relevant operations cannot be successfully executed (limited time; Salthouse, 1996).

In the case of the latter mechanism, the products of information processing may be lost before the processing is completed. As a consequence, the products of early processing may no longer be available when later processing is completed (simultaneous time). The slowed processing speed in elderly people causes difficulties in reaching later stages of information processing or, in other words, in the completion of complex mental operations. Accordingly, the most pronounced differences between the performance of young and elderly adults were visible in difficult mental tasks, engaging complex mental operations that have to be processed within a limited period of time.

## Deficits in Working Memory Function

Another important framework was proposed by Craik and Byrd (1982), who associated age-related declines in mental operations with working memory deterioration.

Accordingly, working memory was defined as "the amount of on-line cognitive resources available at any given moment to process information, and can involve storage, retrieval and transformation of information" (Park, 1999, p. 10). As postulated by Baddeley's (1986) model, working memory can be considered the total amount of "mental energy" required to perform online mental operations.

The declining working memory hypothesis is supported by substantial experimental comparative data on this cognitive function in young and elderly adults (see Baddeley, 2007; Park & Schwarz, 1999, for a review). These studies used procedures in which it was critically important to keep in the subject's mind a high working memory load associated with presented material.

The decline in working memory capacity in elderly individuals can also be reflected in everyday observations, suggesting that for elderly people it usually seems easier when the memory load of either instructions given or processed information is as low as possible. Therefore some environmental supports that can result in improved remembering (e.g., various memory cues or written information) are very important for elderly people.

## Inhibitory Processes

According to some theories, inhibitory mechanisms are important and fundamental to understanding cognitive aging. Hasher and Zacks (1988) postulated that age-related declines in cognitive functioning may result from reduced ability of the elderly to focus attention on primary target information because they diffuse attention between relevant and irrelevant material. Inefficient inhibitory function during processing of incoming information may be a neural basis of deteriorated cognition. Because of inefficient inhibition, irrelevant information enters working memory; moreover, the maintenance of irrelevant information affects subsequent cognitive performance.

The inhibitory hypothesis finds its support in existing aging stereotypes and many everyday situations. The elderly seem to be more susceptible to distraction when they are presented multiple sources of information—for example, during multiple conversations at a party when it is necessary to pay attention to more than one speaker. Reduced inhibition may be also demonstrated in poorer mental control of many social situations. For instance, older adults are more likely to speak their minds or are unable to inhibit inappropriate reactions in social interactions.

## Deficits in Sensory Function

The impairments in sensory function, especially in vision and hearing, are commonly reported in older adults. These deficits may often lead to difficulties in daily activity (functional impairment) and occupational and social functioning and reduced independence in daily life. Although sensory impairments do not affect cognitive functioning per se, in neuropsychological diagnosis it is essential to take into account whether degraded specific modality function could account for some (or all) deficits in cognition.

### Vision
Visual deficits affect a large population of elderly people. Most 70-year-old individuals display poorer vision and only 10% of healthy 80-year-olds have correct vision. The deficits comprise visual acuity loss, stereopsis (binocular vision), slow dark adaptation, decreased scanning efficiency, macular degradation, glaucoma, cataracts, and so forth (Lezak, 1995). They may cause visual loss or visual misperception, which may lead to social isolation or dependence on others in daily life.

### Hearing
Auditory deficits parallel those of vision and are commonly reported in the elderly. Worsened hearing comprises degraded auditory acuity at a level that contradicts processing a typical conversation, peripheral hearing loss (pure tone hearing loss), or central auditory dysfunction. Auditory acuity rapidly decreases between the ages of 50 and 60 and approximately 70% of 70-year-olds suffer some hearing loss. Initially high frequencies alone are affected, which causes increasing difficulty in auditory speech comprehension (difficulties in reception of high-frequency phonemes like /s/, /z/, /c/, etc.).

# HYPOTHESES ON CONTENT-RELATED VERSUS LOGISTIC-RELATED COGNITIVE FUNCTIONING

Neuroimaging methods in studies of cognitive functioning (such as functional magnetic resonance imaging, positron emission tomography, single photon emission computed tomography, electroencephalography, or magnetoencephalography) have been particularly important in cognitive psychology. They have led to several findings on neuroanatomical substrates associated with cognitive declines. Despite abundant evidence on the spatial separation of cognitive functioning in various brain areas (the neuroanatomical basis of recent neuroimaging and clinical data), most neuroscientists endorse the view that complex cognitive functioning has no strict localization, but rather is represented in many brain areas (Frackowiak et al., 2003; Schlösser, Wagner, & Sauer, 2006). Accordingly, the complex functions are reflected by integrative actions of distributed neuronal modules and thus by integrative brain activity (Konorski, 1967). Such distribution of modules that form complex functions encourages inquiry into mechanisms that might possibly link neuronal information from one area to another in such a way that integrated percepts or acts are possible. Current research has suggested that one of the characteristic features of human behavior is temporal information processing. On the basis of substantial experimental data and everyday observations, we might assume that many aspects of human functioning may derive—at least in part—from timing, which constitutes an essential component of memory, language, attention, perception, actions, and decision making (Pöppel, 1978, 1994, 2004; Szymaszek, Sereda, Pöppel, & Szelag, 2009).

Neuropsychological and psychophysiological evidence suggest that timing is not a continuous process, but can more accurately be characterized by different processing systems that employ discrete time sampling in some tens or hundreds of milliseconds, as well as in a few seconds (Pöppel, 1994, 1997, 2004; Szelag, 1997; Szelag, Kanabus, Kolodziejczyk, Kowalska, & Szuchnik, 2004; Szelag & Pöppel, 2000; Szelag, von Steinbüchel, Reiser, de Langen, & Pöppel, 1996; Wittmann, 1999). Accordingly, different "time windows" or "temporal domains" provide different processing platforms crucial for our mental activity.

On the basis of these data, von Steinbüchel and Pöppel (1993) distinguished two classes of functions. According to this classification, one class is responsible for the content of our subjective experiences ("what") and can be responsible for "content-related" processing (e.g., language, memory, actions). The other class can create the logistic prerequisite for our content representation ("how") and thus can constitute "logistic-related" functions, creating a logistical basis for our mental operations. Considering the omnipresence of temporal information processing in our mental activity, we can assume that timing constitutes an example of so-called logistic-related functions.

## AGE-RELATED DIFFERENCES IN TEMPORAL INFORMATION PROCESSING

Although recent studies clearly showed poorer cognitive functioning in elderly people, little is truly known with regard to age-related declines in timing, which provides an essential frame of human cognition (Park & Schwarz, 1999; Pöppel, 1994; Szymaszek et al., in press). Some important findings on declining temporal processing in elderly individuals (aged 65–75) in comparison with younger ones (aged 18–40) were provided by Fitzgibbons and Gordon-Salant (1998) and Gordon-Salant and Fitzgibbons (1999). Their research demonstrated deteriorated sequential abilities in perception of temporal order for three-tone sequences. These declines were primarily observed in more difficult experimental tasks associated with some experimental uncertainty. Deteriorated sequential abilities associated with advancing age were also confirmed in experiments with two-stimuli sequence (Fink, Churan, & Wittmann, 2005; Fink, Ulbrich, Churan, & Wittmann, 2006; Kolodziejczyk & Szelag, 2008; Szymaszek et al., 2009; Szymaszek, Szelag, & Sliwowska, 2006). However, relatively little is known about the age at which the perception of temporal order starts to decline, how it might be related to a cognitive decline, or whether there might be any cross-linguistic differences on age-related deterioration. To answer these questions, we compared temporal perception in Polish and German subjects using an identical experimental procedure.

In our study we identified 168 adult subjects between 20 and 69 years of age (86 Polish and 82 German) divided into five age groups (20–29, 30–39, 40–49, 50–59, 60–69 years). The subjects were either Polish or German native speakers who were free of any history of neurological or psychiatric disorders and past head injuries. The age groups were balanced with respect to gender and level of education. All subjects were right-handed and had normal hearing levels, as evidenced by screening audiometry.

We focused on the temporal order threshold paradigm. In such an experimental setting, subjects were asked to reproduce the order of two clicks presented monaurally in rapid succession with short interstimulus intervals. The temporal order threshold, defined as the shortest time interval at which the temporal order of these stimuli was reported correctly, was analyzed and the results are presented below.

The cross-linguistic comparison revealed a lack of any significant differences between Polish and German subjects in the perception of temporal order. This suggests that the phonological aspects of these two languages have no influence on temporal order perception. There was evidence, however, that temporal order threshold values were influenced by age and cognitive abilities.

A clear pattern of age-related declines was revealed in both the Polish and German subjects. The threshold values remain on a relatively constant level (all differences between particular age groups were nonsignificant) in subjects between 20 and 59 years old.

A significant deterioration in temporal order perception was found in subjects over the age of 59. This age-effect was strongly related to subjects' cognitive abilities. The partial correlation analysis revealed the involvement of intellectual (Mosaik Test, 1991) and attentional resources (Zimmermann & Fimm, 1997) in the performance level on both temporal tasks. Older subjects with higher fluid intelligence level and better alertness level performed temporal tasks more effectively than participants with lower levels of these cognitive abilities. Thus the deterioration in temporal ordering paralleled the decline in intellectual and attentional resources. The results of our study indicate that time perception is not particularly related to subjects' chronological age, but to the level of their intellectual or attentional resources. In other words, elderly individuals above the age of 60 with relatively well-preserved cognitive functioning showed less deteriorated timing than those more declined on these two functions. These results shed a new light on the relationship between age and timing, focusing on the dissociation between chronological age and mental activity.

This relationship was confirmed in our subsequent study conducted exclusively on Polish subjects ($N = 86$) who were divided into five age groups (20–29, 30–39, 40–49, 50–59, 60–69 years). Two different timing tasks were administered. The subjects reported the temporal order of either two clicks presented monaurally or of two tones of different frequencies (400 Hz and 3000 Hz) presented binaurally. Two stimuli (clicks or tones) were presented in rapid succession and subjects were asked to report the order in which they were presented.

In the assessment of cognitive functioning, we concentrated on intellectual (Mosaik Test, 1991) and attentional resources (Zimmermann & Fimm, 1997). Two aspects of attention were considered—alertness (see above) and vigilance, defined as an ability to maintain attention over a long time period. In the vigilance assessment, two tones of different frequencies were presented sequentially and subjects were asked to press a button when two identical tones were presented consecutively.

The results obtained indicated two different patterns of age-related deterioration in temporal processing, depending on the stimulus presentation mode. In the monaural mode (clicks), the pattern of age-related differences was similar to the one reported for the Polish-German baseline comparisons. We observed a relatively stable threshold level until the age of 59; then considerable deterioration was observed beyond 60 years of age. By contrast, the binaural mode (tones) declines were actually found earlier, starting at 40 years of age and progressively deteriorating with advancing age. This dissociation in age-related deterioration in timing may be explained by referring to different neural processes and mechanisms underlying temporal processing in these two tasks. They involved the interplay of both temporal processing and mode-specific nontemporal processing. While the monaural task perhaps provided more insights into the internal timing mechanism, the binaural mode may reflect, by contrast, an auditory streaming and frequency modulation phenomenon. Accordingly, despite the presentation of two tones, subjects' performance on the binaural task was based on one frequency-modulated pattern—either "low-to-high" ("up" direction) or "high-to-low" ("down" direction)—without any temporal separation of sequential elements within a stream. It is probably easier for subjects to judge the order of the presented stimuli; thus the integration of events into one auditory stream may result in significantly lower threshold values (better performance) in the binaural task.

A novel result of this study was a divergent pattern of age-related influences of cognitive functioning on temporal processing depending on the stimulus presentation mode. Although we found important declines in intellectual abilities, alertness, and vigilance in the subjects studied here, the important influences of these resources were revealed only on the performance of the monaural task and only weakly affected the performance of the binaural task. These two different patterns of age-related declines in sequencing abilities support the idea that in addition to temporal processing, temporal tasks also involve the mode-specific processing involving different neural processes and mechanism.

To conclude, the direct comparison of two presentation modes provides new insight into timing mechanisms. Accordingly, temporal processing was strongly influenced by the context of information processed; thus it probably was not governed by a single timing mechanism, free of any procedure-related nontemporal factors. The main finding of our study on temporal order threshold is a relationship between timing and cognition. Since temporal constraints are crucial for many aspects of human cognitive functioning (e.g., perception, memory, motor control, decision making), our findings suggest that attentional and intellectual resources under specific experimental conditions may contribute to time perception (Szymaszek et al., 2009).

Age-related deterioration has been also reported in other studies from the literature using different paradigms related to milliseconds time range—for example, fusion threshold (Chisolm, Willott, & Lister, 2003; Lister & Roberts, 2005; Tun & Lachman, 2008), inspection time (Gregory, Nettelbeck, Howard, & Wilson, 2008; Nettelbeck, & Rabbitt, 1992), duration judgment (Block, Zakay, & Hancock, 1998), or simple reaction time (Fozard et al., 1994; Inui, 1997; Ratcliff, Thapar, & McKoon, 2001).

On one hand, the existing studies may be related not only to deteriorated timing, but also to other critical nontemporal processes—for example, detection of a target stimulus (compare above sensory deficits), decision making at which moment to press a button, preparation for a motor reaction to press a button, or performance of a given motor action. Because of these complex influences, the parallel deterioration in simple reaction time and sequencing abilities is not a rule in existing aging studies. On the other hand, many reaction time experiments showed evidence for the common mechanisms underlying these paradigms. They may involve an internal clock perspective or other cognitive processes strongly related to timing (i.e., attentional resources or working memory). Such a hypothesis may be supported by our data, which showed declining alertness or divided attention in advancing age (compare above). On the basis of these data, it would be difficult to dissociate between timing and attention, since both these functions may have a common biological origin based on neuronal oscillatory activity (e.g., dynamic attending theory; Jones, 1976; Large & Jones, 1999). We argue, however, that temporal pattering acuity may constitute a very basic process crucial for mental functioning.

Support comes from some literature indications suggesting that training in timing improves some aspects of cognition—for example, language abilities (Merzenich et al., 1996; Szelag, 2005; Tallal et al., 1996). Further studies are needed to investigate whether training in timing can also improve the broader aspects of cognition. Studies on this question were recently conducted in our laboratory. The preliminary data might suggest a transfer from time domain not only to language domain, but also to learning abilities and attention.

## TIMING AS A PEDICTOR OF PSYCHOMETRIC INTELLIGENCE

There are converging indications that age-related declines in temporal processing may be related to declining intelligence and cognitive abilities that are often reported in elderly people (Engle et al., 2005).

Such observations encouraged us to study associations between timing and individual differences in intelligence levels, and to consider whether timing can constitute a predictor of psychometric intelligence (Rammsayer & Brandler, 2002, 2007). This led us to inquire if there might be observable differences in temporal processing between superior-intelligent individuals (SIIs) and average-intelligent individuals (AIIs).

In the existing literature, intelligence has several meanings depending on the context in which this term is used (Stankov, 2005, Sternberg, 2000). In neuroscience it is often referred to as Spearman's $g$ factor (Spearman, 1904; Toga & Thompson, 2005). According to John Carroll's (1993) suggestion, the $g$ factor is substantially associated with the speed of information processing, which can be assessed with psychometric tests as well as so-called elementary cognitive tasks (ECTs; e.g., reaction time, inspection time). In the mental speed paradigm, processing speed was considered as an important indicator of intelligence level (Danthiir, Roberts, Schulze, & Wilhelm, 2005; Eysenck, 1987; Jensen, 2006). Jensen (2006) also showed that the $g$ factor is a good predictor of intellectual giftedness in adolescents and may be an excellent criterion for differentiating between gifted and nongifted students. However, only two models were developed to explore potential neural mechanisms that may be associated with individual differences in the intelligence level: (a) the oscillator model (Jensen, 1998), which related superior intelligence to higher frequency of oscillations in the neuronal assemblies; and (b) the neural efficiency hypothesis (see Vernon, 1983, for a review), which considered possible biological substrates of a positive correlation between IQ and the speed of information processing. Compared with these findings, the results of many studies on mental speed are fragmentary, inconsistent, and often ambiguous (see Sternberg, 2000, for a review).

Meta-analyses concerning the relationships between intelligence and inspection time (one of the ECTs indicated above) have led to these conclusions (Grudnik & Kranzler, 2001; Petrill & Deary, 2001). An alternative suggestion is that individual differences in temporal sequencing of elementary cognitive processes are determined by neuronal mechanisms underlying timing—for example, an internal clock (Block, 1990; Fraisse, 1984; Gibbon, 1991; Ivry & Richardson, 2002; Pöppel, 1971, 1994, 2004; Pöppel & Logothetis, 1986). At this point temporal resolution in information processing may be responsible for individual differences in both psychometric intelligence and the level of performance on various ECTs (master clock: Surwillo, 1964; temporal resolution hypothesis: Rammsayer & Brandler, 2002, 2007).

In addition to these data, there are some indications in the literature that may provide indirect support for possible associations between intelligence and temporal processing. Such support comes from experiments on age-related cognitive slowing (Kolodziejczyk & Szelag, 2008; Surwillo, 1968; Vanneste, Pouthas, & Wearden, 2001), mental retardation (Kumai, 1999), or reading disorders (Tiffin-Richards, Hasselhorn, Richards, Banaschewski, & Rothenberger, 2004). At this point it should be stressed that a number of existing studies show associations between intelligence and millisecond timing behaviors (Helmbold & Rammsayer, 2006; Helmbold, Troche, & Rammsayer, 2007; Madison, Forsman, Blom, Karabanov, & Ullén, 2009). For example, Rammsayer and Brandler (2007) revealed that some temporal tasks can be linked to the "temporal $g$" factor and may constitute better predictors of psychometric intelligence than classical speed measures like reaction time. Similarly, Madison et al. (2009), using simple motor tasks such as synchronization-continuation tapping, found that variability in performance in this task constituted another good predictor of psychometric intelligence. Furthermore, in other studies they suggested the same neuroanatomical basis for both intelligence and timing (Ullén, Forsman, Blom, Karabanov, & Madison, 2008).

To explore possible associations between timing and superior intelligence, our studies aimed at investigating individual differences in temporal processing in superior-intelligent and average-intelligent individuals in two temporal domains: (a) some tens of milliseconds (using the temporal order threshold paradigm described above), and (b) some hundreds of milliseconds (using finger tapping). We assumed that intelligence may be defined as a dynamic process or a product of complex system coordination consisting of many elements, which could appear in nonlinear parameters of motor actions.

In our studies two groups of Polish adolescents aged 16–17 were investigated. Group 1 (SII) included 55 individuals (25 boys, 30 girls) recruited from the School for High Ability Students in Torun. Group 2 (AII) comprised 50 individuals (25 boys, 25 girls) from regular schools. Using the Polish-language version of the Wechsler Adult Intelligence Scale–Revised (Wechsler, 1981), the SII group comprised subjects above 130 IQ, whereas the AII group was drawn from adolescents with IQs of 100 to 115.

The Raven's Advanced Progressive Matrices (RAPM; Raven, 1958) were applied as an indicator of fluid reasoning in both groups. According to many authors, the RAPM is one of the best nonverbal tests for measuring "pure $g$" (Toga & Thomson, 2005). SIIs scored 26.43 points and AIIs 14.63 points on RAPM, conducted using a nonstandard time limit of twenty minutes (Frearson & Eysenck, 1986).

In temporal order judgment task, SIIs and AIIs reported the order of two tones presented in rapid succession (see above for details). More efficient performance (smaller number of errors) was observed in SIIs in comparison with AIIs (Figure 6).

Additionally, SII students displayed a higher resistance to the context of presented stimuli. Specifically, they committed fewer errors than AIIs in case of more differentiated interstimulus intervals in consecutive trials (e.g., switches from 30 to 300 ms). These findings support the notion not only of more efficient, but also more flexible performance in SIIs than in AIIs.

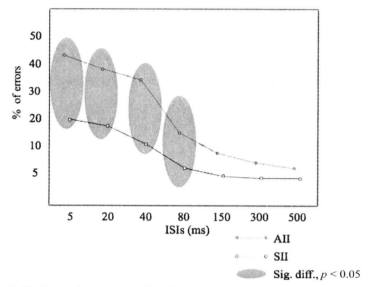

**Figure 6.** The level of performance in SII and AII in temporal order judgment task.

As presented above, sequencing abilities may be strongly associated with cognitive functioning. The relationship between intelligence and attention or working memory was evidenced in our previous studies (Szymaszek et al., 2009). These results are consistent with prior findings described in the literature that classic psychometric intelligence measures may be substituted by working memory measures (Kyllonen & Christal, 1990; Süβ, Oberauer, Wittmann, Wilhelm, & Schulze, 2002). Our results added a novel value to these indications, showing that the millisecond timing may be interpreted as a measure of sequencing ability that is strongly associated with the level of intelligence. Superior intelligence may be based on more efficient timing mechanisms.

Furthermore, in the other study we investigated the effect of intelligence on temporal processing in another time domain, some hundreds of milliseconds. This processing level is usually related to our motor activity—that is, planning and execution of movements. The paradigm of sequential repetitive movements (tapping) performed at the fastest (maximum) and the personally chosen (comfortable) tempo was applied in these studies (Wittmann, von Steinbüchel, & Szelag, 2001). The timing control of voluntary movements, performed at the personal tempo, is conceptualized as a good predictor of cognitive functioning; however, it is rarely described in the existing literature (see Danthiir et al., 2005, for a review). For example, according to Fraisse (1982), spontaneous motor tempo is related directly to the speed of information processing because it appears to be relatively free of any working memory influences (Baudouin, Vanneste, Isingrini, & Pouthas, 2006; Madison et al., 2009).

In our study subjects' performance at these two tapping tempos was analyzed. The results showed that SIIs performed significantly faster than AIIs at both maximum (mean interresponse intervals: 120 ms vs. 139 ms, respectively) and personal (183 vs. 280 ms, respectively) tempos.

Moreover, nonlinear elements for the reconstruction of dynamic properties (Glass, 2001; Higuchi, 1988; Swierkocka-Miastkowska & Osinski, 2007) of personal tapping showed the fractal properties in both SII and AII. Thus in both groups temporal dynamics of sequential movements were characterized by nonlinear structures in which complex patterns of performance associated with specific cycles of mental activity during preparation for consecutive movements were defined. The patterns of these cycles, however, had various structures in SII and AII. In the case of SII, this structure was more condensed (i.e., specific attractor points were easy to detect; Figure 7). By contrast, in AII these attractor points were more scattered. These results can be interpreted in terms of intelligence-related neural activity in motor control — that is, higher resistance in SII in preparation to a given motor action. On this basis we hypothesize (a) that the "internal clock system" determines timing and could have a fractal nature, and (b) that intellectual giftedness could be associated with better synchronization of neural processes controlling repetitive movements.

Return map plot is a display method of temporal structure characterizing obtained results. For each reconstructed attractor, it defined a "basin of attraction" (i.e., a specific region within the reconstructed attractor related to a given behavior). Then a topological structure of each region was calculated on the mean interresponse interval.

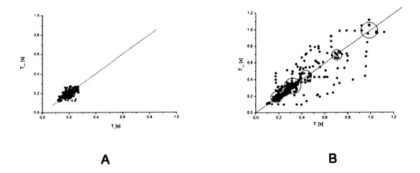

**A**                    **B**

**Figure 7.** Reconstruction of attractor with fractal properties in SII (A) and AII (B).

This method is based on the Kernel Density Estimation formula (Andelić, Schaffőner, Katz, Krüger, & Wendemuth, 2006; Higuchi, 1988):

$$T_{ave} = \frac{1}{n}\sum_{i=1}^{n} K\left(\frac{T - T_i}{\varepsilon}\right)$$

in which $n$ is the number of tapping points, $\varepsilon$ is the minimal value of nearest neighbors on a topology of return map plot reconstruction area strictly compared with delay time, and $K$ is the normalized Gauss distribution function.

## FINAL REMARKS AND OPEN QUESTIONS

The principal points of this overview may be simply summarized. On the basis of existing studies, the strong relationships between deteriorated timing and cognition can be observed. Thus timing should be considered as the logistic brain function that is crucial for other content-related functions, like memory, intelligence, motor control, decision making, or language. Another logistic function may constitute attention; thus distinguishing between timing and attention seems difficult since these two logistic functions may be governed by common neural mechanisms. These arguments lead us to conclude that age-related cognitive declines reported in content-related functions cannot be considered separately because of strong associations with the logistic basis of the brain.

Age-related declines in both cognitive functioning and timing discussed in this chapter reveal a number of key questions that need to be answered in future studies. From these issues we have derived questions regarding the possibility of improvement of cognition (in both elderly and young people) through the application of the specific training focused on improvements within the timing processes. As a result of convincing evidence presented in this chapter on the close relationships between timing and cognition, such training might focus on temporal information processing. This hypothesis needs to be empirically verified not only from a theoretical point of view, but also through the results of studies published in the existing literature (Merzenich et al., 1996; Szelag, 2005; Tallal et al., 1996; Wittmann & Fink, 2004).

On the basis of our ongoing projects, we can anticipate that advances in specific training affecting temporal information processing might be beneficial to both young and elderly individuals.

## Acknowledgments

These studies were supported by grants #PBZ–MIN/001/P05/06, #1082/P01/2006/31, #507N–DFG/2009, #WKP–1/1.4.3.1/2004/11/11/52/2005/U, #N–N402–434633, #N–N106–109636, and #1–H01F–094-30 from the Polish Ministry of Science and Higher Education, and the Fellowship START for Aneta Szymaszek from the Foundation for Polish Science. We wish to thank Ernst Pöppel for encouraging us to perform these studies.

## REFERENCES

Andelić, E., Schafföner, M., Katz, M., Krüger, S. E., & Wendemuth, A. (2006). Kernel least-squares models using updates of the pseudoinverse. *Neural Computation, 18,* 2928–2935.

Baddeley, A. D. (1986). *Working memory.* Oxford, UK: Clarendon Press.

Baddeley, A. D. (2007). *Working memory, thought and action.* Oxford, UK: Oxford University Press.

Balcombe, N. R., & Sinclair, A. (2001). Aging: Definitions, mechanisms and the magnitude of the problem. *Best Practice & Research Clinical Gastroenterology, 15,* 835–849.

Baltes, P. B., & Staundinger, U. (1993). The search for the psychology of wisdom. *Current Directions in Psychological Science, 2,* 75–80.

Baudouin, A., Vanneste, S., Isingrini, M., & Pouthas, V. (2006). Differential involvement of internal clock and working memory in the production and reproduction of duration: A study on older adults. *Acta Psychologica, 121,* 285–296.

Birren, J. E. (1965). Age changes in speed of behavior: Its central nature and physiological correlates. In A. T. Welford & J. E. Birren (Eds.), *Behavior, aging, and the nervous system* (pp. 191–216). Springfield, IL: Charles C. Thomas.

Birren, J. E., & Fisher, L. M. (1995). Aging and speed of behavior: Possible consequences for psychological functioning. *Annual Review of Psychology, 46,* 329–353.

Birren, J. E., & Schaie, K. W. (Eds.). (2001). *Handbook of the psychology of aging.* San Diego, CA: Academic Press.

Block, R. A. (1990). *Cognitive models of psychological time.* Hillsdale, NJ: Erlbaum.

Block, R. A., Zakay, D., & Hancock, P.A. (1998). Human aging and duration judgments: A meta-analytic review. *Psychology of Aging, 13,* 584–596.

Burgess, N., Jeffrey, K., & O'Keefe, J. (Eds.). (1999). *The hippocampal and parietal foundations of spatial cognition.* Oxford, UK: Oxford University Press.

Burke, D. M., & MacKay, D. G. (1997). Memory, language and ageing. *Philosophical Transactions of the Royal Society of London, Series B: Biological Sciences, 352,* 1845–1856.

Cambridge Cognition. (2005a). CANTABeclipse *Software User Guide.* Cambridge, UK: Cambridge Cognition.

Cambridge Cognition. (2005b). CANTABeclipse *Test Administration Guide.* Cambridge, UK: Cambridge Cognition.

Carroll, J. B. (1993). *Human cognitive abilities: A survey of factor-analytic studies.* Cambridge, UK: Cambridge University Press.

Chisolm, T. H., Willott, J. F., & Lister, J. J. (2003). The aging auditory system: Anatomic and physiologic changes and implications for rehabilitation. *International Journal of Audiology, 42* (Suppl. 2), 3–10.

Craik, F. I. M. (1999). Age-related changes in human memory. In D. C. Park & N. Schwarz (Eds.), *Cognitive aging: A primer* (pp. 75–92). Philadelphia: Psychology Press.

Craik, F. I. M., & Byrd, M. (1982). Aging and cognitive deficits: The role of attentional resources. In F. I. M. Craik & S. Trehub (Eds.), *Aging and cognitive processes* (pp. 191–211). New York: Plenum Press.

Craik, F. I. M., & Salthouse, T. A. (Eds.). (1992). *The handbook of aging and cognition.* Hillsdale, NJ: Erlbaum.

Danthiir, V., Roberts, R. D., Schulze, R., & Wilhelm, O. (2005). Mental speed: On frameworks, paradigms, and a platforms for the future. In O. Wilhelm & R. W. Engle (Eds.), *Handbook of understanding and measuring intelligence* (pp. 27–46). Thousand Oaks, CA: Sage.

Engle, R. W., Sedek, G., von Hecker, U., & McIntosh, D. N. (2005). (Eds.) *Cognitive limitations in aging and psychopathology.* Cambridge, UK: Cambridge University Press.

Eysenck, H. J. (1987). Speed of information processing, reaction time, and the theory of intelligence. In P. A. Vernon (Ed.), *Speed of information-processing and intelligence* (pp. 21–67). Norwood, NJ: Ablex.

Fink M., Churan J., & Wittmann, M. (2005). Assessment of auditory temporal order thresholds: A comparison of different measurement procedures and the influence of age and gender. *Restorative Neurology and Neuroscience, 23*, 1–16.

Fink, M., Ulbrich, P., Churan, J., & Wittmann, M. (2006). Stimulus-dependent processing of temporal order. *Behavioural Processes, 71*, 344–352.

Fitzgibbons, P. J., & Gordon-Salant, S. (1998). Auditory temporal order perception in younger and older adults. *Journal of Speech, Language, and Hearing Research, 41*, 1052–1060.

Fowler, K., Saling, M., Conway, E., Semple, J., & Louis, W. (1995). Computerized delayed matching to sample and paired associate performance in the early detection of dementia. *Applied Neuropsychology, 2*, 72–78.

Fowler, K., Saling, M., Conway, L., Semple, J., & Louis, W. (2002). Paired associate performance in the early detection of DAT. *Journal of the International Neuropsychological Society, 8*, 58–71.

Fozard, J. L., Vercryssen, M., Reynolds, S. L., Hancock, P. A., & Quilter, R. E. (1994). Age differences and changes in reaction time: The Baltimore Longitudinal Study of Aging. *Journal of Gerontology, 49*, 179–189.

Frackowiak, R. S. J., Ashburner, J. T., Penny, W. D., Zeki, S., Friston, K. J., Frith, C. D., et al. (Eds.). (2003). *Human brain function* (2nd ed.). Amsterdam: Elsevier Academic Press.

Fraisse, P. (1982). Rhythm and tempo. In D. Deutsch (Ed.), *The psychology of music* (pp. 149–180). New York: Academic Press.

Fraisse, P. (1984). Perception and estimation of time. *Annual Review of Psychology, 35*, 1–36.

Frearson, W., & Eysenck, H. J. (1986). Intelligence, reaction time (RT) and a new "odd-man-out" RT paradigm. *Personality and Individual Differences, 7*, 807–818.

Gibbon, J. (1991). Origin of scalar timing. *Learning and Motivation, 22*, 3–38.

Glass, L. (2001). Synchronization and rhythmic processes in physiology. *Nature, 410*, 277–284.

Gordon-Salant, S., & Fitzgibbons, P. J. (1999). Profile of auditory temporal processing in older listeners. *Journal of Speech, Language, and Hearing Research, 42*, 300–311.

Gregory, T., Nettelbeck, T., Howard, S., & Wilson, C. (2008). Inspection time: A biomarker for cognitive decline. *Intelligence, 36*, 664–671.

Grudnik, J. L., & Kranzler, J. H. (2001). Meta–analysis of the relationship between intelligence and inspection time. *Intelligence, 29*, 523–535.

Hartley, A. A. (1992). Attention. In F. I. M. Craik & T. A. Salthouse (Eds.), *The handbook of aging and cognition* (pp. 3–49). Hillsdale, NJ: Erlbaum.

Hasher, L., & Zacks, R. T. (1988). Working memory, comprehension, and aging: A review and a new view. In G. H. Bower (Ed.), *The psychology of learning and motivation* (pp. 193–225). San Diego, CA: Academic Press.

Helmbold, N., & Rammsayer, T. H. (2006). Timing performance as a predictor of psychometric intelligence as measured by speed and power tests. *Journal of Individual Differences, 27*, 20–37.

Helmbold, N., Troche, S., & Rammsayer, T. H. (2007). Processing of temporal and non-temporal information as predictors of psychometric intelligence: A structural-equation-modeling approach. *Journal of Personality, 75*, 985–1006.

Higuchi, T. (1988). Approach to an irregular time series on the basis of the fractal theory. *Physica D, 31*, 277–283.

Inui, N. (1997), Simple reaction times and timing of serial reactions of middle-aged and old men. *Perceptual and Motor Skills, 84*, 219–225.

Ivry, R. B., & Richardson, T. C. (2002). Temporal control and coordination: The multiple timer model. *Brain and Cognition, 48*, 117–132.

Jensen, A.R. (1998). *The g factor: The science of mental ability*. Westport, CT: Praeger.

Jensen, A. R. (2006). *Clocking the mind: Mental chronometry and individual differences*. Amsterdam: Elsevier.

Jones, M. R. (1976). Time, our lost dimension: Toward a new theory of perception, attention, and memory. *Psychological Review, 83*, 323–355.

Klein, C., Fischer, B., Harnegg, K., Heiss, W. H., & Roth, M. (2000). Optomotor and neuropsychological performance in old age. *Experimental Brain Research, 135*, 141–154.

Kolodziejczyk, I., & Szelag, E. (2008). Auditory perception of temporal order in centenarians in comparison with young and elderly subjects. *Acta Neurobiologiae Experimentalis, 68*, 373–381.

Konorski, J. (1967). *Integrative activity of the brain*. Chicago: University of Chicago Press.

Kumai, M. (1999). Relation between self-paced and synchronized movement in persons with mental retardation. *Perceptual and Motor Skills, 89*, 395–402.

Kyllonen, P. C., & Christal, R. E. (1990). Reasoning ability is (little more than) working-memory capacity?! *Intelligence, 14*, 389-433.

Large, E. W., & Jones, M. R. (1999). The dynamics of attending: How we track time-varying events. *Psychological Review, 106*, 119–159.

Lehman, E. B., & Mellinger, J. C. (1984). Effects of aging on memory for presentation modality. *Developmental Psychology, 20*, 1210–1217.

Lezak, M. D. (1995). *Neuropsychological assessment* (3rd ed.). New York: Oxford University Press.

Lezak, M. D., Howieson, D., & Loring, D. (2004). *Neuropsychological assessment* (4th ed.). New York: Oxford University Press.

Lister, J. J., & Roberts, R. A. (2005). Effects of age and hearing loss on gap detection and the precedence effect: Narrow-band stimuli. *Journal of Speech, Language, and Hearing Research, 48*, 482-493.

Luo, L., & Craik, F. I. M. (2008). Aging and memory: A cognitive approach. *La Revue Canadienne de Psychiatrie, 53*, 346–353.

Madden, D. J. (2001). Speed and timing of behavioral processes. In J. E. Birren & K. W. Schaie (Eds.), *Handbook of the psychology of aging* (pp. 288–312). San Diego, CA: Academic Press.

Madison, G., Forsman, L., Blom, Ö., Karabanov, A., & Ullén, F. (2009). Correlation between intelligence and components of serial timing variability. *Intelligence, 37*, 68–75.

Maguire, E., Frith, C., Burgess, N., Donnett, J., & O'Keefe, J. (1998). Knowing where things are: Parahippocampal involvement in encoding object locations in virtual large-scale space. *Journal of Cognitive Neuroscience, 10*, 61–76.

McDowd, J. M., & Shaw, R. J. (2000). Attention and aging: A functional perspective. In F. I. M. Craik & T. A. Salthouse (Eds.), *The handbook of aging and cognition* (2nd ed., pp. 221–292). Hillsdale, NJ: Erlbaum.

Merzenich, M. M., Jenkins, W. M., Johnston, P., Schreiner, C., Miller, S. L., & Tallal, P. (1996). Temporal processing deficits of language-learning impaired children ameliorated by training. *Science, 271,* 77–81.

Metcalfe, J. (1998). *The brain: Degeneration, damage and disorder.* Berlin: Springer-Verlag.

Mishkin, M., & Pribram, K. (1956). Analysis of the effects of frontal lesions in monkeys: Variations in delayed response. *Journal of Comparative and Physiological Psychology, 49,* 36–40.

Morris, R., Evenden, J., Sahakian, B., & Robbins, T. (1987). Computer-aided assessment of dementia: Comparative studies of neuropsychological deficits in Alzheimer-type dementia and Parkinson's disease. In S. M. Stahl, S. D. Iversen, & E. C. Goodman (Eds.), *Cognitive neurochemistry* (pp. 21–36). Oxford, UK: Oxford University Press.

Mosaik Test (1991). Göttingen, Germany: Hawie-R, Verlag Hans Huber.

Nettelbeck, T., & Rabbitt, P. M. A. (1992). Aging, cognitive performance, and mental speed, *Intelligence 16,* 189–205.

O'Connell, H., Coen, R., Kidd, N., Warsi, M., Chin, A. V., & Lawlor, B. A. (2004). Early detection of Alzheimer's disease (AD) using the CANTAB Paired Associate Learning Test. *International Journal of Geriatric Psychiatry, 19,* 1207–1208.

Park, D. C. (1999). The basic mechanisms accounting for age-related decline in cognitive function. In D. C. Park & N. Schwarz (Eds.), *Cognitive aging: A primer* (pp. 3–21). Philadelphia: Psychology Press.

Park, D. C., & Schwarz, N. (Eds.). (1999). *Cognitive aging: A primer.* Philadelphia: Psychology Press.

Petrill, S. A., & Deary, I. (2001). Inspection time and intelligence: Celebrating 25 years of research. *Intelligence, 29,* 441–442.

Pöppel, E. (1971). Oscillations as possible basis for time perception. *Studium Generale, 24,* 85–107.

Pöppel, E. (1978). Time perception. In R. Held, H. W. Leibowitz, & H.-L. Teuber (Eds.), *Handbook of sensory physiology: Vol. 8. Perception* (pp. 713–729). Berlin: Springer-Verlag.

Pöppel, E. (1994). Temporal mechanisms in perception. *International Review of Neurobiology, 37,* 185–202.

Pöppel, E. (1997). A hierarchical model of temporal perception. *Trends in Cognitive Sciences, 1,* 56–61.

Pöppel, E. (2004). Lost in time: A historical frame, elementary processing units and the 3-s window. *Acta Neurobiologiae Experimentalis, 64,* 295–301.

Pöppel, E., & Logothetis, N. (1986). Neuronal oscillations in the brain: Discontinuous initiation of pursuit eye movements indicate a 30–Hz temporal framework for visual information processing. *Naturwissenschaften, 73,* 267–268.

Rammsayer, T. H., & Brandler, S. (2002). On the relationship between general fluid intelligence and psychophysical indicators of temporal resolution in the brain. *Journal of Research in Personality, 36,* 507–530.

Rammsayer, T. H., & Brandler, S. (2007). Performance on temporal information processing as an index of general intelligence. *Intelligence, 35,* 123–139.

Ratcliff, R., Thapar, A., & McKoon, G. (2001). The effects of aging on reaction time in a signal detection task. *Psychology of Aging, 16,* 323-341.

Raven, J. C. (1958). *Advanced progressive matrices.* London: H. K. Lewis.

Rogers, W. A., & Fisk, A. D. (2001). Understanding the role of attention in cognitive aging research. In J. E Birren & K. W. Schaie (Eds.), *Handbook of the psychology of aging* (pp. 267–287). San Diego, CA: Academic Press.

Salthouse, T. A. (1991). *Theoretical perspectives on cognitive aging.* Hillsdale, NJ: Erlbaum.

Salthouse, T. A. (1996). The processing-speed theory of adult age differences in cognition. *Psychological Review, 103*, 403–428.

Salthouse, T. A. (1999). Pressing issues in cognitive aging. In D. C. Park & N. Schwarz (Eds.), *Cognitive aging: A primer* (pp. 43–54). Philadelphia: Psychology Press.

Schlösser, R. G., Wagner, G., & Sauer, H. (2006). Assessing the working memory network: Studies with functional magnetic resonance imaging and structural equation modeling. *Neuroscience, 139*, 91–103.

Smith, M., & Milner, B. (1981). The role of the right hippocampus in the recall of spatial location. *Neuropsychologia, 19*, 781–793.

Spearman, C. (1904). General intelligence objectively determined and measured. *American Journal of Psychology, 15*, 201–293.

Stankov, L. (2005). g factor: Issues of design and interpretation. In O. Wilhelm & R. W. Engle (Eds.), *Handbook of understanding and measuring intelligence* (pp. 279–294). Thousand Oaks, CA: Sage.

Sternberg, R. J. (2000). (Ed.). *Handbook of intelligence.* Cambridge, UK: Cambridge University Press.

Surwillo, W. W. (1964). Age and the perception of short intervals of time. *Journal of Gerontology, 19*, 322–324.

Surwillo, W. W. (1968). Timing of behavior in senescence and the role of the central nervous system. In G. A. Talland (Ed.), *Human aging and behavior: Recent advances in research and theory* (pp. 1–35). New York: Academic Press.

Süß, H. M., Oberauer, K., Wittmann, W. W., Wilhelm, O., & Schulze, R. (2002). Working-memory capacity explains reasoning ability—and a little bit more. *Intelligence, 30*, 261–288.

Swainson, R., Hodges, J. R., Galton, C. J., Semple, J., Michael, A., Dunn, B. D., et al. (2001). Early detection and differential diagnosis of Alzheimer's Disease and depression with neuropsychological tasks. *Dementia and Geriatric Cognitive Disorders, 12*, 265–280.

Swierkocka-Miastkowska, M., & Osinski, G. (2007). Nonlinear analysis of brain spirography signals: The way to new non-invasive diagnostic tool. *Cerebrovascular Diseases, 23* (Suppl. 2), 138–139.

Szelag, E. (1997). Temporal integration of the brain as studied with the metronome paradigm. In H. Atmanspacher & E. Ruhnau (Eds.), *Time, temporality, now: Experiencing time and concepts of time in an interdisciplinary perspective* (pp. 121–132). Berlin: Springer-Verlag.

Szelag, E. (2005). Nowe tendencje w terapii logopedycznej w świetle badań nad mózgiem [New horizons in speech therapy]. In T. Galkowski, E. Szelag, & G. Jastrzebowska (Eds.), *Podstawy neurologopedii. Opole: Wydawnictwo Uniwersytetu Opolskiego.*

Szelag, E., Kanabus, M., Kolodziejczyk, I., Kowalska, J., & Szuchnik, J. (2004). Individual differences in temporal information processing in humans. *Acta Neurobiologiae Experimentalis, 64*, 349–366.

Szelag, E., & Pöppel, E. (2000). Temporal perception: A key to understanding language. *Behavioral and Brain Sciences, 23*, 52.

Szelag, E., von Steinbüchel, N., Reiser, M., de Langen, E., & Pöppel, E. (1996). Temporal constraints in processing of nonverbal rhythmic patterns. *Acta Neurobiologiae Experimentalis, 56*, 215–225.

Szymaszek, A. Sereda, M., Pöppel, E., & Szelag, E. (2009). Individual differences in the perception of temporal order: The effect of age and cognition. *Cognitive Neuropsychology, 26*, 135–147.

Szymaszek, A., Szelag, E., & Sliwowska, M. (2006). Auditory perception of temporal order in humans: The effect of age, gender, listener practice and stimulus presentation mode. *Neuroscience Letters, 403*, 190–194.

Tallal, P., Miller, S. L., Bedi, G., Byma, G., Wang, X., Nagarajan, S. S., et al. (1996). Language comprehension in language-learning impaired children improved with acoustically modified speech. *Science, 271*, 81–84.

Tiffin-Richards, M. C., Hasselhorn, M., Richards, M. L., Banaschewski, T., & Rothenberger, A. (2004). Time reproduction in finger tapping tasks by children with attention-deficit hyperactivity disorder and/or dyslexia. *Dyslexia, 10*, 299–315.

Tisserand, D. J., & Jolles, J. (2003). On the involvement of prefrontal networks in cognitive aging. *Cortex, 39*, 1107–1128.

Toga, A. W., & Thompson, P. M. (2005). Genetics of brain structure and intelligence. *Annual Review of Neuroscience, 28*, 1–23.

Tun, P. A., & Lachman, M. E., (2008). Age differences in reaction time and attention in a national telephone sample of adults: Education, sex, and task complexity matter. *Developmental Psychology, 44*, 1421-1429.

Ullén, F., Forsman, L., Blom, Ö., Karabanov, A., & Madison, G. (2008). Intelligence and variability in a simple timing task share neural substrates in the prefrontal white matter. *Journal of Neuroscience, 28*, 4238–4243.

Vanneste, S., Pouthas, V., & Wearden, J. H. (2001). Temporal control of rhythmic performance: A comparison between young and old adults. *Experimental Aging Research, 27*, 83–102.

Vernon, P. A. (1983). Speed of information processing and general intelligence. *Intelligence, 7*, 53–70.

von Steinbüchel, N., & Pöppel, E. (1993). Domains of rehabilitation: A theoretical perspective. *Behavioural Brain Research, 56*, 1–10.

Wechsler, D. (1981). *WAIS-R manual: Wechsler Adult Intelligence Scale–Revised.* New York: Psychological Corporation.

Wittmann, M. (1999). Time perception and temporal processing levels of the brain. *Chronobiology International, 16*, 17–32.

Wittmann, M., & Fink, M. (2004). Time and language-critical remarks on diagnosis and training methods of temporal-order judgment. *Acta Neurobiologiae Experimentalis, 64*, 341–348.

Wittmann, M., von Steinbüchel, N., & Szelag, E. (2001). Hemispheric specialisation for self-paced motor sequences. *Cognitive Brain Research, 10*, 341–344.

Zimmermann, P., & Fimm, B. (1997). *TAP: Test for Attentional Performance.* Hetzongernath, Germany: PSYTEST.

CHAPTER 6

# The Mismatch Negativity
## *A Unique Window on Central Auditory Processing*

## Risto Näätänen

### INTRODUCTION

The mismatch negativity (MMN; Näätänen, Gaillard, & Mäntysalo, 1978; for a review see Näätänen, Paavilainen, Rinne, & Alho, 2007) is a negative displacement peaking at 150–250 ms from change onset—in particular at the frontocentral and central scalp electrodes—in the difference wave obtained by subtracting the event-related potential (ERP) to frequent, "standard" stimuli from that to deviant stimuli (see Figure 1). However, one has to take into account the possible differences in the obligatory ERPs between standards and deviants caused by differences in physical stimulus between the two stimuli, and those in the refractoriness of the neural populations activated by the two stimuli due to the difference in probability. These differences in the obligatory components are, however, usually rather small in amplitude and mainly involve the N1 (the most prominent obligatory ERP response peaking at approximately 100–150 ms from stimulus onset) in ignore conditions, with subjects not paying attention to this stimulus sequence. Therefore post-N1 measurements usually provide quite reliable estimates of the "genuine" MMN.

The MMN is generated by two intracranial processes: (a) a bilateral supratemporal process generating the supratemporal MMN subcomponent and (b) a predominantly right-hemisphere frontal process generating the frontal MMN subcomponent (Giard, Perrin, Pernier, & Bouchet, 1990; Rinne, Alho,

*Personality from Biological, Cognitive, and Social Perspectives* edited by Tomasz Maruszewski, Małgorzata Fajkowska, and Michael W. Eysenck. Eliot Werner Publications, Clinton Corners, New York, 2010.

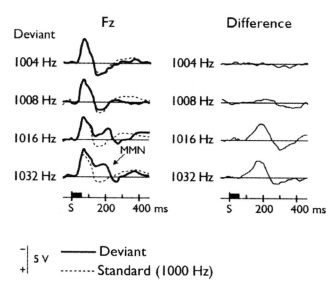

**Figure 1.** MMN as a function of frequency change. (a) Frontal (Fz) ERPs (averaged across subjects) to randomized 1000 Hz standard (80%, black line) and deviant (20%, thick line) stimuli of different frequencies (as indicated on the left side). (b) The difference waves obtained by subtracting the standard stimulus ERP from that of the deviant stimulus for the different deviant stimuli. Subjects were reading a book. Adapted from "Auditory Frequency Discrimination and Event-Related Potentials" by M. Sams, P. Paavilainen, K. Alho, and R. Näätänen, 1985, *Electroencephalography and Clinical Neurophysiology, 62*, pp. 440, 441. Copyright 1985 by Elsevier. Reprinted with permission.

Ilmoniemi, Virtanen, & Näätänen, 2000; for a review see Deouell, 2007). The supratemporal component is associated with preperceptual change detection, whereas the frontal component appears to be related to the initiation ("call"; Öhman 1979) of involuntary attention switch caused by auditory change (Escera, Alho, Winkler, & Näätänen, 1998; Giard et al., 1990; Näätänen & Michie, 1979; Rinne et al., 2000; Schröger, 1997).

## MEMORY DEPENDENCE

As indicated above, a prerequisite of MMN elicitation is that the central auditory system has been able to form a representation of the repetitive aspects of auditory stimulation before the occurrence of the deviant stimulus (Winkler, Karmos, & Näätänen, 1996), with an MMN being elicited when a stimulus violates this representation. Most studies have employed a simple "oddball" paradigm (e.g., the standard-stimulus tone of 500 Hz and deviant-stimulus tone of 550 Hz). The MMN, however, is also elicited by changes in complex stimuli such as speech sounds (Dehaene-Lambertz, 1997; Näätänen et al., 1997) and even by stimuli that deviate from an abstract rule followed by the ongoing auditory stimulation, such as a tone repetition in a sequence of descending tones with no constant standard stimulus (Tervaniemi, Maury, & Näätänen, 1994).

Hence the MMN depends on the presence of a short-term memory trace of a few seconds in duration in the auditory cortex representing the repetitive aspects of the preceding auditory events. The memory-trace interpretation is in particular supported by the MMN elicited by an infrequent shortening of the interstimulus interval (ISI; Rüsseler, Altenmüller, Nager, Kohlmetz, & Münte, 2001) or one elicited by stimulus omission (Yabe, Tervaniemi, Reinikainen, & Näätänen, 1997; Yabe et al., 1998). Nor can new afferent elements account for the fact that the MMN peak latency strongly depends on the magnitude of the difference between the deviant and standard stimuli (Näätänen et al., 1988; Tiitinen, May, Reinikainen, & Näätänen, 1994; see Figure 2). The sensory information carried by the sensory-memory traces underlying the MMN generation indeed corresponds to sound perception and memory (and thus provides the central sound representation) rather than just to the acoustic elements composing the stimulus (Näätänen & Winkler, 1999).

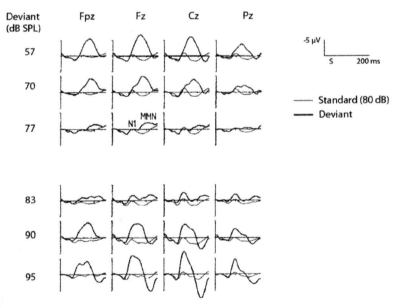

**Figure 2.** MMN to instensity decrement and increment. Grand-average frontal-pole (Fpz), frontal (Fz), central (Cz), and parietal (Pz) difference waves obtained by subtracting the response elicited by the 80-dB standard tone from the responses elicited by deviant tones of six different intensity levels presented in separate blocks. The N1 latency is marked to point out that whereas the N1 amplitude increases with increasing deviant-tone intensity (independent of the standard-tone intensity), the MMN amplitude increases and the MMN peak latency decreases with increasing magnitude of deviation from the standard (i.e., for deviants being both louder and softer than the standard). From *Attention and Brain Function* by R. Näätänen, 1992, p. 142. Copyright 1992 by Lawrence Erlbaum Associates. Reprinted with permission.

Further, traces involved in MMN generation are of a relatively short duration. In young subjects these traces usually last for about 5–10 seconds, judging from the ISIs that still permit MMN elicitation (Böttscher-Gandor & Ullsperger, 1992), but with aging the trace duration becomes shorter (Pekkonen et al., 1996). Moreover, this age-dependent shortening of the memory trace is expedited by chronic alcoholism (Polo, Escera, Gual, & Grau, 1999) and, in particular, by neurodegenerative diseases such as Alzheimer's disease (Pekkonen, Jousmäki, Könönen, Reinikainen, & Partanen, 1994).

The MMN amplitude is decreased with an increasing deviant-stimulus probability (Ritter et al., 1992). This is partially due to the standard stimulus being more often replaced by the deviant stimulus (the standard stimulus then being unable to contribute to the trace strength), but with shorter deviant-stimulus intervals, deviant stimuli may also develop a trace of their own—which in turn might inhibit the MMN generation process for the initial standard (Rosburg, 2004; Sams, Alho, & Näätänen, 1984). In fact, Näätänen (1984) explained the MMN phenomenon in terms of the input from the eliciting deviant stimulus "starting" to develop the representation of its own in the auditory sensory-memory system already engaged by the representation of the standard stimulus.

## RELATIONSHIP WITH ATTENTION

As already mentioned, MMN generation is an automatic brain process in the sense that its occurrence does not depend on attention (Alain & Woods, 1994; Alho, Sams, Paavilainen, Reinikainen, & Näätänen, 1989; Näätänen & Michie, 1979; see also Muller-Gass, Stelmack, & Campbell, 2005). Hence the MMN is elicited even when attention is strongly focused on a concurrent auditory stimulus stream, although its amplitude may be somewhat attenuated (Trejo, Ryan-Jones, & Kramer, 1995; Woldorff, Hackley, & Hillyard, 1991; Woldorff, Hillyard, Gallen, Hampson, & Bloom, 1998).

It is assumed that the activation of the auditory change-detection mechanism reflected by the MMN may also trigger the switching of attention to potentially important events in the unattended auditory environment (Giard et al., 1990; Näätänen & Michie, 1979). Several studies (e.g., Escera et al., 1998; Schröger, 1997) indeed showed that sound changes (eliciting an MMN) in irrelevant auditory background stimulation distract task performance and also elicit a subsequent P3a response (Squires, Squires, & Hillyard, 1975) thought to be associated with the actual orienting of attention to the deviant stimulus (Escera et al. 1998; Escera, Yago, & Alho, 2001; Ford, Roth, & Kopell, 1976; for reviews see Friedman, Cycowicz, & Gaeta, 2001; Ranganath & Rainer 2003). Furthermore, the MMN may also be followed by autonomic nervous system responses associated with the involuntary orienting of attention, such as heart rate deceleration and the skin-conductance response (Sokolov, Spinks, Näätänen, & Lyytinen, 2002).

## INDEX OF AUDITORY DISCRIMINATION

Several studies have shown that the MMN sensitivity to small stimulus changes corresponds quite well, in general, to the behavioral discrimination thresholds. Furthermore, this holds both with normal subjects and clinical populations. For example, it was found by Lang et al. (1990) that the behavioral discrimination accuracy for a frequency difference between two successively presented tone stimuli strongly correlated with the MMN amplitude (recorded in a separate, passive session; see Figure 3).

In addition, in studying school children who were successful and unsuccessful in discriminating between the /ba/ and /da/ syllables, Kraus et al. (1996) found a distinct MMN for these syllables in the children with good behavioral discrimination only. Importantly, children with speech-discrimination difficulties had learning problems. This suggests a role for these discrimination difficulties in the emergence of learning or other problems at school.

The MMN can also reflect improvement in discrimination performance as a result of training. For example, Näätänen Schröger, Karakas, Tervaniemi, and

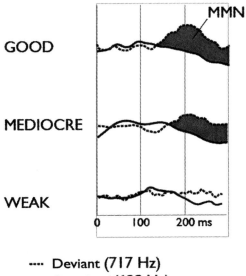

···· Deviant (717 Hz)
— Standard (698 Hz)

**Figure 3.** MMN as a function of behavioral pitch-discrimination accuracy. The MMN (recorded in a separate reading condition) was larger in amplitude in school children classified as "good" in a behavioral pitch-discrimination task (Seashore's test of musicality) than those who were "mediocre" or "weak" in this task. Adapted from "Pitch Discrimination Performance and Auditory Event-Related Potentials" by H. A. Lang, T. Nyrke, M. Ek, O. Aaltonen, I. Raimo, and R. Näätänen, 1990. In C. H. M. Brunia, A. W. K. Gaillard, A. Kok, G. Mulder, and M. N. Verbaten (Eds.), *Psychophysiological Brain Research* (Vol. 1), p. 296. Copyright 1990 by Tilburg University Press. Reprinted with permission.

Paavilainen (1993), using a complex spectrotemporal stimulus pattern as the standard stimulus, found that subjects who were able to detect a slightly deviant pattern in a behavioral discrimination task showed an MMN to this deviant stimulus in a subsequent passive condition. In contrast, no MMN was elicited in those subjects who were not able to behaviorally discriminate the stimuli in the preceding discrimination condition. However, an MMN was elicited by the deviant patterns in the subsequent passive conditions after they had learned behaviorally to discriminate them during the course of the session. Subsequently, Atienza and Cantero (2001), using identical stimuli, showed that this MMN training effect could even be obtained in REM sleep three days after training.

## COMPLEX STIMULI

The MMN (and its magnetic equivalent, the MMNm) is also elicited when speech sounds are presented in a passive oddball paradigm (Aaltonen, Niemi, Nyrke, & Tuhkanen, 1987; Cheour et al. 1998). In addition, several studies also found that with the MMN one can probe the permanent language-specific speech-sound memory traces. In one of these studies, Näätänen et al. (1997; see also Dehaene-Lambertz, 1997) found that an infrequent vowel deviant presented in a sequence of native-language vowel standards elicited a larger amplitude MMN when it was a typical exemplar of a vowel category of the subject's native language (Finnish) than when it was not typical of a vowel in this language (the /õ/ in Estonian does not exist in Finnish). The subsequent magnetoencephalographic (MEG) recordings showed that the vowel-related MMN enhancement originated from the left posterior auditory cortex, suggesting this as the probable locus of the language-specific vowel traces. Näätänen et al. (1997) further proposed that these long-term — or permanent — traces serve as recognition patterns activated by the corresponding speech sounds, enabling one to correctly perceive them, and further that these traces provide reference information for pronunciation. In addition, using a similar Finnish-Estonian cross-linguistic design, Cheour et al. (1998) obtained results suggesting that the language-specific speech-sound memory traces develop between six and twelve months of age.

Furthermore, with the MMN one can also probe the memory representations of higher order linguistic phenomena. For example, Shtyrov et al. (1998) obtained MMN evidence for memory traces of mother-tongue syllables. In addition, Korpilahti, Krause, Holoainen, and Lang (2001) and Pulvermüller et al. (2001) found that even the memory traces of mother-tongue words can be probed with the MMN; moreover, Pulvermüller and Shtyrov (2003) found that the MMN can also reflect the automatic processing of grammar. As suggested by the authors, these data demonstrated that the brain detects grammatical violations even when subjects direct their attention away from the language input. This would mean that early syntax processing in the human brain may take place outside the focus of attention.

In the so-called abstract-feature MMN studies, there is no physically identical, repetitive standard stimulus but rather a class of several physically different "standard" stimuli united by some common rule that they all obey. Saarinen, Paavilainen, Schröger, Tervaniemi, and Näätänen (1992) presented their subjects with a sequence of tone pairs randomly varying over a wide frequency range. Hence there was no physically identical, repetitive standard stimulus. All the standard pairs were ascending (i.e., the second tone of a pair was higher in frequency than the first one), whereas the deviant pairs were descending pairs. Nevertheless the MMN was elicited by the direction-deviant pairs in an ignore condition, showing that the preattentively formed sensory representations encoded a common invariant feature (ascending pair) from a set of individual varying physical events. Subsequently, Korzyukov, Winkler, Gumenyuk, and Alho (2003), using a similar paradigm, localized the source of the abstract feature MMN with electroencephalographic and MEG recordings at the auditory cortex. Furthermore, such abstract-feature MMNs can be recorded even in newborns (Carral et al., 2005; Ruusuvirta, Huotilainen, Fellman, & Näätänen, 2003).

Moreover, Tervaniemi et al. (1994) found that even extrapolatory traces— that is, those representing the forthcoming stimuli on the basis of the regularities or trends detected in the immediate auditory past—can be automatically formed in sensory memory. Their standard stimuli consisted of a long sequence of steadily descending tones, occasionally interrupted by an ascending tone or a tone repetition. It was found that both types of these deviant events elicited an MMN. Again, all standard stimuli were physically different and the deviant events were composed of physically identical stimuli that had occurred in the immediate auditory past. Hence it appeared that the automatic comparison process used as a reference an extrapolatory trace, one automatically anticipated on the basis of the trend detected in the sequence of the preceding stimuli.

These MMN studies indicate that the central auditory system performs complex cognitive operations, such as generalization leading to simple concept formation, rule extraction, and the anticipation of the next stimulus at the preattentive level, demonstrating the presence of "primitive sensory intelligence" in the auditory cortex (for a review see Näätänen, Tervaniemi, Sussman, Paavilainen, & Winkler, 2001). Furthermore, the information extracted by the sensory-memory mechanisms often seems to be in an implicit form, not directly available to conscious processes and difficult to express verbally (Paavilainen, Arajärvi, & Takegata, 2007). These results suggest that an important function of the MMN process is to adjust neural models maintained in auditory sensory memory to the various regularities of the auditory environment. This would enable the central auditory system to process a large part of the subsequent input automatically—that is, without requiring the limited resources of the controlled-processing system (Winkler et al., 1996).

## Acknowledgments

Preparation of this chapter was supported by grant #12275 from the Academy of Finland.

## REFERENCES

Aaltonen, O., Niemi, P., Nyrke, T., & Tuhkanen, M. (1987). Event-related brain potentials and the perception of a phonetic continuum. *Biological Psychology, 24*, 197–207.

Alain, C., & Woods, D. L. (1994). Brain indices of automatic pattern processing. *NeuroReport, 6*, 140–144.

Alho, K., Sams, M., Paavilainen, P., Reinikainen, K., & Näätänen, R. (1989). Event-related brain potentials reflecting processing of relevant and irrelevant stimuli during selective listening. *Psychophysiology, 26*, 514–528.

Atienza, M., & Cantero, J. L. (2001). Complex sound processing during human REM sleep by recovering information from long-term memory as revealed by the mismatch negativity (MMN). *Brain Research, 901*, 151–160.

Böttcher-Gandor, C., & Ullsperger, P. (1992). Mismatch negativity in event-related potentials of auditory stimuli as a function of varying interstimulus interval. *Psychophysiology, 29*, 546–550.

Carral, V., Huotilainen, M., Ruusuvirta, T., Fellman, V., Näätänen, R., & Escera, C. (2005). A kind of auditory "primitive intelligence" already present at birth. *European Journal of Neuroscience, 21*, 3201–3204.

Cheour, M., Ceponiene, R., Lehtokoski, A., Luuk, A., Allik, J., Alho, K., et al. (1998). Development of language-specific phoneme representations in the infant brain. *Nature Neuroscience, 1*, 351–353.

Dehaene-Lambertz, G. (1997). Electrophysiological correlates of categorical phoneme perception in adults. *NeuroReport, 8*, 919–924.

Deouell, L. (2007). The frontal generator of the mismatch negativity revisited. *Journal of Psychophysiology, 21*, 188–203.

Escera, C., Alho, K., Winkler, I., & Näätänen, R. (1998). Neural mechanisms of involuntary attention switching to novelty and change in the acoustic environment. *Journal of Cognitive Neuroscience, 10*, 590–604.

Escera, C., Yago, E., & Alho, K. (2001). Electrical responses reveal the temporal dynamics of brain events during involuntary attention switching. *European Journal of Neuroscience, 14*, 877-883.

Ford, J. M., Roth, W. T., & Kopell, B. S. (1976). Attention effects on auditory evoked potentials to infrequent events. *Biological Psychology, 4*, 65–77.

Friedman, D., Cycowicz, Y. M., & Gaeta, H. (2001). The novelty P3: An event-related brain potential (ERP) sign of the brain's evaluation of novelty. *Neuroscience and Biobehavioral Reviews, 25*, 355–373.

Giard, M. H., Perrin, F., Pernier, J., & Bouchet, P. (1990). Brain generators implicated in processing of auditory stimulus deviance: A topographic event-related potential study. *Psychophysiology, 27*, 627–640.

Korpilahti, P., Krause, C. M., Holopainen, I., & Lang, A. H. (2001). Early and late mismatch negativity elicited by words and speech-like stimuli in children. *Brain and Language, 76*, 332–339.

Korzyukov, O., Winkler, I., Gumenyuk, V. I., & Alho, K. (2003). Processing abstract auditory features in the human auditory cortex. *NeuroImage, 20*, 2245–2258.

Kraus, N., McGee, T. J., Carrell, T. D., Zecker, S. G., Nicol, T. G., & Koch, D. B. (1996). Auditory neurophysiologic response and discrimination deficits in children with learning problems. *Science, 273*, 971–973.

Lang, H. A., Nyrke, T., Ek, M., Aaltonen, O., Raimo, I., & Näätänen, R. (1990). Pitch discrimination performance and auditory event-related potentials. In C. H. M. Brunia, A. W. K. Gaillard, A. Kok, G. Mulder, & M. N. Verbaten (Eds.), *Psychophysiological brain research* (Vol. 1, pp. 294–298). Tilburg, The Netherlands: Tilburg University Press.

Muller-Gass, A., Stelmack, R. M., & Campbell, K. B. (2005). ". . . and were instructed to read a self-selected book while ignoring the auditory stimuli": The effects of task demands on the mismatch negativity. *Clinical Neurophysiology, 116*, 2142–2152.

Näätänen, R. (1984). In search of a short-duration memory trace of a stimulus in the human brain. In L. Pulkkinen & P. Lyytinen (Eds.), *Human action and personality: Essays in honour of Martti Takala* (pp. 29–43). Jyväskylä, Finland: University of Jyväskylä.

Näätänen, R. (1992). *Attention and brain function.* Hillsdale, NJ: Erlbaum.

Näätänen, R., Gaillard, A.W.K., & Mäntysalo, S. (1978). Early selective-attention effect on evoked potential reinterpreted. *Acta Psychologica, 42*, 313–329.

Näätänen, R., Lehtokoski, A., Lennes, M., Cheour, M., Huotilainen, M., Iivonen, A., et al. (1997). Language-specific phoneme representations revealed by electric and magnetic brain responses. *Nature, 385*, 432–434.

Näätänen, R., & Michie, P. T. (1979). Early selective attention effects on the evoked potential: A critical review and reinterpretation. *Biological Psychology, 8*, 81–136.

Näätänen, R., Paavilainen, P., Rinne, T., & Alho, K. (2007). The mismatch negativity (MMN) in basic research of central auditory processing: A review. *Clinical Neurophysiology, 118*, 2544–2590.

Näätänen, R., Sams, M., Alho, K., Paavilainen, P., Reinikainen, K., & Sokolov, E. N. (1988). Frequency and location specificity of the human vertex N1 wave. *Electroencephalography and Clinical Neurophysiology, 69*, 523–531.

Näätänen, R., Schröger, E., Karakas, S., Tervaniemi, M., & Paavilainen, P. (1993). Development of a memory trace for a complex sound in the human brain. *NeuroReport, 4*, 503–506.

Näätänen, R., Tervaniemi, M., Sussman, E., Paavilainen, P., & Winkler, I. (2001). "Primitive intelligence" in the auditory cortex. *Trends in Neurosciences, 24*, 283–288.

Näätänen, R., & Winkler, I. (1999). The concept of auditory stimulus representation in neuroscience. *Psychological Bulletin, 125*, 826–859.

Öhman, A. (1979). The orienting response, attention and learning: An information-processing perspective. In H. D. Kimmel, E. H. van Olst, & J. F. Orlebeke (Eds.), *The orienting reflex in humans* (pp. 443–471). Hillsdale, NJ: Erlbaum.

Paavilainen, P., Arajärvi, P., & Takegata, R. (2007). Preattentive detection of nonsalient contingencies between auditory features. *NeuroReport, 18*, 159–163.

Pekkonen, E., Jousmäki, V., Könönen, M., Reinikainen, K., & Partanen, J. (1994). Auditory sensory memory impairment in Alzheimer's disease: An event-related potential study. *NeuroReport, 5*, 2537–2540.

Pekkonen, E., Rinne, T., Reinikainen, K., Kujala, T., Alho, K., & Näätänen, R. (1996). Aging effects on auditory processing: An event-related potential study. *Experimental Aging Research, 22,* 171–184.

Polo, M. D., Escera, C., Gual, A., & Grau, C. (1999). Mismatch negativity and auditory sensory memory in chronic alcoholics. *Alcoholism: Clinical and Experimental Research, 23,* 1744–1750.

Pulvermüller, F., Kujala, T., Shtyrov, Y., Simola, J., Tiitinen, H., Alku, P., et al. (2001). Memory traces for words as revealed by the mismatch negativity. *NeuroImage, 14,* 607–616.

Pulvermüller, F., & Shtyrov, Y. (2003). Automatic processing of grammar in the human brain as revealed by the mismatch negativity. *NeuroImage, 20,* 159–172.

Ranganath, C., & Rainer, G. (2003). Neural mechanisms for detecting and remembering novel events. *Nature Reviews Neuroscience, 4,* 193–202.

Rinne, T., Alho, K., Ilmoniemi, R.J., Virtanen, J., & Näätänen, R. (2000). Separate time behaviors of the temporal and frontal mismatch negativity sources. *NeuroImage, 12,* 14–19.

Ritter, W., Paavilainen, P., Lavikainen, J., Reinikainen, K., Alho, K., Sams, M., et al. (1992). *Electroencephalography and Clinical Neurophysiology, 83,* 306–321.

Rosburg T. (2004). Effects of tone repetition on auditory evoked neuromagnetic fields. *Clinical Neurophysiology, 115,* 898–905.

Rüsseler, J., Altenmüller, E., Nager, W., Kohlmetz, C., & Münte, T. F. (2001). Event-related brain potentials to sound omissions differ in musicians and non-musicians. *Neuroscience Letters, 308,* 33–36.

Ruusuvirta, R., Huotilainen, M., Fellman, V., & Näätänen, R. (2003). The newborn human brain binds sound features together. *NeuroReport, 14,* 2117–2119.

Saarinen, J., Paavilainen, P., Schröger, E., Tervaniemi, M., & Näätänen, R. (1992). Representation of abstract stimulus attributes in the human brain. *NeuroReport, 3,* 1149–1151.

Sams, M., Alho, K., & Näätänen, R. (1984). Short-term habituation and dishabituation of the mismatch negativity of the ERP. *Psychophysiology, 21,* 434–441.

Sams, M., Paavilainen, P., Alho, K., & Näätänen, R. (1985). Auditory frequency discrimination and event-related potentials. *Electroencephalography and Clinical Neurophysiology, 62,* 437–448.

Schröger, E. (1997). On the detection of auditory deviants: A pre-attentive activation model. *Psychophysiology, 34,* 245–257.

Shtyrov, Y, Kujala, T., Ahveninen, J., Tervaniemi, M., Alku, P., Ilmoniemi, R. J., et al. (1998). Background acoustic noise and the hemispheric lateralization of speech processing in the human brain: Magnetic mismatch negativity study. *Neuroscience Letters, 251,* 141–144.

Sokolov, E. N., Spinks, J. A., Näätänen, R., & Lyytinen, H. (2002). *The orienting response in information processing.* Mahwah, NJ: Erlbaum.

Squires, N. K., Squires, K. C., & Hillyard, S. A. (1975). Two varieties of long-latency positive waves evoked by unpredictable auditory stimuli in man. *Electroencephalography and Clinical Neurophysiology, 38,* 387–401.

Tervaniemi, M., Maury, S., & Näätänen, R. (1994). Neural representations of abstract stimulus features in the human brain as reflected by the mismatch negativity. *NeuroReport, 5,* 844–846.

Tiitinen, H., May, P., Reinikainen, K., & Näätänen, R. (1994). Attentive novelty detection in humans is governed by pre-attentive sensory memory. *Nature, 370*, 90–92.

Trejo, L. J., Ryan-Jones, D. L., & Kramer, A. F. (1995). Attentional modulation of the mismatch negativity elicited by frequency differences between binaurally presented tone bursts. *Psychophysiology, 32*, 319–328.

Winkler, I., Karmos, G., & Näätänen, R. (1996). Adaptive modeling of the unattended acoustic environment reflected in the mismatch negativity event-related potential. *Brain Research, 742*, 239–252.

Woldorff, M. G., Hackley, S. A., & Hillyard, S. A. (1991). The effects of channel-selective attention on the mismatch negativity wave elicited by deviant tones. *Psychophysiology, 28*, 30–42.

Woldorff, M. G., Hillyard, S. A., Gallen, C. C., Hampson, S. R., & Bloom, F. E. (1998). Magnetoencephalographic recordings demonstrate attentional modulation of mismatch-related neural activity in the human auditory cortex. *Psychophysiology, 35*, 283–292.

Yabe, H., Tervaniemi, M., Reinikainen, K., & Näätänen, R. (1997). Temporal window of integration revealed by MMN to sound omission. *NeuroReport, 8*, 1971–1974.

Yabe, H., Tervaniemi, M., Sinkkonen, J., Huotilainen, M., Ilmoniemi, R. J., & Näätänen, R. (1998). Temporal window of integration of auditory information in the human brain. *Psychophysiology, 35*, 615–619.

# PART III

# Social Context
## *From Within Persons to Among Persons*

CHAPTER 7

# Environmental and Genetic Determinants of Sociopolitical Attitudes

## Urszula Jakubowska
## Wlodzimierz Oniszczenko

### INTRODUCTION

Sociopolitical attitudes have been studied since the 1930s when the rapidly spreading Nazi and Communist ideologies encouraged researchers to investigate the determinants of antidemocratic attitudes (cf. Reich, 1975). In subsequent years the focus on this problem yielded many empirical studies and theories that strove to provide a better understanding of individual differences in such ideological dimensions as conservatism-liberalism (e.g., Adorno, Frenkel-Brunswik, Levinson, & Sanford, 1950; Amodio, Jost, Master, & Yee, 2007), conservatism-radicalism (e.g., Eysenck, 1954; Tesser, 1993), leftism-rightism (e.g., Oniszczenko & Jakubowska, 2005; Rokeach, 1960, 1973; Tomkins, 1963), attitudes toward specific social phenomena (e.g., religion, divorce, abortion, the death penalty; Altemeyer, 1996; Altemeyer & Hunsberger, 2005; Tesser, 1993) and political events (e.g., Hahn & Emory, 2002), and also attitudes toward specific political objects (e.g., politicians, political parties, political institutions; e.g., Campus, 2002; Sears, 1969).[1]

The search for determinants of sociopolitical attitudes has focused on two different domains, social and biological.

*Personality from Biological, Cognitive, and Social Perspectives* edited by Tomasz Maruszewski, Małgorzata Fajkowska, and Michael W. Eysenck. Eliot Werner Publications, Clinton Corners, New York, 2010.

# ENVIRONMENTAL DETERMINANTS OF SOCIOPOLITICAL ATTITUDES

The traditional and still dominant explanation of sociopolitical attitudes is that these attitudes are environmentally determined. We can analyze the social influences on the macrosocial, institutional, group, and family level.

## Macrosocial Influences

The broadest social context to determine sociopolitical attitudes is the political system. According to the psychoanalytic approach, restrictive social norms (largely embodied in religion) imposed by authoritarian political systems by means of the family (Fromm, 1941) lead to the repression of primary biological impulses (particularly sexual needs) and hence to the development of antidemocratic and ethnocentric attitudes. These attitudes are expressions of repressed sexuality, which is associated with aggression (Reich, 1975).

    Macrosocial, group, and individual research findings suggest that a crisis of the political system in the form of economic decline and intensification of sociopolitical tension generates symptoms of authoritarianism, a condition that predisposes people to adopt profascist, ethnocentric, and xenophobic attitudes (Fromm, 1941), manifest political prejudice and cynicism (Doty, Peterson, & Winter, 1991), and express extreme political conservatism (Doty et al., 1991; Duckitt & Fischer, 2003).

## Institutional Influences

There is also another way in which the political system affects the development of sociopolitical attitudes: it provides a framework for the implementation of possible models of education oriented toward the formation of specific sociopolitical attitudes (e.g., civic, prodemocratic ones; Campbell, 2006; Ichilov, 2003). These are deliberate, intentional forms of socialization as opposed to the vicarious environmental effects mentioned earlier (i.e., ones that are not introduced deliberately in order to foster the development of specific sociopolitical attitudes). The media also undertake intentional actions whose aim is to form and/or change sociopolitical attitudes. Toward this end they adopt specific instruments of propaganda. For example, they use special symbols to trigger loyalty and patriotism

---

[1] These examples show that the concept of attitudes is used in numerous meanings (see, for example, consideration of the attitude definitions and attitude assessment in Krosnick, Judd, & Wittenbrink, 2005). We will use the term "sociopolitical attitude" as the evaluation of social and political phenomena such as divorce, abortion, egalitarianism, the economy, foreign policy, and so on. The evaluation of social and political phenomena contains cognitive, affective, and behavioral components (Albarracin, Zanna, Johnson, & Kumkale, 2005; Clarkson, Tormala, & Rucker, 2008). Sociopolitical attitudes are relatively stable through situations and are regulated by more general standards—that is, a system of values (Feldman, 2003).

(Sears, 1993), ethnic hostility (Kaufman, 2004), or a particular attitude toward politicians and political parties (Campus, 2002).

## Group Influences

Other communities—albeit narrower ones—that shape sociopolitical attitudes toward the political system and institution are the peer group, neighborhood, and friendship network (see Blazak, 2001; Hahn & Emory, 2002; Tam Cho, Gimpel, & Dyck, 2006). For example, ethnographic research using guided interviews has shown that racism in teenagers develops under the influence of indoctrination by older Nazi skinheads, but this process only takes place when teenage anomie is high (Blazak, 2001). Other findings suggest that attitudes toward politicians and political parties, as well as various political issues, can emerge and change under the influence of discussions with friends and acquaintances (e.g., Tam Cho et al., 2006).

## Family Influences

However, the socialization agenda that is thought to play the greatest role in the development of sociopolitical attitudes is the family. The family is where sociopolitical attitudes are transmitted directly from generation to generation or indirectly through the value system, which is primary with respect to attitudes (Feldman, 2003; Rokeach, 1973). It has been found, for example, that children acquire political opinions largely from their parents (e.g., Austin & Pinkleton, 2001; Frątczak-Rudnicka, 1990; Furnham, 2001; Sears, 1969; ter Bogt, Meeus, & Raaijmakers, 2001; Ventura, 2001), albeit from their father rather than their mother (Austin & Pinkleton, 2001). Transmission of party identification follows a similar pattern (Frątczak-Rudnicka, 1990; Niemi, Ross, & Alexander, 1978; Sears, 1969). Children and their parents tend to share the same collectivistic versus individualistic values and mental orientations (Furnham, 2001). This parent-offspring similarity has also emerged from longitudinal studies measuring the level of conservatism, defined as degree of tolerance for alternative lifestyles—a measure of so-called cultural conservatism—and level of acceptance of equality of income and property, a measure of so-called economic conservatism (ter Bogt et al., 2001). Although similarity with their parents of adolescents' cultural conservatism was reduced in favor of similarity with their peers' opinions (ter Bogt et al., 2001), when Sears (1969) conducted a meta-analysis of the congruence of parent-offspring political attitudes, he found similarity in more than half the respondents (from about 50% to 68%) in each sample studied.

The effect of the family on the formation of sociopolitical attitudes is largely vicarious. The effect may be direct or indirect. Sociopolitical attitudes are directly acquired through the learning process by means of modeling, punishment, and reward or association. For example, parents may model ethnocentric attitudes by making derogatory and hostile remarks about "foreigners" and blaming them for problems in the country (although the empirical data on this are inconsistent; cf. Rieker, 1999). Parents may apply a complex system of punishments and rewards—for example by expressing disapproval or approval of expressions of hedonistic needs (e.g., sexual permissiveness exemplified by acceptance of contraceptives, abortion, or divorce), aggressive impulses (expressed in negativity toward ethnic minorities, acceptance of the death penalty, condoning of war), or their control (see Eysenck, 1954).

The most elementary way of acquiring sociopolitical attitudes from one's parents is through repeated association of a political object with either positive or negative affect. According to symbolic politics theory, children are very often exposed to adults' affect (unconditioned stimulus) toward particular objects or their symbols (conditioned stimulus), and these stimuli evoke and mobilize a child's emotions (unconditioned response). Thus previously neutral stimuli (object symbols) associated with emotion acquire an individual affective meaning that is positive or negative (Sears, 1993). Affective responses to particular symbols and linked symbols combine to form specific attitudinal ("symbolic") predispositions. Some of them are very strong and remain stable over time; each exposure to pertinent objects or relevant symbols automatically evokes the previously learned affect and influences the processes of consistent evaluation and cognition (see numerous data described by Brader & Valentino, 2004; Sears, 1993; Sears & Henry, 2000a, 2000b; and the discussion on alternative explanation of political preferences by Sears, 1997).

The indirect effect of the family on the formation of sociopolitical attitudes has been associated largely with parenting and its effect on the development of personality traits that underlie the tendency to adopt specific sociopolitical attitudes. For example, restrictive parenting based on punishment rather than reward, lack of affection, and lack of intimacy in parent-child relationships leads to the development of the authoritarian/dogmatic personality (Adorno et al., 1950; Altemeyer, 1996; Oesterreich, 1999; Rokeach, 1960). Based on well-documented empirical findings, it has been suggested that right-wing authoritarianism is a predictor of pseudoconservative (Adorno et al., 1950) and conservative (Bouchard et al., 2004) attitudes, nationalistic attitudes (Altemeyer, 1996), fundamentalist religious attitudes (Altemeyer and Hunsberger, 2004, 2005; Danso, Hunsberger, & Pratt, 1997; Hunsberger, Owosu, & Duck, 1999), racist (Wylie & Forest, 1992) and sexist (Laythe, Finkel, & Kirkpatrick, 2001; Hunsberger et al., 1999) attitudes, separatist attitudes toward sexual minorities (Hunsberger, 1996; Hunsberger et al., 1999; Laythe, Finkel, & Kirkpatrick, 2001; Wylie & Forest, 1992), punitiveness (Wylie & Forest, 1992), and belligerence (Tibon & Blumberg, 1999). Dogmatism coexists with extreme right-wing (Jakubowska, 2005; Rokeach, 1960) and extreme left-wing (Rokeach, 1960) attitudes.

According to Tomkins (1963), normative upbringing—that is, one that focuses on instilling obedience to social norms—leads to the development of a normative personality. This personality tends to experience negative affect and perceive the world in terms of threat. Humanistic upbringing, meanwhile (i.e., one that focuses on encouraging the child to express needs freely), leads to the development of a humanistic personality. This personality has a dominant positive emotional script. A large body of research findings suggests that these two different personality types lead to the adoption of the specific sociopolitical attitudes that typify the right-wing/left-wing dimension. The normative personality predisposes the individual to adopt right-wing attitudes, whereas the humanistic personality predisposes the individual to adopt left-wing attitudes (Tomkins, 1963; cf. the extensive review by Stone, 1986).

It follows from the data presented that personality mediates the generation of sociopolitical attitudes (see also Olson, Vernon, Harris, & Jang, 2001). The popular belief that personality is determined by nurture alone is being questioned more and more frequently in view of recent neuropsychological findings and the work of behavior geneticists, whose observations suggest that some of the personality traits that are responsible for the adoption of sociopolitical attitudes are biologically determined to a considerable extent. However, the mediating role of personality in the formation of sociopolitical attitudes has been questioned in analyses demonstrating the relationships between person-specific neurohormonal brain work (Winkielman & Berridge, 2003) and areas of arousal in response to the same stimuli (Amodio et al., 2007) on the one hand, and the contribution of biological factors to the formation of sociopolitical attitudes on the other.

## GENETIC DETERMINANTS OF SOCIOPOLITICAL ATTITUDES

Due to recent advancements in behavior genetics, it is now possible to study the determinants of sociopolitical attitudes more thoroughly and to consider the contribution of both biological and social factors—including the family and extrafamily environment—to their development.

Assessment of biological and social factors is largely based on comparing monozygotic and dizygotic twins, parents with their biological offspring, and members of adoptive families. The basic purpose of behavior genetic research is to determine the degree to which a specific behavior is genetically determined and the degree to which that behavior is environmentally determined. These two factors are not completely independent because environmental factors may affect gene expression and because the human genotype that expresses itself in genetically determined characteristics of the human genotype affects various elements of a person's environment. The genetic factor includes both the effects of gene transmission from parents to their offspring (the so-called additive effect) and the effects of interaction of genes in the offspring (the nonadditive factor). As far as research on the determinants of attitudes is concerned, the general genetic contribution to their variance—that is, heritability broadly understood—is particularly important. Heritability tells us which portion of individual differences in the attitude or attitudes under study may be attributed to the combined additive and nonadditive effect of genetic factors. This indicator can vary from 0 (no genetic effect) to 1 (the entire variance is accounted for by genetic factors) or from 0% to 100%.

Environmental effects include the effect of the shared environment and the specific environment. By shared environment we mean all the factors characterizing the living environment of the family, both the biological family and the adoptive family. The shared environment includes both factors relating to the family's material conditions of living and traditional or shared relationships among family members. This factor facilitates increasing similarity between members of the same family. By specific environment we mean those environmental factors (within and without the family) that contribute to the differentiation of family members. These factors may be understood as a person's set of individual, unique environmental experiences that is the effect (among other things) of person-specific interactions and correlations between the genotype on the one hand, and the family and extrafamily environment on the other. In this sense specific environment can be viewed as the individual's life history.

Assuming that sociopolitical attitudes are acquired and that personality mediates the acquisition of sociopolitical attitudes, it has also been pointed out (a) that social perception and learning proceed differently depending on the organism's biological endowment (Eysenck, 1954; Winkielman & Berridge, 2003), and (b) that some personality traits have a strong genetic component. For example, McLeod (in his studies described by Eysenck, 1954) compared the levels of extraversion/introversion in monozygotic and dizygotic twins and found that the heritability of this personality trait was about 70–80%. Although the biological dynamics of the inheritance of personality traits have yet to be explained, it has now been established that extraverts and introverts have different patterns of arousal and inhibition of nervous processes, properties that are responsible for response acquisition and extinction. Learning is slower in extraverts, who need more intense stimuli than introverts to develop habits and also need more stimulus-response association repetitions within a given time. Hence Eysenck (1954) posited that extraverts are more resistant to social influence, less socialized, and more prone to adopt sociopolitical stances supporting ideologies that refer to hedonistic impulses (associated with material assets, power, and prestige) and enable discharge of aggressive impulses (e.g., support war or the death penalty) and sexual impulses (e.g., support the loosening of legal restrictions concerning divorce and abortion) than introverts. This hypothesis has been confirmed by Eaves and Eysenck (1974) in a study of several hundred pairs of monozygotic and dizygotic twins. The authors of this study found that sociopolitical attitudes, conceptualized in terms of conservatism-radicalism and the associated personality syndrome called tough-mindedness/tender-mindedness (a political projection of extraversion and introversion, respectively), are largely inherited. The genetic factor was 65% for conservatism-radicalism and 54% for tough-mindedness/tender-mindedness.

## Heritability of Sociopolitical Attitudes

The high genetic factor for conservatism—measured in terms of attitudes toward the death penalty, gay rights, censorship, and so forth—has also emerged systematically in other studies (Abrahamson, Baker, & Caspi, 2002; Bouchard et al., 2003, 2004). Tesser (1993) conducted a meta-analysis of the research literature on the heritability of various attitudes and managed to identify a group of attitudes that were most genetically determined and another group that were least genetically determined. The following attitudes had a high heritability index (at least 0.40): toward the death penalty, royalty, apartheid, censorship, white superiority, divorce, and military drill. The following attitudes had the lowest heritability index: toward socialism (0.26), biblical truth (0.25), flogging (0.21), and coeducation (0.07).

The high genetic factor for attitudes relating, for example, to Eysenck's conservatism-radicalism has been confirmed in a series of experiments. Tesser (1993, 2002) and Tesser, Whitaker, Martin, and Ward (1998) hypothesized that attitudes with a high heritability index—that is, ones with stronger biological bases—are stronger in the psychological sense (i.e., are difficult to change). People experience discomfort when we try to change their attitudes and they develop psychological mechanisms to maintain them (Olson et al., 2001). One such mechanism is so-called "niche-building": people seek environments that are compatible with respect to attitudes or even strive to change or construct such environments to facilitate freedom of attitude expression (Tesser, 2002). Tesser and associates (Crelia & Tesser, 1996; Tesser, 1993; Tesser & Crelia, 1994; Tesser et al., 1998) found that the greater the contribution of genetic factors to attitude changeability, the quicker people reacted to information relating to the attitude in question—and that the attitude itself was more difficult to change. Attempts to change attitudes with a high heritability index led to more intense electrodermal responses and increased heart rate (Tesser et al., 1998). This work, conducted within the behavior genetic and experimental paradigms, lends powerful support to the hypothesized biological determination of sociopolitical attitudes but tells us nothing about the psychological, physiological, and social mechanisms whereby such attitudes develop.

## Biological Foundations of Sociopolitical Attitudes

The research findings demonstrating that people with normative and humanistic personalities have different types of lateralization may shed some light on the relationships between biological factors and personality (Tomkins, 1963). The right cerebral hemisphere (which is responsible for intuition and the emotions) is the dominant hemisphere in the humanistic type, whereas the left hemisphere (which is responsible for rational thinking) is dominant in the normative type (cf. a series of studies reported by Stone, 1986).[2] The different sociopolitical attitudes described along the liberal-conservative (i.e., left-wing/right-wing) dimension are

---

[2] Estimates of hemisphericity were based on the measurement of eye movements (see Stone, 1986).

congruent with the special functions of the two hemispheres. Liberal attitudes and people who endorse them are typical for right-hemisphere functioning: openness to experience, trust, creativity, value-free attitudes, and high regard for egalitarianism. Conservative attitudes are typical for left-hemisphere functioning: skepticism, resistance to change and novelty, defense of the status quo, and the tendency to make evaluative judgements (see Stone, 1986).

Additional empirical evidence for the physiological determinants of sociopolitical attitudes has been gathered by Amodio et al. (2007), who conducted an experiment in which conservatives and liberals were required to react very quickly to a computer-differentiated stimulus. It appeared that conservatives made significantly more errors than liberals. The authors revealed that conservatives and liberals differed also in activity of the anterior cingulate, which is responsible for recognizing novel situations and altering a habitual response pattern (Amodio et al., 2007). There is convincing evidence, which has been observed for many years, that conservatives and liberals have different cognitive styles. Conservatives are less tolerant of ambiguity and have more stable cognitive structures, and their structures are more organized (cf. Amodio et al., 2007; Chirumbolo, 2002; Eysenck, 1954; Frenkel-Brunswik, 1949; Golec, 2001; McAllister & Anderson, 1991; Stone, 1986). Liberals, meanwhile, are more open to experience and more tolerant of novel and unanticipated situations (e.g., Stone, 1986). Traditionally, these differences have been interpreted in terms of different levels of anxiety resulting from different socialization experiences in the family (Budner, 1962; Frenkel-Brunswik, 1949).

The authoritarianism/dogmatism/normative personality syndrome is a personality formation whose function is to protect the individual from anxiety. This syndrome is responsible for closure, rigidity, and intolerance of ambiguity in the cognitive structures (Budner, 1962; Eysenck, 1954; Frenkel-Brunswik, 1949; Rokeach, 1960). It was not until Amodio et al. (2007) scanned the brains of individuals experimentally confronted with the demand to respond to novel and mutable stimuli that it was found that anterior cingulate activity is several times lower in conservatives than in liberals. This is why conservatives ignored the incoming, mutable information and liberals responded appropriately to this information. This finding explains the observed differences in cognitive styles and sociopolitical attitudes. Conservatism is more easily accommodated by less cerebrally active individuals, whereas liberalism is more likely to appeal to individuals who are biologically disposed to process complex and rapidly changing information. However, these new findings concerning the plasticity of brain processes prompt us to ask whether the differences in brain arousal are genetically determined (by anterior cingulated activity or dominance of left or right cerebral hemisphere) or whether they result from changes in response to specific environmental factors — that is, the differential anxiety-arousing experiences of conservatives and liberals (see Adorno et al., 1950; Budner, 1962; Frenkel-Brunswik, 1949; Stone, 1986; Tomkins, 1963). Future behavior genetic work may help answer this question.

## Anxiety and Sociopolitical Attitudes

It is generally well known that anxiety—a key factor in the development of specific personality traits and sociopolitical attitudes—always has a significant genetic component, although how powerful this genetic effect actually is remains to be determined. Most empirical data suggest that it contributes considerably (from about 45% to 76%) to the variance of trait anxiety (Legrand et al., 1999; Jakubowska & Oniszczenko, in press), sensitivity to anxiety-provoking stimuli (Stein, Jang, & Livesley, 1999), symptoms of social anxiety (Beatty, Heisel, Hall, Levine, & LaFrance, 2002), panic disorder, social phobias, and separation anxiety (Eley, 1999; Ogliari et al., 2006; Topolski, 1998), and anxious depression (Boomsma, van Beijstervaldt, & Hudziak, 2005). It is worth noting, however, that the contribution of genetic factors to generalized anxiety disorders is much smaller (about 15–20%; Hettema, Prescott, & Kendler, 2001; Ogliari et al., 2006).

The significance of anxiety for biological survival may explain why the contribution of genetic factors to the variance of anxiety is so high. Anxiety is a mechanism that has evolved to signal danger and enable the organism to defend itself (e.g., Beck, Emery, & Greenberg, 1985). Our own work with monozygotic and dizygotic twins (Jakubowska & Oniszczenko, in press) has demonstrated that trait anxiety is 60% genetically determined. We also found that anxiety is a statistically significant predictor of fundamentalist religious attitudes (religious ethnocentrism), measured with the abbreviated version of the scale constructed by Altemeyer and Hunsberger (2004). Our analyses also revealed a considerable genetic contribution to fundamentalist religious attitudes (38%) but the effect of the environment on the formation of such attitudes was much stronger (62%). The findings for the Polish sample are similar to observations from Anglo-Saxon countries, where the contribution of the genetic factor to (variously defined) fundamentalist religious attitudes varies from about 26% (e.g., Carver & Udry, 1997) to 43% (Bouchard, McGue, Lykken, & Tellegen, 1999). This finding lends support to the claim that some personality traits, viewed as mediators of sociopolitical attitudes, as well as sociopolitical attitudes—which are important for biological survival (anxiety) and social adaptation (religiousness)—may be genetically transmitted from generation to generation.

## The Big Five and Sociopolitical Attitudes

This conclusion is also suggested by the results of research on the biological and environmental determinants of the Big Five personality traits, whose relationships with sociopolitical attitudes are quite well documented. Extraversion, agreeableness, conscientiousness, neuroticism, and openness/intellect all play an important role in natural selection and reproduction. This process can also be observed in animal species (Bouchard & Loehlin, 2001). As far as humans are concerned, the Big Five personality traits represent the basic dimensions of social adjustment such as the ability to be liked (extraversion), to be kind and supportive (agreeableness), to maintain sustained effort and direction (conscientious-ness), emotional undependability (neuroticism), and the ability to generate ideas (openness/intellect). The results of meta-analyses conducted by Bouchard & Loehlin (2001) suggest high heritability (over 0.40) of the Big Five personality traits (cf. also, e.g., Jang, Livesley, & Vernon, 1996; Jang, McCrae, Angleitner, Riemann, & Livesley, 1998; Riemann, Angleitner, & Strelau, 1997).

Several of the Big Five traits correlate significantly with sociopolitical atti-tudes. For example, conscientiousness correlates positively with religiousness (McCullough, Tsang, & Brion, 2003), while low openness to experience predicts fundamentalist religious attitudes (Saraglou, 2002; Streyffeler & McNally, 1998), conservative attitudes (e.g., Chirumbolo, 2002; McAllister & Anderson, 1991), and conservatism understood as attachment to the political past (in Communist countries this means sentimental attachment to Communist ideology; see Golec, 2001).

Our own study (Oniszczenko & Jakubowska, 2005) of monozygotic and dizygotic twins has led us to conclude that economic attitudes (represented along the free market-state interventionism dimension) are determined to a considerable extent by the level of neuroticism and agreeableness. Regression analyses have shown that the more pronounced these traits, the higher the observed support for state domination in the economy. In other words, a high level of anxiety (neuroti-cism) paired with striving for friendly relations with other people (agreeableness) leads people to support systems that ensure social security (well-developed social welfare, a regulated market, egalitarian values, an egalitarian standard of living) and reduce the discomfort of social inequality. On the other hand, the Big Five personality traits were not significant predictors of attitudes relating to moral issues (the test items referred to loosening the restrictions on divorce, division of roles between men and women, lifestyle, and open-door immigration policies; Oniszczenko and Jakubowska 2005). We also found that 28% of the variance of moral attitudes was determined by the additive genetic factor, whereas genetic factors had no significant effect on the development of economic attitudes. Although the contribution of genetic factors to the development of moral attitudes is not high, the difference between moral and economic attitudes lends support to the claim that attitudes which are important for social adjustment and biological survival are the ones that are more genetically determined.

The failure to find any significant relationship between the Big Five and moral attitudes suggests that we should look for other predictors of moral atti-tudes, such as temperament traits (e.g., sensation seeking) or personality traits—albeit ones that are differently defined. For example, when a different categoriza-tion of personality traits was adopted (Olson et al., 2001), a significant positive relationship was found between attitudes toward equality (racial discrimination, separate roles for men and women, open-door immigration policies, and getting along well with others) on the one hand and sociability, one of several personal-ity traits assessed in this study (aggressiveness, sociability, dependence, persist-ence, and obsessiveness), on the other. This study also showed that higher obsessiveness correlates with support for severe punishment. It is important to remember that in these studies the aforementioned sociopolitical attitudes had a strong genetic component (over 0.40).

The findings on the relationships between personality traits with a large genetic component and sociopolitical attitudes are rather inconclusive. The presented results suggest that different personality traits with a large genetic component predict different types of sociopolitical attitudes. What is more, many of these findings also point to low and statistically insignificant correlations or no correlations at all between personality traits and sociopolitical attitudes. Therefore it is not yet possible to formulate any universal laws concerning the role of personality as a mediator of sociopolitical attitudes. The biological mechanism of inheritance of personality and sociopolitical attitudes is just as enigmatic.

## EMERGING CONCLUSIONS

Behavior genetic research is shedding new light on the development of sociopolitical attitudes. It is providing empirical evidence of the diversity of attitudes with respect to their social and biological determinants. We now know that some attitudes — in accordance with popular beliefs — are formed in response to environmental factors, whereas others are biologically determined to a greater or lesser extent. The relationship between genes and sociopolitical attitudes is not direct, however. The existing research has shown that sociopolitical attitudes are largely environmentally determined. How a person experiences social events, however, depends on that person's biologically determined sensory structures, memory processes, and the physiology of the brain as processor of informational input (cf. Olson et al., 2001; Winkielman & Berridge, 2003). In other words, the formation of sociopolitical attitudes is a holistic psychophysiological process (see Figure 1).

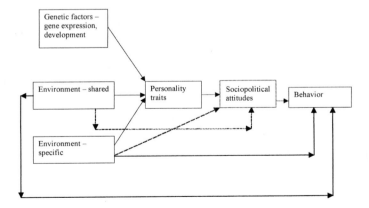

**Figure 1.** Environmental and genetic determinants of sociopolitical attitudes.

As Figure 1 shows, biological factors predispose the adoption of certain attitudes by means of such structures as personality. But as the findings presented have demonstrated, the environment plays the leading role in their expression.

## Acknowledgments

This chapter was funded by grant #BST–1340–01–2008 from the Faculty of Psychology, University of Warsaw.

## REFERENCES

Adorno, T. W., Frenkel-Brunswik, E., Levinson, D. J., & Sanford, R. N. (1950). *The authoritarian personality*. New York: Harper & Brothers.

Abrahamson, A., Baker, L., & Caspi, A. (2002). Rebellious teens? Genetic and environmental influences on the social attitudes of adolescents. *Journal of Personality and Social Psychology, 83*, 1392–1408.

Albarracin, D., Zanna, M., Johnson, B. T., & Kumkale, G. T. (2005). Attitudes: Introduction and scope. In D. Albarracin, B. T. Johnson, & M. P. Zanna (Eds.), *The handbook of attitudes* (pp. 3–19). Mahwah, NJ: Erlbaum.

Altemeyer, B. (1996). *The authoritarian specter*. Cambridge, MA: Harvard University Press.

Altemeyer, B., & Hunsberger, B. (2004). A revised Religious Fundamentalism Scale: The short and sweet of it. *International Journal for the Psychology of Religion, 14*, 47–54.

Altemeyer, B., & Hunsberger, B. (2005). Fundamentalism and authoritarianism. In R. F. Palotzian & C. L. Park (Eds.), *Handbook of the psychology of religion and spirituality* (pp. 378–393). New York: Guilford Press.

Amodio, D., Jost, J. T., Master, S. L., & Yee, C. M. (2007). Neurocognitive correlates of liberalism and conservatism. *Nature Neuroscience, 10*, 1246–1247.

Austin, E. W., & Pinkleton, B. F. (2001). The role of parental mediation in the political socialization process. *Journal of Broadcasting & Electronic Media, 45*, 221–240.

Beatty, M. J., Heisel, A. D., Hall, A. E., Levine, T. R., & La France, B. H. (2002). What can we learn from the study of twins about genetic and environmental influences on interpersonal affiliation, aggressiveness, and social anxiety? A meta-analytic study. *Communication Monographs, 69*, 1–18.

Beck, A. T., Emery, G., & Greenberg, R. L. (1985). *Anxiety disorders and phobias: A cognitive perspective*. New York: Basic Books.

Blazak, R. (2001). White boys to terrorist men: Target recruitment of Nazi skinheads. *American Behavioral Scientist, 44*, 982–1000.

Boomsma, D. I., van Beijstervaldt, C. E. M., & Hudziak, J. J. (2005). Genetic and environmental influences on anxious/depression during childhood: A study from the Netherlands Twin Register. Genes, *Brain and Behavior, 4*, 466–481.

Bouchard, T. J., Jr., & Loehlin, J. C. (2001). Genes, evolution, and personality. *Behavior Genetics, 31*, 243 – 273.

Bouchard, T. J., Jr., McGue, M., Lykken, D., & Tellegen, A. (1999). Intrinsic and extrinsic religiousness: Genetic and environmental influences and personality correlates. *Twin Research, 2*, 88–98.

Bouchard, T. J., Jr., Segal, N. L., Tellegen, A., McGue, M., Keyes, M., & Krueger, R. (2003). Evidence for the construct validity and heritability of the Wilson–Patterson Conservatism Scale: A reared twins study of social attitudes. *Personality and Individual Differences, 34*, 959–969.

Bouchard, T. J., Jr., Segal, N. L., Tellegen, A., McGue, M., Keyes, M., & Krueger, R. (2004). Genetic influence on social attitudes: Another challenge to psychology from behavior genetics. In L. F. Dilalla (Ed.), *Behavior genetics principles: Perspectives in development, personality, and psychopathology* (pp. 89–104). Washington, DC: American Psychological Association.

Brader, T., & Valentino, N. (2004, April). Cueing emotions and identity: The power of group threats in American politics. Paper presented at the annual meeting of the Midwestern Political Science Association, Chicago.

Budner, S. (1962). Intolerance of ambiguity as a personality variable. *Journal of Personality, 30*, 29–50.

Campbell, D. E. (2006). *Why we vote: How schools and communities shape our civic life.* Princeton, NJ: Princeton University Press.

Campus, D. (2002). Leaders, dreams and journeys: Italy's new political communication. *Journal of Modern Italian Studies, 7*, 171–191.

Carver, K., & Udry, J. R. (1997, August). The biosocial transmission of religious attitudes. Paper presented at the annual meeting of the American Sociological Association, Toronto.

Chirumbolo, A. (2002). The relationship between need for cognitive closure and political orientation: The mediating role of authoritarianism. *Personality and Individual Differences, 32*, 603–610.

Clarkson, J. J., Tormala, Z. L., & Rucker, D. D. (2008). A new look at the consequences of attitude certainty: The amplification hypothesis. *Journal of Personality and Social Psychology, 95*, 810–825.

Crelia, R. A., & Tesser, A. (1996). Attitude heritability and attitude reinforcement: A replication. *Personality and Individual Differences, 21*, 803–808.

Danso, H., Hunsberger, B., & Pratt, M. (1997). The role of parental religious fundamentalism and right-wing authoritarianism in child-rearing goals and practices. *Journal for the Scientific Study of Religion, 36*, 496–511.

Doty, R. M., Peterson, B. E., & Winter, D. (1991). Threat and authoritarianism in the United States, 1978–1987. *Journal of Personality and Social Psychology, 61*, 629–640.

Duckitt, J., & Fisher, K. (2003). The impact of social threat on worldview and ideological attitudes. *Political Psychology, 24*, 199–222.

Eaves, L., & Eysenck, H. J. (1974). Genetics and the development of social attitudes. *Nature, 249*, 288–289.

Eley, T. C. (1999). Behavioral genetics as a tool for developmental psychology: Anxiety and depression in children and adolescents. *Clinical Child and Family Psychology Review, 2*, 21–36.

Eysenck, H. J. (1954). *The psychology of politics.* London: Routledge & Kegan Paul.

Feldman, S. (2003). Values, ideology, and the structure of political attitudes. In D. O. Sears, L. Huddy, & R. Jervis (Eds.), *Oxford handbook of political psychology* (pp. 477–508). Oxford, UK: Oxford University Press.

Frątczak-Rudnicka, B. (1990). *Socjalizacja polityczna w rodzinie w warunkach kryzysu* [Political socialization in conditions of political crisis]. Warsaw: Warsaw University.

Frenkel-Brunswik, E. (1949). Intolerance of ambiguity as an emotional and perceptual personality variable. *Journal of Personality, 18*, 108–143.

Fromm, E. (1941). *Escape from freedom*. New York: Farrar & Rinehart.

Furnham, A. (2001). Internalizing values and virtues. In F. Columbus (Ed.), *Advances in psychology research* (Vol. 6, pp. 229–254). Hauppaugauge, NY: Nova Science Publishers.

Golec, A. (2001). Konserwatyzm polityczny a potrzeba poznawczego domknięcia w badaniach polskich [Political conservatism and the need for closure in a Polish investigation]. *Studia Psychologiczne, 1*, 41–58.

Hahn, C. L., & Emory, U. (2002). Implications of September 11 for political socialization research. *Theory and Research in Social Education, 30*, 158–162.

Hettema, J. M., Prescott, C. A., & Kendler, K. S. (2001). A population-based twin study of generalized anxiety disorder in men and women. *Journal of Nervous and Mental Disease, 189*, 413–420.

Hunsberger, B. (1996). Religious fundamentalism, right-wing authoritarianism, and hostility toward homosexuals in non-Christian religious groups. *International Journal for the Psychology of Religion, 6*, 39–49.

Hunsberger, B., Owusu, V., & Duck, R. (1999). Religion and prejudice in Ghana and Canada: Religious fundamentalism, right-wing authoritarianism, and attitudes toward homosexuals and women. *International Journal for the Psychology Religion, 9*, 181–194.

Ichilov, O. (2003). Education and democratic citizenship in a changing world. In D. O. Sears, L. Huddy, & R. Jervis (Eds.), *Oxford handbook of political psychology* (pp. 637–669). Oxford, UK: Oxford University Press.

Jakubowska, U. (2005). *Ekstremizm polityczny* [Political extremism]. Gdańsk, Poland: Gdańskie Wydawnictwo Psychologiczne.

Jakubowska, U., & Oniszczenko, W. (in press). The role of personality, cognitive, environmental and genetic factors as determinants of religious fundamentalism: A twin study in a Polish sample. *Studia Psychologica*.

Jang, K. L., Livesley, W. J., & Vernon, P. A. (1996). Heritability of the Big Five personality dimensions and their facets: A twin study. *Journal of Personality, 64*, 577–591.

Jang, K. L., McCrae, R. R., Angleitner, A., Riemann, R., & Livesley, W. J. (1998). Heritability of facet-level traits in a cross-cultural twin sample: Support for a hierarchical model of personality. *Journal of Personality and Social Psychology, 74*, 1556–1565.

Kaufman, S. J. (2004, September). Myth and symbols in violent mobilization: The Palestinian-Israeli case. Paper presented at the annual meeting of the American Political Science Association, Chicago.

Krosnick, J. A., Judd, C. M., & Wittenbrink, B. (2005). The measurement of attitudes. In D. Albarracin, B. T. Johnson, & M. P. Zanna (Eds.), *The handbook of attitudes* (pp. 21–76). Mahwah, NJ: Erlbaum.

Laythe, B., Finkel, D., & Kirkpatrick, L. A. (2001). Predicting prejudice from religious fundamentalism and right-wing authoritarianism: A multiple regression approach. *Journal for the Scientific Study of Religion, 40*, 1–10.

Legrand, L. N., McGue, M., & Iacono, W. G. (1999). A twin study of state and trait anxiety in childhood and adolescence. *Journal of Child Psychology and Psychiatry, 40*, 953–958.

McAllister, P., & Anderson, A. (1991). Conservatism and the comprehension of implausible text. *European Journal of Social Psychology, 21*, 147–167.

McCullough, M., Tsang, J-A., & Brion, S. (2003). Personality traits in adolescence as predictors of religiousness in early adulthood; Findings from the Terman Longitudinal Study. *Personality and Social Psychology Bulletin, 29*, 980–991.

Niemi, R. G., Ross, R. D., & Alexander, J. (1978). The similarity of political values of parents and college-age youth. *Public Opinion Quarterly, 42*, 503–523.

Oesterreich, D. (1999, July). Authoritarian personality and parental socialization: Theoretical consideration and empirical results. Paper presented at the annual meeting of the International Society of Political Psychology, Berlin.

Ogliari, A., Cittero, A., Zanoni, A., Fagnani, C., Patriarca, V., Cirrincione, R., et al. (2006). Genetic and environmental influences on anxiety dimensions in Italian twins evaluated with the SCARED questionnaire. *Journal of Anxiety Disorders, 20*, 760–777.

Olson, J., Vernon, P. A., Harris, J. A., & Jang, K. L. (2001). The heritability of attitudes: A study of twins. *Journal of Personality and Social Psychology, 80*, 845–860.

Oniszczenko, W., & Jakubowska, U. (2005). Genetic determinants and personality correlates of sociopolitical attitudes in a Polish sample. *Twin Research and Human Genetics, 2*, 47–52.

Reich, W. (1975). *The mass psychology of fascism*. London: Penguin Books.

Rieker, P. (1999, July). Ethnocentrism and youth: A multiperspective contribution to research in socialization. Paper presented at the annual meeting of the International Society of Political Psychology, Amsterdam.

Riemann, R., Angleitner, A., & Strelau, J. (1997). Genetic and environmental influences on personality: A study of twins reared together using the self- and peer report NEO-FFI scales. *Journal of Personality, 65*, 449–475.

Rokeach, M. (1960). *The open and closed mind*. New York: Basic Books.

Rokeach. M. (1973). *The nature of human values*. New York: Free Press.

Saraglou, V. (2002). Religion and the five factors of personality: A meta-analytic review. *Personality and Individual Differences, 32*, 15–25.

Sears, D. O. (1969). Political behavior. In G. Lindzey & E. Aronson (Eds.), *The handbook of social psychology: Vol. 5. Applied social psychology* (2nd ed., pp. 315–458). Reading, MA: Addison-Wesley.

Sears, D. O. (1993). Symbolic politics: A socio-psychological theory. In S. Iyenga & W. J. McGuire (Eds.), *Explorations in political psychology* (pp. 114–149). Durham, NC: Duke University Press.

Sears, D. O. (1997). The impact of self-interest on attitudes—a symbolic politics perspective on differences between survey and experimental findings: Comment on Crano (1997). *Journal of Personality and Social Psychology, 72*, 492-496.

Sears, D. O., & Henry, P. J. (2000a, July). The theory of symbolic racism after thirty years: A current appraisal. Paper presented at the annual meeting of the International Society of Political Psychology, Seattle.

Sears, D. O., & Henry, P. J. (2000b, July). The origins of symbolic racism: The "blend" of antiblack affect and individualism is more than the sum of parts. Paper presented at the annual meeting of the International Society of Political Psychology, Seattle.

Stein, M. B., Jang, K. L., & Livesley, W. J. (1999). Heritability of anxiety sensitivity: A twin study. *American Journal of Psychiatry, 156*, 246–251.

Stone, W. F. (1986). Personality and ideology: Empirical support for Tomkins' Polarity Theory. *Political Psychology, 4*, 689–708.

Streyffeler, L., & McNally, R. (1998). Fundamentalists and liberals: Personality characteristics of Protestant Christians. *Personality and Individual Differences, 24*, 579–580.

Tam Cho, W. K., Gimpel, J. G., & Dyck, J. (2006). Residential concentration, political socialization, and voter turnout. *Journal of Politics, 68*, 156–167.

ter Bogt, T. F. M., Meeus, W. H. J., & Raaijmakers, Q. A. W. (2001). Youth centrism and the formation of political orientations in adolescence and young adulthood. *Journal of Cross-Cultural Psychology, 32*, 229–240.

Tesser, A. (1993). The importance of heritability in psychological research: The case of attitudes. *Psychological Review, 100*, 129–142.

Tesser, A. (2002). Constructing a niche for the self: A bio-social, PDP approach to understanding lives. *Self and Indentity, 1*, 185–190.

Tesser, A., & Crelia, R. (1994). Attitude heritability and attitude reinforcement: A test of the niche building hypothesis. *Personality and Individual Differences, 16*, 571–577.

Tesser, A., Whitaker, D., Martin, L., & Ward, D. (1998). Attitude heritability, attitude change and physiological responsivity. *Personality and Individual Differences, 24*, 89–96.

Tibon, S., & Blumberg, H. H. (1999). Authoritarianism and political socialization in the context of the Arab-Israeli conflict. *Political Psychology, 20*, 581–591.

Tomkins, S. (1963). Left and right: A basic dimension of ideology and personality. In R. W. White (Ed.), *The study of lives* (pp. 388–411). New York: Atherton Press.

Topolski, T. D. (1998). A twin study of genetic and environmental influences on anxiety during childhood and adolescence. *Dissertation Abstracts International, 58*, 3936.

Ventura, R. (2001). Family political socialization in multiparty systems. *Comparative Political Studies, 34*, 666–691.

Winkielman, P., & Berridge, K. (2003). Irrational wanting and subrational liking: How rudimentary motivational and affective process shape preferences and choices. *Political Psychology, 24*, 657–680.

Wylie, L., & Forest, J. (1992). Religious fundamentalism, right-wing authoritarianism and prejudice. *Psychological Reports, 71*, 1291–1298.

CHAPTER 8

# The Cognitive Nature of Prejudiced Individuals

## Kinga Piber-Dabrowska
## Grzegorz Sedek
## Miroslaw Kofta

### INTRODUCTION

Over the past fifty years, prejudice theorists have put forward a number of explanations for "the nature of prejudice" (Allport, 1954). In the last two decades, prejudice theory has been dominated by the cognitive approach (Nelson, 2002; Schneider, 2004). Following his seminal 1969 paper "Cognitive Aspects of Prejudice," Henri Tajfel was especially influential in establishing a social cognitive perspective for the domain of stereotypes and prejudice. This cognitive view has underscored the importance of social categorization to the prejudiced style of information processing: prejudice, like stereotypes, is the result of social categorization. Social categorization occurs when instead of thinking about a given person as a unique individual, people perceive that person as a typical member of a given social group. However, people do not always categorize other people; they might opt to either categorize or individuate other persons depending on their available time or degree of interest in obtaining deeper knowledge (Brewer, 1988; Fiske, 1998).

According to the classic cognitive efficiency perspective developed by Allport (1954), using such social categories as stereotypes helps people cope with a

*Personality from Biological, Cognitive, and Social Perspectives* edited by Tomasz Maruszewski, Małgorzata Fajkowska, and Michael W. Eysenck. Eliot Werner Publications, Clinton Corners, New York, 2010.

complex social environment. As stressed by Hamilton and Trolier (1986), the crucial aspect of this perspective is that "if we, as social perceivers, were to perceive each individual as an individual, we would be confronted with an enormous amount of information that would quickly overload our cognitive processing and storage capabilities" (p. 128).

An adaptive response to this situation, therefore, is to treat individuals as being indistinguishable from other members of the same social category, classified based on their physical characteristics (e.g., age, gender, or race) or other socially created categories (e.g., nationality, social roles, social status). Categorization of a target is therefore informative, in the sense that it provides information about the characteristics of that individual (Lee, Jussim, & McCauley, 1995). Once an individual is recognized as belonging to a specific category, perceivers may infer that the target has many of the qualities shared by other members of that category. Hence categorization reduces the need to form an individuated impression of each category member (Brewer, 1988; Fiske & Neuberg, 1990; Hamilton & Sherman, 1994). As a consequence, when perceivers categorize a target, "they automatically tend to feel, think, and behave toward that individual in the same way they tend to feel, think, and behave toward members of the social category" (Fiske, Lin, & Neuberg, 1999, p. 234). In other words, the social cognitive approach maintains that assigning an individual to a specific category leads that individual to be perceived through the automatically activated stereotypes and prejudices associated with that category. This process is considered to be natural, unavoidable, and universal (Ashmore & Del Boca, 1981; Hamilton, 1981; Hamilton & Trolier, 1986).

In sum, the cognitive approach leads to the quite pessimistic conclusion that possessing prejudices—like stereotypes—is rather inevitable, since prejudice is seen as resulting from automatic categorization. Devine's (1989) frequently cited model of automatic and controlled processes in prejudice is the prototypical example of this pessimistic view. According to this model, stereotypes are well-learned associations between a set of characteristics and a group label. Through the socialization process, people learn a lot of cultural stereotypes that become part of their associative network, connected further with either congruent or incongruent personal beliefs. In the case of stereotypes regarding blacks, for instance, high-prejudice persons hold beliefs that are highly congruent with their knowledge of the black stereotype, whereas low-prejudice persons have rejected the stereotype and learned a different set of personal beliefs about blacks. However, empirical evidence has shown (Devine, 1989, Study 2) that low-prejudice persons' rejection of stereotypes does not delete those stereotypes from their associative network. On the contrary, high- and low-prejudice individuals were not found to differ in the level of automatic stereotype activation.

Nevertheless this pessimistic view is now being increasingly challenged. Researchers have demonstrated that not all persons share such so-called social stereotypes; rather, people turn out to differ in terms of how they anticipate the content of such a stereotype. Furthermore, as argued by Devine (1989), knowledge of (social) stereotypes is not universal within society; rather, such knowledge is influenced by the perceiver's level of prejudice (Gordijn, Koomen, & Stapel, 2001; Krueger, 1996). For example, high-prejudice individuals believe that the content of cultural stereotypes are more strongly negative and more strongly positive, compared with low-prejudice persons (Gordijn et al., 2001).

## NOT ALL PERSONS ARE PREJUDICED

The title of this chapter, closely linked to the titles of classic works by Allport (1954) and Tajfel (1969), reflects our particular interest in gaining a better understanding of the cognitive mechanisms underlying prejudice. However, in what follows we will be seeking to synthesize the traditional approach with the latest findings, which suggest increasingly that the traditional view of the nature of prejudice needs to be modified. While many factors identified in classic prejudice research do indeed remain quite relevant, this traditional approach is adequate for describing selected (but not all) members of a given community—that is, only those who are prejudiced.

Although some research has pointed to a lack of differences in prejudice on the implicit (automatic) level between individuals high and low in explicit prejudice (see Brauer, Wasel, & Niedenthal, 2000, for a review), other studies have yielded more conclusive evidence pointing in the opposite direction (for a review see Bodenhausen, Mussweiler, Gabriel, & Moreno 2001). Specifically, recent research has demonstrated that people high and low in explicit prejudice might differ in their automatic stereotype activation and implicit prejudice (Augoustinos, Ahrens, & Innes, 1994; Dovidio, Kawakami, Johnson, Johnson, & Howard, 1997; Kawakami, Dion, & Dovidio, 1998; Lepore & Brown, 1997, 1999, 2002; Moskowitz, Gollwitzer, Wasel, & Schaal, 1999; Neumann & Seibt, 2001; Spencer, Fein, Wolfe, Fong, & Dunn, 1998; Wittenbrik, Judd, & Park, 1997).

There has been vigorous debate over whether individuals low in prejudice never activate stereotypes or whether they control prejudiced reactions once a negative stereotype has been activated. Indeed, compared with high-prejudice individuals, those low in prejudice have been found to be less sensitive to subliminal primes intended to activate stereotypes (Lepore & Brown, 1997). However, other findings show that even in cases when stereotypes are automatically activated (regardless of levels of prejudice), low-prejudice individuals may not apply such stereotypes, in part due to their personal (egalitarian) values and belief systems (e.g., Monteith, Devine, & Zuwerink, 1993; Plant & Devine, 1998). In other words, high-prejudice individuals tend to make more stereotypical judgments than low-prejudice individuals (Monteith, 1993).

Substantial empirical evidence for the importance of differentiating between high- and low-prejudice persons is being gathered in terms of the suppression of stereotypical thoughts. Well-known research by Macrae, Bodenhausen, Milne, and Jetten (1994) has elegantly demonstrated that intentional suppression of stereotypical thoughts does not reduce automatic stereotypes, but may rather amplify them. Following the initial demonstration of such stereotype rebound effects, researchers have begun seeking potential moderators of them. Many of these research programs have examined the possibility that only low-prejudice individuals may be successful in circumventing stereotype rebound effects (Gordijn, Hindriks, Koomen, Dijksterhuis, & van Knippenberg, 2004; Monteith, Spicer, & Tooman, 1998b). For example, Monteith et al. (1998b) found rebound effects following the suppression of homosexual stereotypes, but only among participants who were prejudiced against homosexuals (see also Hodson & Dovidio, 2001). This suggests that low-prejudice persons are much more likely to actively inhibit stereotypical thinking and responding than are high-prejudice persons (e.g., Monteith, Sherman, & Devine, 1998a). In contrast to those high in prejudice, low-prejudice individuals may be able and motivated to suppress prejudiced reactions to negative stereotypes and monitor their reactions and behavior toward outgroup members (Blascovich, Wyer, Swart, & Kibler, 1997; Fazio, Jackson, Dunton, & Williams, 1995; Monteith et al., 1993).

If we assume, therefore, that people differ in terms of the degree to which they are prejudiced toward specific social categories, this raises a range of questions. Does the cognitive functioning of high-prejudice persons differ from that of low-prejudice persons? Do negatively prejudiced persons process information differently than nonprejudiced persons? Does such information processing differ based on the individual whom the information is about (is processing the same for targets or nontargets of prejudice) and does it depend on the information content (whether it is consistent with the prejudice or neutral)?

The remainder of this chapter reviews existing research, including recent evidence gathered in our own laboratory, which seeks to shed more light on these and other questions about the cognitive characteristics of prejudiced persons. First we will look at the two different perspectives on prejudice, the information-processing style versus the phenomenological approach. Next we will turn to research on various memory and integrating processes in prejudice and its effect on executive functions. And then we will look at the relationship between prejudice and personality, noting that prejudice seems to be a consequence (not a cause) of the specific cognitive functioning of prejudiced individuals.

## TWO SOCIAL COGNITIVE PERSPECTIVES ON PREJUDICED INDIVIDUALS: INFORMATION-PROCESSING STYLES VERSUS PHENOMENOLOGY OF INTERGROUP EXPERIENCE

Contemporary social cognitive research on the prejudiced personality is developing along two lines. One line, broadly addressed in this chapter, focuses on individual differences in the processing of social information. The other line attempts to understand the processes involved in imparting meaning to intergroup relations (e.g., a person's effort to mentally construct the outgroup as a meaningful whole with collective intentionality). Within the latter context, prejudiced responses are linked to a subjective image of these relationships in the mind of a social perceiver.

Adherents of the first approach especially analyze differences in attention allocation, categorization processes, accessibility of attitudes and stereotypes, impression formation style (e.g., piecemeal vs. category based), memory encoding and retrieval for stereotypical versus nonstereotypical content, and mental model formation and operation in the prejudiced domain—all of which are processes that presumably account for prejudiced intergroup judgments and discriminatory behavior. Within this framework several important personality dimensions have been identified that might codetermine the aforementioned individual differences in processing style, such as the need for cognition, need for cognitive closure, need for structure, or uncertainty orientation.

The second approach, illustrated by our own research on conspiracy stereotypes, is more phenomenological: as we have already noted, its adherents seek to identify the meaning imposed upon ingroup-outgroup relations and individual differences in this regard. Whereas some researchers here seem more interested in identifying the formal features of a group image (e.g., group entitativity and essentialism), others focus more on its content. The fact that the outgroup is perceived as an entity (as a clearly defined group of people seen as similar, intensely interacting with one another, sharing common views and goals, and behaving in a highly coordinated way) promotes more stereotypical and prejudiced responses to outgroup members. Interestingly, a general disposition to view another person in entity (trait-like) terms was also shown to increase stereotypicality of judgments (Plaks, Stroessner, Dweck, & Sherman, 2001). In addition to entitativity, category essentialism (a tendency to perceive group traits as inborn, shared by all group members, unchangeable, and highly predictive of behavior) is also important for intergroup cognition: it is widely established that high essentialism of a category promotes unified (usually negative) attitudes and stereotypical judgments about category members.

However, in addition to the form of representation, its content also matters: growing interest in studying the content of outgroup representation has recently been observed among phenomenologically oriented researchers. According to one stereotype content model (Fiske, Cuddy, Glick, & Xu, 2002), the combination of low- versus high-competence traits and warm versus cold traits allows for the construction of four qualitatively different types of outgroups, each of which instigates different intergroup emotions and behavioral tendencies. In a similar vein, the image theory proposes that to understand the meaning and nature of outgroup behavior, people may map their knowledge about interpersonal relations onto intergroup relations (e.g., Alexander, Brewer, & Hermann, 1999). Due to this process, they may create holistic images of outgroups as collective "allies," "enemies," "imperialists," or "barbarians," largely determining attitudes, emotions, and behavioral tendencies aroused by the group.

Our own research on conspiracy theories, belonging to the same family of approaches, assumes that people may develop a relatively stable image of certain group targets as collective, conspiring enemies (conspiracy stereotypes). Such a causal theory of outgroups has a dynamic nature: we will provide some evidence that a conspiracy stereotype may be activated in a specific political context and may play a considerable role as a group-defensive ideology (alleviating a threat to the ingroup's positive image).

## COGNITIVE FUNCTIONING OF PREJUDICED INDIVIDUALS

As already mentioned, there is a long tradition of regarding stereotyping and prejudice as an inevitable consequence of categorization (Allport, 1954; Tajfel, 1969). Such (often) automatic categorization has been regarded as an adaptive and functional process to deal effectively with the complexities of the social world.

Yet the efficiency of prejudiced cognitive functioning can be assessed in a different vein, specifically in terms of time and accuracy in information processing. Quick processing time is the most frequently cited characteristic of social categorization. As summarized by Fiske et al. (1999; see also Brewer, 1988; Fiske, 1998), once a perceiver categorizes a target, the category works quickly and efficiently, making its associated affective, cognitive, and behavioral responses immediately accessible without requiring the perceiver to engage in much effortful thought.

The next section will overview our recent research not only about processing time in high- and low-prejudice persons, but also about their accuracy in memory and reasoning tasks.

## Attention to and Encoding of Prejudice-Relevant and Prejudice-Irrelevant Information

Encoding is often divided into different stages or types of processes, beginning with preattentive analysis and ending with elaborative processing (Sternberg, 1996). In social psychological and social cognition research, however, recognition accuracy is assumed to be a measure of encoding effort. This measure is a sensitive test of whether a given piece of information has been encoded into memory (Stangor & McMillan, 1992). The amount of attention paid to encoding certain information reflects how much time is spent on reading that information.

One important way in which prejudice may influence stereotyping is by affecting the amount of attention paid to stereotypical and counterstereotypical behaviors, and consequently the extent to which those behaviors are carefully encoded. The recognition tests used in such research do not require subjects to reproduce any of the test stimuli on their own, but rather to identify which pieces of information were previously encountered and which were not. Such recognition tests measure the extent to which information has been encoded sufficiently well to discriminate it from information that has not been encountered (Stangor & McMillan, 1992).

A long history of research on selective attention attests that people often attend to information that is consistent or compatible with their existing attitudes and beliefs (see Frey, 1986, for a review). Low-prejudice persons often have strong internal motivations to form nonbiased impressions (Plant & Devine, 1998). A motivation to be accurate leads to equal encoding efforts for all types of available information, irrespective of whether that information is consistent or inconsistent with a preexisting expectation. This would occur if these persons gave no weight to expectations (e.g., Brewer, 1988).

## Memory and Integrating Processes in Prejudice I: Trait Judgments About Target Individuals

Recent research on memory processes (Sherman, Stroessner, Conrey, & Azam, 2005) had high- and low-prejudice participants read stereotype-consistent and stereotype-inconsistent information about an individual from a given group (e.g., about a gay man), and then gauged encoding quality by later assessing recognition memory for this material. After the recognition test, participants made trait judgments about the target individual. The study examined whether judgments were based on information that was most thoroughly encoded (e.g., "studied interpretive dance in college"), and its findings demonstrated that high-prejudice participants made more stereotypical judgments of the target than low-prejudice participants.

At the same time, recognition results showed that high-prejudice persons encoded stereotype-inconsistent information more thoroughly than stereotype-consistent information. Participants low in prejudice appeared to have integrated the information into individuated impressions of the target. By contrast, high-prejudice participants showed no relationship between recognition and judgment, although high-prejudice participants encoded stereotype-inconsistent information almost as thoroughly as low-prejudice participants. In other words, they were able—with nearly perfect accuracy—to correctly discriminate old stereotype-inconsistent information from new stereotype-inconsistent information. However, high-prejudice participants encoded stereotype-consistent information less thoroughly than low-prejudice participants, being unable to correctly discriminate old stereotype-consistent information from new stereotype-consistent information.

These findings suggest that high-prejudice participants "were not forming systematic, individuated impressions on the basis of the behaviors they attended to and encoded" (Sherman et al., 2005, p. 611). Generally results showed that low-prejudice but not high-prejudice people formed individuated impressions.

High levels of prejudice seem to be characterized by biased encoding and judgment about stereotyped targets.

## Memory and Integrating Processes in Prejudice II: Linear Orders About Target and Nontarget Individuals

Similar findings about the difficulties of high-prejudice persons in integrating pieces of information into more coherent mental structures were found in our recent studies applying the linear order paradigm (Sedek, Piber-Dabrowska, Maio, & von Hecker, 2009; see Sedek & von Hecker, 2004, for a detailed description of the paradigm). In this task the participants were first presented with some relations between persons. Next they were tested on their recollection of the relations just presented (a memory test) and on their reasoning ability (with the correct answer requiring appropriate integration of the relations presented).

To illustrate this task (in the simplest version), let us assume that the participants obtained the following information about three Polish individuals (Rafal, Leszek, Jacek) and one German individual (Hans).

- Hans is more aggressive than Rafal.
- Rafal is more aggressive than Leszek.
- Leszek is more aggressive than Jacek.

The participants studied each piece of such pairwise information at their own pace. The subsequently posed questions "Who is more aggressive, Hans or Leszek?" or "Who is more aggressive, Jacek or Rafal?" will then be reasoning tests because merely remembering the information presented is not enough; participants need to linearly integrate two premises to derive the correct answers. Deriving the first correct answer ("Hans") demands the integration of two pairs of relations between individuals, one involving a German individual (a target of prejudice). Arriving at the second correct answer ("Rafal") demands the integration of two pairs of relations between nontarget individuals. The results (see Figure 1) showed the main effect of prejudice: persons with negative prejudice toward Germans were generally less efficient in reasoning compared with nonprejudiced participants. However, the planned comparisons showed no significant effect of prejudice for reasoning involving a target individual (see left set of bars in Figure 1) but highly significant differences between prejudiced (poorer performance) and nonprejudiced participants for reasoning about nontarget individuals (the right set of bars). Additionally, we did not observe any relationships between prejudice and performance with respect to the differences between memory tasks for the relations involving the target outgroup member (the German individual).

However, we were also able to examine whether correct judgments concerning the target relation were based on logical reasoning (integration of premises) or on inferences from negative stereotypes. If reasoning about the relation is

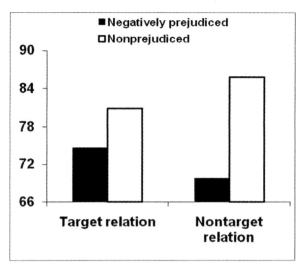

**Figure 1.** Accuracy of linear order reasoning (percentage of correct answers) as a function of prejudice and target.

involved, participants should generate a mental model to make a correct judgment. Using ">" to denote the relation "more aggressive," the hierarchical order of aggressiveness (Hans > Rafal > Leszek) follows from the premises "Hans is more aggressive than Rafal" and "Rafal is more aggressive than Leszek." As a result, there should be a significant correlation between the accuracy for the relation that demands integrative reasoning (Hans > Leszek) and the accuracies for this relation's constituent elements (i.e., Hans > Rafal and Rafal > Leszek). If there is a lack of reliable correlations, we might conclude that the correct answer was based more on the negative stereotype than on integrative reasoning, because the German (outgroup) target was most negative on all traits.

The results indeed showed a strong and significant correlation between memory and reasoning in the nonprejudiced group ($r = 0.74$) and no significant relationship in the negatively prejudiced group ($r = 0.02$). These results support the prediction that negatively prejudiced participants made inferences based on their stereotype, whereas neutral participants clearly integrated the well-remembered premises for correct linear order reasoning. Our findings are highly consistent with the above-noted findings of Sherman et al. (2005) that highly prejudiced participants based their judgments about target individuals (belonging to the prejudiced category) mostly by applying preexisting stereotypes, whereas low-prejudice participants carefully integrate the incoming information about target individuals.

Interestingly, the evidence gathered within this linear order paradigm also supported the efficiency conceptions about prejudice (see Sedek et al., 2009, for more details). For target relations (including relations involving a target German), negatively prejudiced participants spent less time studying the relations than neutral participants. By contrast, negatively prejudiced and neutral participants did not differ in their (nearly perfectly accurate) memory of previously presented relations. Together these two findings support the view that negative prejudices might constitute efficient knowledge structures (Macrae et al., 1994; Sherman, Lee, Bessenoff, & Frost, 1998): less time was needed by negatively prejudiced persons to correctly encode the relations presented about target objects.

However, a completely different pattern of results emerged when nontarget relations were considered. Negatively prejudiced participants were less accurate than they were for relations involving the target members, especially when those relations had to be logically inferred (see Figure 1, right set of bars). To conclude, negative prejudice seems to be a relatively effective mental tool when it comes to encoding—but not reasoning—about prejudiced target individuals. However, negative prejudice impairs memory encoding and reasoning when nontarget members are also involved.

## Memory and Integrating Processes in Prejudice III: Social Cliques Models Including Target and Nontarget Members

Most of the previous study's results were conceptually replicated while applying a different integrative mental model paradigm—the mental model of social cliques (Sedek & Piber-Dabrowska, 2009). Within this social cliques paradigm (for a review see von Hecker & Sedek, 1999), we employed a process-tracing method to study the construction of social mental models, focusing on mental models about a set of perceived sentiment relations (Heider, 1958). There is experimental evidence showing that sets of sentiment relations like "A and B like each other," "A and C dislike each other," and so on are simultaneously represented in memory by means of so-called mental cliques—that is, mental models in which people perceived as liking each other are placed into the same clique, whereas people disliking each other are placed into different cliques. These structures, as can be shown, are constructed from piecemeal information (i.e., from single relations) in a process guided by a step-by-step integration of more diagnostic or less diagnostic information. For example, consider the simple sets of relations shown in Figure 2 (the actual experimental material was more complex because it contained a mix of diagnostic and nondiagnostic information).

Let each pair of names (two target German names, Hans and Ulrich, and four nontarget Polish names—Rafal, Piotr, Jacek, and Leszek) represent one particular piecemeal sentiment relation, presented in isolation, whereby "+" and "–" stand for "like each other" and "dislike each other," respectively. It can be easily seen from the diagram that there is always exactly one relation (e.g., the one between individuals Piotr and Leszek) that is most diagnostic or critical for the kind of overall representation that may be constructed for the whole set of sentiment relations. If and only if individuals Piotr and Leszek like each other is it possible to arrange the whole set of relations in this figure into exactly two cliques of people who mutually like each other. The first of these cliques (model A)

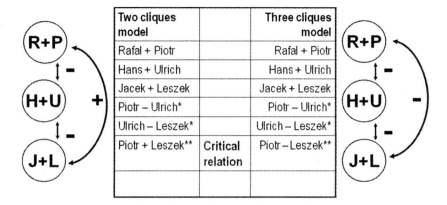

| | Two cliques model | | Three cliques model | |
|---|---|---|---|---|
| | Rafal + Piotr | | Rafal + Piotr | |
| | Hans + Ulrich | | Hans + Ulrich | |
| | Jacek + Leszek | | Jacek + Leszek | |
| | Piotr – Ulrich* | | Piotr – Ulrich* | |
| | Ulrich – Leszek* | | Ulrich – Leszek* | |
| | Piotr + Leszek** | Critical relation | Piotr – Leszek** | |
| | | | | |

**Figure 2.** Exemplary mental models of two and three social cliques.

would have individuals Rafal, Piotr, Jacek, and Leszek as members, and the other one would include Hans and Ulrich as members. This holds for the left part of Figure 2. However, the very same social cliques might be constructed perfectly well by relying not on logic, but on the simple assumptions that Poles and Germans will be in different cliques and will not like each other. This inferring of separate ethnic groups should be especially evident for negatively prejudiced participants, and hence we expected that the construction of social cliques (of separate ethnic groups) by such participants should be rapid and correct.

However, once the information about the sentiment between individuals Piotr and Leszek is changed to a "dislike" between them, as in the right part B of Figure 2, the only clique arrangement now possible is one of exactly three cliques (model B). The first of these is formed by individuals Rafal and Piotr (the first nontarget group), the second comprises individuals Hans and Ulrich (the second target group), and the third has individuals Jacek and Leszek (the second nontarget group) as members. In this configuration participants have to differentiate the nontarget individuals, determining which of them belongs to which of the two different social cliques wholly composed of Poles. According to the previous findings on linear orders, participants negatively prejudiced toward Germans should have compelling difficulties in such a situation because of their nearly complete attentional preoccupation with the target (German) individuals.

The third model (not presented in Figure 2) required that participants completely ignore nationality-related information because it was irrelevant to classifying the individuals into social cliques. We expected that for prejudiced participants suppressing the information about nationality would prove to be the most difficult task, and that their construction of such social cliques (model C) would be most impaired. Our experimental procedure involved the step-by-step learning of relation sets of the kind just described; participants were asked to study one relation at a time on a computer screen, at a self-paced presentation rate.

The first set of results (see Figure 3) confirmed once again that negatively prejudiced participants showed rapid performance and ignored the importance of most diagnostic information: only for the participants not prejudiced (toward Germans) was there a significant increase of studying time connected with special attention devoted to the critical relation. Remember that it was full assimilation of this critical relation that enabled a participant to answer correctly the number-of-cliques question based on logical reasoning.

An inspection of accuracy (see Figure 4) showed that the first model (model A) of social cliques (with Germans and Poles in separate groups) was solved

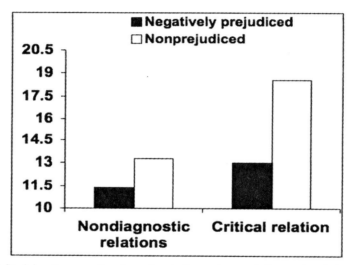

**Figure 3.** Studying time as a function of prejudice and type of diagnostic relation.

nearly perfectly by negatively prejudiced participants. It is when the experimental design fits the expectations of prejudiced persons that they have no difficulties reconstructing the proper grouping (that is, identifying that ingroup members are fully separated from outgroup members).

However, when constructing social cliques demanded that the participant differentiate nontarget individuals (model B) or completely ignore the ethnic category of the individuals presented (model C), negatively prejudiced participants showed a significantly lower ability to properly construct social cliques (see Figure 4) based on logical rules of transitivity (three-cliques model) and antitransitivity (two-cliques model).

Taken together, then, the results of our studies using the linear order and social cliques mental model paradigms contribute some new and somewhat counterintuitive findings to the psychological study of prejudices and stereotypes. Negative prejudice might facilitate the processing of information about target individuals, but at the same time it might substantially impair the memory and

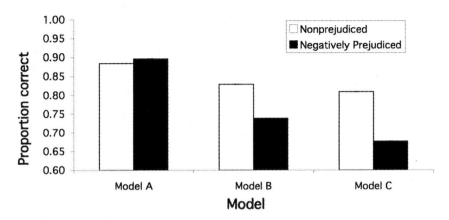

**Figure 4.** Accuracy of integration of sentiment relations into mental models of social cliques as a function of prejudice and type of mental models.

reasoning processes about nontarget individuals (i.e., about ingroup members). These results underscore the necessity of seeing the target outgroup individual in the context of broader social groups that might consist of outgroup and ingroup members, in order to better understand the cognitive and emotional processes among prejudiced and nonprejudiced people.

## Negative Prejudice and Executive Function: Application of Classic Stroop Test

In our previous studies, negatively prejudiced persons exhibited a specific cognitive style: they responded quickly and committed many errors when dealing with nonemotional materials (information about ingroup members). However, negatively prejudiced persons were relatively efficient in processing the relations involving outgroup individuals.

Another of our studies (Sedek et al., 2009) aimed at better understanding this more general mechanism of the cognitive style of negatively prejudiced persons by addressing a broader issue: that participants holding strong negative prejudice had generally poorer cognitive control (i.e., executive attention and resistance to interference) when dealing with emotionally neutral tasks. To examine the possibility of such general dysfunction in executive attention, we applied a classic Stroop test (for a review of multiple experimental and clinical applications, see Engle, Sedek, von Hecker, & McIntosh, 2005; MacLeod, 1991).

The common finding for the Stroop test is that it takes longer to name the ink color of a word (and more errors are committed) if the word itself names an incompatible color (e.g., the word "green" printed in red ink). A remaining issue is whether these impairments are rooted in more general limitations in executive functions, such as attention and memory. Recent research by Richeson and associates (Richeson et al., 2003; Richeson & Shelton, 2003; Richeson & Trawalter, 2005) has demonstrated that interracial interactions impair executive functions, leading to greater inhibitory problems for persons who are negatively prejudiced toward their interaction partners. All the studies showed a convincing effect: the more negative prejudice the subjects had exhibited toward blacks, the greater the interference on their performance of a Stroop task (i.e., the greater the impairment in task performance).

Our Stroop test study explored the hypothesis of the existence of a specific trade-off between accuracy and speed among negatively prejudiced persons on an emotionally neutral task. They might have a general tendency to react quickly but commit more errors. If this hypothesis is true, there should be different scores for latency and accuracy measures: negative prejudice should decrease the latency for correct response and increase the proportion of errors.

The pattern for errors and response time in the classic Stroop test was clear-cut. There is no evidence for a general failure of negatively prejudiced participants (again toward Germans) in this demanding executive task, since they showed relatively better correct response time compared with participants from the nonprejudiced group. However, the negatively prejudiced persons committed more errors, thus bearing out the hypothesis of a trade-off between speed and errors among negatively prejudiced students.

The findings from our study indicating the quick response time for the emotionally neutral but complex Stroop task among high-prejudice participants are in line with the findings of Locke, MacLeod, and Walker (1994). In their work high- and low-prejudice persons also performed a Stroop task, although this was an emotional Stroop task: they were required to name the color of a word that was related versus unrelated to the stereotype of Aborigines. Low-prejudice persons did not evidence reliable differences in color-naming latencies between stereotype-related words and stereotype-unrelated words, while high-prejudice persons were indeed found to demonstrate longer color-naming latencies for stereotype-related words than for stereotype-unrelated words. Although no significant difference was found between high- and low-prejudice individuals in color-naming latencies for stereotype-related words, high-prejudice individuals exhibited shorter color-naming latencies for stereotype-unrelated words than for stereotype-related words.

## PROCESSING TIME, ENCODING, MEMORY, AND REASONING IN PREJUDICE: AN INTERIM SUMMARY

This review has shown a clear pattern of information processing by high-prejudice persons. Such people tended to accept information that is consistent with their beliefs with little examination but set a higher threshold for accepting belief-inconsistent information. Therefore, compared with stereotype-consistent information, high-prejudice persons studied stereotype-inconsistent information very carefully because they are motivated to uphold their stereotypes and are threatened by such inconsistency (Sherman et al., 2005). However, their effort was not directed toward gaining an unbiased, individuating impression, but rather to inspecting the information for some means by which the impact of stereotype-inconsistent information might be minimized or explained away. For individuals low in prejudice, on the other hand, there was no evidence that they studied information in a stereotype-disconfirming way (Sherman et al., 2005). The low-prejudice participants demonstrated no differences in processing time for stereotype-consistent and -inconsistent information.

When all information obtained about a target is stereotype-consistent, high-prejudice persons devote less time to it than low-prejudice persons (our research with linear orders and social cliques; Sherman et al., 2005). A high-prejudice person gives shallow processing to information that is consistent with his or her beliefs, as being obvious ("I already know that, so I do not have to study it"). This seems to be an expression of the "cognitive efficiency" that is ascribed to prejudice (Allport, 1954). But that is the limit of the "efficiency" in the processing of prejudice-consistent information by high-prejudice persons, because this lack of attention in fact entails cognitive losses: such quickly processed information gets integrated by high-prejudice persons to a lesser degree than by low-prejudice persons.

Nevertheless high-prejudice persons devote less time not just to prejudice-consistent or prejudice-neutral information about a target individual. They also devote little time to information concerning other individuals co-occurring with the target individual, even if these are individuals from their own ingroup (again our research with linear orders and social cliques). And once again such information not only attracts the attention of high-prejudice persons to a lesser degree, it also gets recalled and integrated less well by high-prejudice persons than by individuals low in prejudice.

How can it be explained that prejudiced persons have shown a rather counterintuitive limitation—problems with reasoning tasks (both linear orders and social cliques) that demand the integration of information about nontarget (i.e., ingroup) members? A plausible explanation might be offered in terms of associative links (Lepore & Brown, 1997; Locke et al., 1994; Wittenbrink et al., 1997). The linear order and social cliques tasks involve combinations of target and nontarget persons. High- and low-prejudice participants' representation of such mixed groups may differ not necessarily in terms of content (at least for stereotype knowledge), but because stronger evaluative links may have developed for target characteristics. Stronger endorsed connections between the target and the (most probably) automatically activated strong negative characteristics should be observable only for high-prejudice people. For the low-prejudice group, the activation of category-negative characteristics should be much weaker. Therefore, only for high-prejudice persons can the rapid and strong activation of negatively loaded knowledge about the characteristics of target individuals interfere with the cognitively demanding task of memorizing and integrating information about emotionally neutral nontarget persons. The mechanism of cognitive interference postulated here is quite similar to the associative difficulties found for the emotional version of the Stroop test (MacLeod, 1991), in the sense that the emotionally activating content of the specific words for a given population (for example, threatening words for anxious people) might interfere with the emotionally neutral task of naming the color of such words.

It seems, therefore, that high-prejudice persons generally exhibit a tendency to devote less attention to all information that is not controversial (i.e., which does not contradict their prejudice). This conclusion is supported by the results of our classic Stroop task study discussed above, where high-prejudice participants showed a shorter response time than low-prejudice participants. In other words, high-prejudice persons spent less time concentrating not only on targets that were prejudice-irrelevant, but also on those that occurred outside of any context-triggering prejudice.

Generally it seems that high-prejudice persons have a tendency for rapid processing of information. This is evident not only in the above-described research on attention, memory, and reasoning, but also in research on decision making. For instance, in a study by Chiu, Ambady, and Deldin (2004), high- and low-prejudice persons were shown successive faces of white and black men on a computer screen, their facial expressions either happy or angry. The task set for the high- and low-prejudice participants was to determine for each face whether they would enjoy working with that individual. No difference in response performance ("yes" vs. "no") was obtained. High-prejudice persons, in turn, generally responded more quickly than low-prejudice persons, although this effect was only significant for angry faces.

The study by Piber-Dabrowska (2006) noted an analogous tendency for high-prejudice persons to exhibit rapid and shallow information processing. In this study Polish students high and low in prejudice against Germans were asked to anticipate how much time they would need to recognize scientists from eight different social categories based on their outward appearance. The individuals to be categorized were listed alphabetically, with a German appearing fifth and a Pole appearing seventh (see Kwiatkowska, 1995, for a detailed description of the paradigm). The recognition time for the German was found to be significantly shorter for high-prejudice persons than low-prejudice persons. Intriguingly, however, the time anticipated by high-prejudice persons was in general significantly shorter with respect to nearly all the targets. Only with respect to the Pole (the ingroup member) were there no differences in the anticipated time of recognition.

This recurring pattern of results again points to the conclusion that high-prejudice persons are characterized by a specific style of cognitive functioning: rapid and at the same time shallow processing of "convenient" information (prejudice-consistent, neutral, or irrelevant), plus rapid but also shallow processing of prejudice-inconsistent information. It seems, therefore, that the cognitive functioning of a high-prejudice person involves not only striving for accuracy, but rather striving for the fastest possible processing of information. If this style pertained solely to information about a target of prejudice or about targets co-occurring with a target of prejudice, it would then be an argument in favor of the influence of prejudice upon cognitive distortions: an activated prejudice regulates the processing of information. Nonetheless the results obtained for information that is entirely unrelated to prejudice encourage us to postulate a different direction of the dependency between cognitive functioning and prejudice—that it is not the course of cognitive processes in high-prejudice persons that is a consequence of the activation of their prejudice, but rather it is prejudice that is a consequence of a specific kind of cognitive functioning. This conclusion runs counter to the currently dominant interpretation under the cognitive approach: the notion of prejudice as an effect of cognitive processes (for more on this, see Park & Judd, 2005). Nevertheless, as we will see in what follows, this conclusion is indeed consistent with forgotten proposals made by the pioneers of the cognitive approach (Allport, 1954; Tajfel, 1981), and especially with the personality approach, which is now experiencing a renaissance in psychology—the notion of prejudice as a manifestation of more fundamental personality dimensions.

## PREJUDICED PERSONALITY?

The concept of the prejudiced personality (Allport, 1954), in its contemporary interpretation (Altemeyer, 1998; Ekehammar & Akrami, 2003), has been intensively explored in recent years. Allport himself previously noted that if some people harbor a prejudice toward one social group, they are likely to be prejudiced against another group. So-called generalized prejudice, "a composite of different kinds of prejudice" (Akrami & Ekehammar, 2006, p. 123), is being demonstrated empirically using various paradigms. For example, Ekehammar and associates (Ekehammar and Akrami, 2003, 2007; Ekehammar, Akrami, Gylje, & Zakrisson, 2004) used a battery of questionnaires, each of which measured prejudice toward a specific social category (e.g., homosexuals, women, the mentally disabled, African Americans). Well-replicated data indicated that levels of participants' different prejudices were strongly correlated, emerging to form a single factor: generalized prejudice.

### The Research on Conspiracy Stereotypes

We obtained similar findings in our research on conspiracy stereotypes (Kofta & Sedek, 2005). What is a conspiracy stereotype? Our proposal is that it is a causal, holistic theory of the functioning of an outgroup, ascribing to its members (a) a collective goal—permanently and obsessively striving for power and dominance over other groups; (b) collective behavior—a secret (hidden) way of doing things (e.g., involvement in plots, subversive activities, acting in disguise); and (c) a high degree of group egoism and solidarity (high supportiveness for ingroupers combined with complete disregard for the well-being of outgroupers).

The results of a social survey taken in 1995 with a representative national sample of adult Poles ($N = 1,198$) are highly pertinent to discussions about the generality of ethnic prejudice. A primary aim of this survey was to diagnose the conspiracy representations of Jews in comparison with collective representations of five nationalities (Americans, French, Germans, Japanese, and Russians). In this study three items diagnosed the existence of a conspiracy stereotype.

- How do you assess the influence of (various social agents listed, including Jews and the other five nationalities) on what happens in Poland—too small, adequate, or too strong?

- Do you agree or disagree with the opinion that this nationality (the same list including Jews and the other five nationalities) aspires to dominate the world?

- Do you agree or disagree with the opinion that people of this nationality (the same list including Jews and the other five nationalities) want to have a leading say in international financial institutions?

The results showed that the conspiracy stereotypes of different nationalities were highly correlated. The factor analysis of conspiracy scores about the six nationalities showed the existence of only one factor. As in the case of "generalized prejudice" discussed above, the conspiracy-based way of thinking also generalized across many ethnic relations among some persons.

Other findings (Kofta & Sedek, 2004) strongly suggest that two formerly discussed dimensions of a social group's cognitive representation are reliable predictors of conspiracy stereotyping: groups high in entitativity and essentialism are more likely to be seen as "conspiring against us." This means that to be mentally transformed into a conspiring enemy, an outgroup should be perceived as an internally integrated, clearly defined collective entity and should be ascribed some fundamental, unchangeable, inheritable traits and goals (e.g., "to destroy our culture and society"; see Moscovici, 1987).

We assume, however, that a tendency to develop conspiracy theories should not just be reduced to a trait (even if it does show some trait-like features—for example, high generality across different group targets). Rather, it is a naive theory of intergroup relations, ascribing significance to the outgroup's real intentions ("to destroy us") and its typical modus operandi (secret, covert, subversive). Such a theory has a dynamic nature (it activates under some circumstances) and plays an important role in group life. To illustrate this point, let us now turn to two further studies.

In one study (Kofta & Sedek, 2005), we found that a conspiracy stereotype of Jews was activated before the parliamentary elections and deactivated afterward. With high school students in a technical channel of education as participants, we first measured the given stereotype and then, two weeks later, their prejudiced attitudes toward people of Jewish origin and contacts with Israel. The measurements were conducted just before and then shortly after parliamentary elections. We found (see Figure 5) that the conspiracy theory of Jews was a strong and systematic predictor of prejudice prior to the election, whereas the theory

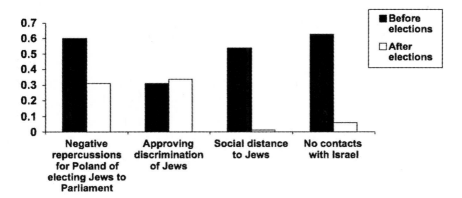

**Figure 5.** Conspiracy stereotype of Jews as a predictor of prejudice toward Jewish targets before and after elections: results of regression analysis (standardized betas).

ceased to function in this way afterward. The election campaign situation presumably raised fears among stereotype holders about the elections being won by a "collective enemy" (e.g., parties that "represent non-Polish interests," "people of Jewish background"), rendering the conspiracy representation of Jews more accessible and augmenting its impact on their attitudes. Thus it seems that a conspiracy theory may help activate ingroup goals (to alleviate a threat from a collective enemy) and concentrate collective efforts on their achievement.

To illustrate the functional meaning of conspiracy stereotypes, let us finally refer to a study in which we asked how an awareness of the historical fact that some Poles were engaged in cruel actions toward Jews (pogroms) soon after World War II affects Polish students' perception of the victims of those events, as well as their attitudes toward present-day Jews living in Israel (Slawuta & Kofta, 2007). In the first experimental group, we found that this awareness led to a significant rise in acceptance for a conspiracy theory of Jews. Clearly the theory functioned as a group-defending ideology ("the victims belonged to a hostile group that had persecuted us in the past"), a way of coping with a threat posed to the morally positive image of the ingroup. Interestingly, when a sense of cultural closeness of Poles and Jews was aroused in the second experimental group (which was exposed to the same information about pogroms), acceptance for the conspiracy theory dropped to the level of the control (baseline) group. Thus a recategorization process, subsuming "us" and "them" into a common superordinate category, may switch off the conspiracy theory of the outgroup.

The findings of the studies we have described so far suggest that high-prejudice persons evidence a characteristic, highly general information-processing style (regardless of whether information is relevant or irrelevant to the prejudiced judgment or attitude). That is why their prejudice seems to be a consequence (rather than a cause) of their specific cognitive functioning. In the next section, we will review further research supporting the view that differences in degree of prejudice are a consequence of personality factors.

## Right-Wing Authoritarianism and Social Dominance Orientation

Right-wing authoritarianism (RWA) and social dominance orientation (SDO) are the personality characteristics that have most often been linked to prejudice research. According to Altemeyer (1998), high-RWA persons are characterized by an adherence to conventional norms and values, uncritical submission to authorities, and aggressive feelings toward people violating conventional norms. High-SDO persons, in turn, support a hierarchically structured social system and believe in inequality among groups (Sidanius & Pratto, 1999). Previous research has documented that both high-RWA persons and high-SDO persons are characterized by generalized prejudice, a composite measure of various types of prejudice (Ekehammar et al., 2004).

Although both high-SDO individuals and high-RWA individuals tend to express prejudices toward a variety of groups, the causes for their prejudice-related beliefs may differ (Esses & Hodson, 2006). High social dominance-oriented individuals tend to view the world as a competitive place in which groups are constantly fighting for dominance. Thus their prejudicial attitudes are likely to be based on perceptions of group competition and conflict. High right-wing authoritarians also hold prejudices toward a variety of groups. These prejudices, however, may be based more on fear and perceived threat to established societal order than on perceived competition. In addition, high right-wing authoritarians tend to see other groups—particularly those who propose social change—as threatening. As a result, high right-wing authoritarians may feel justified holding negative prejudice toward those whom they see as potentially threatening their way of life.

However, the research evidence is not fully consistent concerning the relative roles of RWA and SDO in predicting prejudicial attitudes. RWA seems to be a particularly strong predictor of prejudice in some studies (Altemeyer, 1998; Hodson & Esses, 2005; Verkuyten & Hagendoorn, 1998; Whitley, 1999), while SDO appears to be in others (Heaven & Quintin, 2003). Nevertheless the role of RWA and SDO in explaining prejudicial attitudes has recently been challenged (Kreindler, 2005; Reynolds, Turner, Haslam, & Ryan, 2001). Such criticism is not limited to pointing out that SDO and RWA account for around 50% of the variance in prejudice (Altemeyer, 1998), since no other factor has been shown to be stronger. Rather, the criticism questions the very theoretical constructs of RWA and SDO. For instance, as Reynolds et al. (2001) pointed out, "[I]t is surprising that none of the questions [in the RWA questionnaire] asks specifically about the psychology of the person or is framed in terms of personality characteristics" (p. 430). Reynolds et al. and Duckitt (2001) argued that scales like SDO and RWA are measures of ideological beliefs, not personality traits or dimensions.

That is why the findings of research that uses more valid measures of individual differences are somewhat more convincing. To date there have been few such studies, but their findings support the view that prejudice is associated with certain specific cognitive styles. As Hodson and Esses (2005) have shown, prejudice negatively correlates with a cognitive style like need for cognition (NFC): the stronger the prejudice, the less need for cognition. This finding is consistent with predictions, because persons low in NFC exhibit little interest in abstract thought or working on mental puzzles (Cacioppo & Petty, 1982). Even stronger evidence in favor of the prejudiced personality has been gathered by Ekehammar and associates (Ekehammar & Akrami, 2003, 2007; Ekehammar et al., 2004). Their replicated results suggest that we can distinguish persons characterized by a prejudiced attitude toward people in general (generalized prejudice toward various social groups), and moreover that high levels of prejudice can be predicted quite precisely by Big Five personality traits (McCrae & Costa, 1999), especially by two dimensions: low level of agreeableness and low level of openness to experience.

## CONCLUSIONS

To summarize our discussion, it seems to be a fully justified view (Duckitt, Wagner, du Plessis, & Birum, 2002; Park & Judd, 2005) that understanding the nature of the cognitive functioning of a high-prejudice person requires the integration of different theoretical approaches. Our review of the existing state of research suggests that two approaches to prejudice are key in this regard: the cognitive and personality approaches. In keeping with the cognitive approach, it does indeed seem that (high) prejudice — as a derivative of the natural process of categorization — facilitates and simplifies the processing of information about other people (the systematic ordering of the complex stimulus environment into cognitive heuristics that effectively simplify social reality). However, this simplistic (albeit sometimes effective) method of cognitive functioning only characterizes persons who in general have a tendency to take cognitive shortcuts, are relatively quick in making their judgments, and tend to ignore their social environment (our own research on linear orders and social cliques) when focused on stereotype targets. Recent personality research on conspiracy stereotypes, right-wing authoritarianism, social dominance orientation, and other personality characteristics has supplemented our existing knowledge about the cognitive sources of prejudices and stereotypes and suggests the need for a more interdisciplinary approach in this domain.

In conjunction with research presenting the negative consequences of prejudices, there has been intensive study of psychological mechanisms that may limit their impact on information processing about other people (e.g., research on instructions to suppress unwanted thoughts). Most of the relevant research has concentrated on the possibilities of reducing stereotypes. This line of research has its justification in the common assumption in social cognition research that prejudice is a result of stereotyping, and more broadly of categorization. As recently pointed out by Park and Judd (2005), social cognitive theories are based on the problematic assumption that stereotypes would need to be eliminated or changed if intergroup prejudice were to be reduced. However, there is very little evidence that prejudice might be reduced by eliminating stereotypes. Therefore a certain renaissance can be observed in the popularity of Allport's concept (1954), subsequently developed and promoted by Tajfel (1969), that stereotyping may in fact be a consequence of prejudice—as a form of rationalization or justification of the strong antipathy (or negative affect) that may exist between groups (Jost, Banaji, & Nosek, 2004; Rutland & Brown, 2001; Sherman et al., 2005). They indicated that eliminating outgroup stereotypes without trying to eliminate negative affect (prejudice) might be futile because new sets of negative stereotypical beliefs would quickly be produced.

Our review of the literature suggests that the reduction of prejudices may indeed be difficult: when we look from the personality domain, it seems that on the one hand prejudice is based on specific personality characteristics, while on the other it simultaneously satisfies specific cognitive needs stemming from such personality attributes (sharing conspiracy stereotyping, right-wing authoritarianism, social dominance orientation). Moreover, when we look from the cognitive domain, prejudice facilitates the rapid processing of information, additionally giving one a sense of subjective certainty in making judgments. Hence high-prejudice individuals do not perceive their own mistakes and cognitive limitations that might serve as cues for the self-revision of how they process information about members of outgroups.

## Acknowledgments

Preparation of this chapter was supported by grants #N–N106–040534 to Grzegorz Sedek and #GR–2526 to Miroslaw Kofta from the Polish Ministry of Science and Higher Education.

## REFERENCES

Akrami, N., & Ekehammar, B. (2006). Right-wing authoritarianism and social dominance orientation: Their roots in Big-Five personality factors and facets. *Journal of Individual Differences, 27*, 117–126.

Alexander, M. G., Brewer, M. B., & Hermann, R. K. (1999). Images and affect: A functional analysis of out-group stereotypes. *Journal of Personality and Social Psychology, 77*, 78–93.

Allport, G. W. (1954). *The nature of prejudice*. Reading, MA: Addison-Wesley.

Altemeyer, B. (1998). The other "authoritarian personality." In M. P. Zanna (Ed.), *Advances in experimental social psychology* (Vol. 30, pp. 47–92). Orlando, FL: Academic Press.

Ashmore, R. D., & Del Boca, F. K. (1981). Conceptual approaches to stereotypes and stereotyping. In D. L. Hamilton (Ed.), *Cognitive processes in stereotyping and intergroup behavior* (pp. 1-35). Hillsdale, NJ: Erlbaum.

Augoustinos, M., Ahrens, C., & Innes, J. M. (1994). Stereotypes and prejudice: The Australian experience. *British Journal of Social Psychology, 33*, 125–141.

Blascovich, J., Wyer, N. A., Swart, L. A., & Kibler, J. L. (1997). Racism and racial categorization. *Journal of Personality and Social Psychology, 72*, 1364–1372.

Bodenhausen, G. V., Mussweiler, T., Gabriel, S., & Moreno, K. N. (2001). Affective influences on stereotyping and intergroup relations. In J. P. Forgas (Ed.), *Handbook of affect and social cognition* (pp. 319–343). Mahwah, NJ: Erlbaum.

Brauer, M., Wasel, W., & Niedenthal, P. (2000). Implicit and explicit components of prejudice. *Review of General Psychology, 4*, 79–101.

Brewer, M. B. (1988). A dual process model of impression formation. In T. K. Srull & R. S. Wyer, Jr (Eds.), *Advances in social cognition* (Vol. 1, pp. 1–36). Hillsdale, NJ: Erlbaum.

Cacioppo, J. T., & Petty, R. E. (1982). The need for cognition. *Journal of Personality and Social Psychology, 42*, 116–131.

Chiu, P., Ambady, N., & Deldin, P. (2004). Contingent negative variation to emotional in- and out-group stimuli differentiates high- and low-prejudiced individuals. *Journal of Cognitive Neuroscience, 16*, 1830–1839.

Devine, P. G. (1989). Stereotypes and prejudice: Their automatic and controlled components. *Journal of Personality and Social Psychology, 56*, 5–18.

Dovidio, J. F., Kawakami, K., Johnson, C., Johnson, B., & Howard, A. (1997). On the nature of prejudice: Automatic and controlled processes. *Journal of Experimental Social Psychology, 33*, 510–540.

Duckitt, J. (2001). A dual-process cognitive-motivational theory of ideology and prejudice. In M. P. Zanna (Ed.), *Advances in experimental social psychology* (Vol. 33, pp. 41–113). San Diego, CA: Academic Press.

Duckitt, J., Wagner, C., du Plessis, & Birum, I. (2002). The psychological bases of ideology and prejudice: Testing a dual process model. *Journal of Personality and Social Psychology, 83*, 75–93.

Ekehammar, B., & Akrami, N. (2003). The relation between personality and prejudice: A variable- and person-centered approach. *European Journal of Personality, 17*, 449–464.

Ekehammar, B., & Akrami, N. (2007). Personality and prejudice: From Big Five personality factors to facets. *Journal of Personality, 75*, 899–925.

Ekehammar, B., Akrami, N., Gylje, M., & Zakrisson, I. (2004). What matters most to prejudice: Big Five personality, social dominance orientation, or right-wing authoritarianism? *European Journal of Personality, 18*, 463–482.

Engle, R. W., Sedek, G., von Hecker, U., & McIntosh, D. N. (Eds.). (2005). *Cognitive limitations in aging and psychopathology*. Cambridge, UK: Cambridge University Press.

Esses, V. M., & Hodson, G. (2006). The role of lay perceptions of ethnic prejudice in the maintenance and perpetuation of ethnic bias. *Journal of Social Issues, 62*, 453–468.

Fazio, R. H., Jackson, J. R., Dunton, B. C., & Williams, C. J. (1995). Variability in automatic activation as an unobtrusive measure of racial attitudes: A bona fide pipeline? *Journal of Personality and Social Psychology, 69*, 1013–1027.

Fiske, S. T. (1998). Stereotyping, prejudice, and discrimination. In D. T. Gilbert, S. T. Fiske, & G. Lindzey (Eds.), *The handbook of social psychology: Vol. 2* (4th ed., pp. 357–411). New York: McGraw-Hill.

Fiske, S. T., Cuddy, A. J. C., Glick, P., & Xu, J. (2002). A model of (often mixed) stereo-type content: Competence and warmth respectively follow from perceived status and competition. *Journal of Personality and Social Psychology, 82*, 878–902.

Fiske, S. T., Lin, M., & Neuberg, S. L. (1999). The continuum model: Ten years later. In S. Chaiken & Y. Trope (Eds.), *Dual-process theories in social psychology* (pp. 231–254). New York: Guilford Press.

Fiske, S. T., & Neuberg, S. L. (1990). A continuum model of impression formation, from category-based to individuating processes: Influences of information and motivation on attention and interpretation. In M. P. Zanna (Ed.), *Advances in experimental social psychology* (Vol. 23, pp. 1–74). New York: Academic Press.

Frey, D. (1986). Recent research on selectively exposure to information. In L. Berkowitz (Ed.), *Advances in experimental social psychology* (Vol. 19, pp. 41–80). New York: Academic Press.

Gordijn, E. H., Hindriks, I., Koomen, W., Dijksterhuis, A., & van Knippenberg, A. (2004). Consequences of stereotype suppression and internal suppression motivation: A self-regulation approach. *Personality and Social Psychology Bulletin, 30*, 212–224.

Gordijn, E. H., Koomen, W., & Stapel, D. A. (2001). Level of prejudice in relation to knowledge of cultural stereotypes. *Journal of Experimental Social Psychology, 37*, 150–157.

Hamilton, D. L. (1981). Stereotyping and intergroup behavior: Some thoughts on the cog-nitive approach. In D. L. Hamilton (Ed.), *Cognitive processes in stereotyping and intergroup behavior* (pp. 333–354). Hillsdale, NJ: Erlbaum.

Hamilton, D. L., & Sherman, J. W. (1994). Stereotypes. In R. S. Wyer, Jr. & T. K. Srull (Eds.), *Handbook of social cognition* (Vol. 2, pp. 1–68). Hillsdale, NJ: Erlbaum.

Hamilton, D. L., & Trolier, T. K. (1986). Stereotypes and stereotyping: An overview of the cognitive approach. In J. F. Dovidio, & S. L. Gaertner (Eds.), *Prejudice, discrimina-tion, and racism* (pp. 127–163). San Diego, CA: Academic Press.

Heaven, P. C., & Quintin, D. (2003). Personality factors predict racial prejudice. *Person-ality and Individual Differences, 34*, 625–634.

Heider, F. (1958). *The psychology of interpersonal relations*. New York: Wiley.

Hodson, G., & Dovidio, J. F. (2001). Racial prejudice as a moderator of stereotype rebound: A conceptual replication. *Representative Research in Social Psychology, 25*, 1–8.

Hodson, G., & Esses, V. M. (2005). Lay perceptions of ethnic prejudice: Causes, solutions, and individual differences. *European Journal of Social Psychology, 35*, 329–344.

Jost, J. T., Banaji, M. R., & Nosek, B. A. (2004). A decade of System Justification Theo-ry: Accumulated evidence of conscious and unconscious bolstering of the status quo. *Political Psychology, 25*, 881–920.

Kawakami, K., Dion, K. L., & Dovidio, J. F. (1998). Racial prejudice and stereotype acti-vation. *Personality and Social Psychology Bulletin, 24*, 407–416.

Kofta, M., & Sedek, G. (2004). Essentialism, entitativity, and conspiracy stereotypes. Unpublished data, Faculty of Psychology, Warsaw University.

Kofta, M., & Sedek, G. (2005). Conspiracy stereotypes of Jews during systemic transfor-mation in Poland. *International Journal of Sociology, 35*, 40–64.

Kreindler, S. A. (2005). A dual group processes model of individual differences in preju-dice. *Personality and Social Psychology Review, 9*, 90–107.

Krueger, J. (1996). Personal beliefs and cultural stereotypes about racial characteristics. *Journal of Personality and Social Psychology, 71*, 536–548.

Kwiatkowska, A. (1995). Cognitive distinctness of self-we-others schemata and the tendency to social categorization. In A. Oosterwegel & R. A. Wicklund (Eds.), *The self in European and North American culture: Development and processes* (pp. 257–275). Dordrecht, The Netherlands: Kluwer Academic Publishers.

Lee, Y., Jussim, L. J., & McCauley, C. R. (Eds.) (1995). *Stereotype accuracy: Toward appreciating group differences*. Washington, DC: American Psychological Association.

Lepore, L., & Brown, R. (1997). Category and stereotype activation: Is prejudice inevitable? *Journal of Personality and Social Psychology, 72*, 275–287.

Lepore, L., & Brown, R. (1999). Exploring automatic stereotype activation: A challenge to the inevitability of prejudice. In D. Abrams & M. A. Hogg (Eds.), *Social identity and social cognition* (pp. 141–163). Oxford, UK: Blackwell.

Lepore, L., & Brown, R. (2002). The role of awareness: Divergent automatic stereotype activation and implicit judgment correction. *Social Cognition, 20*, 321–351.

Locke V., MacLeod, C., & Walker, I. (1994). Automatic and controlled activation of stereotypes: Individual differences associated with prejudice. *British Journal of Social Psychology, 33*, 29–46.

MacLeod, C. M. (1991). Half a century of research on the Stroop effect: An integrative review. *Psychological Bulletin, 109*, 163–203.

Macrae, C. N., Bodenhausen, G. V., Milne, A. B., & Jetten, J. (1994). Out of mind but back in sight: Stereotypes on the rebound. *Journal of Personality and Social Psychology, 67*, 808–817.

McCrae, R. R., & Costa, P. T., Jr. (1999). A five-factor theory of personality. In L. A. Pervin & O. P. John (Eds.), *Handbook of personality: Theory and research* (2nd ed., pp. 139–153). New York: Guilford Press.

Monteith, M. J. (1993). Self-regulation of prejudiced responses: Implications for progress in prejudice-reduction efforts. *Journal of Personality and Social Psychology, 65*, 469–485.

Monteith, M. J., Devine, P. G., & Zuwerink, J. R. (1993).Self-directed versus other-directed affect as a consequence of prejudice-related discrepancies. *Journal of Personality and Social Psychology, 64*, 198–210.

Monteith, M., Sherman, J., & Devine, P. (1998a). Suppression as a stereotype control strategy. *Personality and Social Psychology Bulletin, 1*, 63–82.

Monteith, M., Spicer, C. V., & Tooman, G. D. (1998b). Consequences of stereotype suppression: Stereotypes on AND not on the rebound. *Journal of Experimental Social Psychology, 34*, 355–377.

Moscovici, S. (1987). The conspiracy mentality. In C. F. Graumann & S. Moscovici (Eds.), *Changing conceptions of conspiracy* (pp. 151–169). New York: Springer-Verlag.

Moskowitz, G. B., Gollwitzer, P. M., Wasel, W., & Schaal, B. (1999). *Journal of Personality and Social Psychology, 77*, 167–184.

Nelson, T. D. (2002). *The psychology of prejudice*. Boston, MA: Allyn & Bacon.

Neumann, R., & Seibt, B. (2001). The structure of prejudice: Associative strength as a determinant of stereotype endorsement. *European Journal of Social Psychology, 31*, 609–620.

Park, B., & Judd, C. M. (2005). Rethinking the link between categorization and prejudice within the social cognition perspective. *Personality and Social Psychology Review, 9*, 108–130.

Piber-Dabrowska, K. (2006). Prejudice and the tendency to social categorization. Unpublished data, Department of Psychology, Warsaw School of Social Sciences and Humanities.

Plaks, J. E., Stroessner, S. J., Dweck, C. S., & Sherman, J. W. (2001). Person theories and attention allocation: Preferences for stereotypic versus counterstereotypic information. *Journal of Personality and Social Psychology, 80*, 876–893.

Plant, E. A., & Devine, P. G. (1998). Internal and external motivation to respond without prejudice. *Journal of Personality and Social Psychology, 75*, 811–832.

Reynolds, K. J., Turner, J. C., Haslam, S. A., & Ryan, M. K. (2001). The role of personality and group factors in explaining prejudice. *Journal of Experimental Social Psychology, 37*, 421–434.

Richeson, J. A., Baird, A. A., Gordon, H. L., Heatherton, T. F., Wyland, C. L., Trawalter, S., et al. (2003). An fMRI investigation of the impact of interracial contact on executive function. *Nature Neuroscience, 6*, 1323–1328.

Richeson, J. A., & Shelton, J. N. (2003). When prejudice does not pay: Effects of interracial contact on executive function. *Psychological Science, 14*, 287–290.

Richeson, J. A., & Trawalter, S. (2005).Why do interracial interactions impair executive function? A resource depletion account. *Journal of Personality and Social Psychology, 88*, 934–947.

Rutland, A., & Brown, R. (2001). Stereotypes as justifications for prior integroup discrimination: Studies of Scottish national stereotyping. *European Journal of Social Psychology, 31*, 127–141.

Schneider, D. J. (2004). *The psychology of stereotyping*. New York: Guilford Press.

Sedek, G., & Piber-Dabrowska, K. (2009). Prejudice and mental model of social cliques. Manuscript submitted for publication.

Sedek, G., Piber-Dabrowska, K., Maio, G., & von Hecker, U. (2009). Effects of prejudice on memory and linear order reasoning about outgroup and ingroup members. Manuscript submitted for publication.

Sedek, G., & von Hecker, U. (2004). Effects of subclinical depression and aging on generative reasoning about linear orders: Same or different processing limitations? *Journal of Experimental Psychology: General, 133*, 237–260.

Sherman, J. W., Lee, A. Y., Bessenoff, G. R., & Frost, L. A. (1998). Stereotype efficiency reconsidered: Encoding flexibility under cognitive load. *Journal of Personality and Social Psychology, 75*, 589–606.

Sherman, J. W., Stroessner, S. J., Conrey, F. R., & Azam, O. A. (2005). Prejudice and stereotype maintenance processes: Attention, attribution, and individuation. *Journal of Personality and Social Psychology, 89*, 607–622.

Sidanius, J., & Pratto, F. (1999). *Social dominance: An integoup theory of social hierarchy and oppression*. Cambridge, UK: Cambridge University Press.

Slawuta, P., & Kofta, M. (2007, January). You shall not kill . . . your brother: Collective guilt, cultural affinity of the victimized group, and intergroup relations. Poster presented at the SPSP Preconference on Group Processes and Intergroup Relations, Memphis, TN.

Spencer, S. J., Fein, S., Wolfe, C. T., Fong, C., & Dunn, M. (1998). Automatic activation of stereotypes: The role of self-image threat. *Personality and Social Psychology Bulletin, 24*, 1139–1152.

Stangor, C., & McMillan, D. (1992). Memory for expectancy-congruent and expectancy-incogrunt information: A review of the social and social developmental literatures. *Psychological Bulletin, 111*, 42–61.

Sternberg, R. J. (1996). *Cognitive psychology.* Orlando, FL: Harcourt Brace College Publishers.

Tajfel, H. (1969). Cognitive aspects of prejudice. *Journal of Social Issues, 25*, 79–97.

Tajfel, H. (1981). *Human groups and social categories.* Cambridge, UK: Cambridge University Press.

Verkuyten, M., & Hagendoorn, I. (1998). Prejudice and self-categorization: The variable role of authoritarianism and in-group stereotypes. *Personality and Social Psychology Bulletin, 24*, 99–110.

von Hecker, U., & Sedek, G. (1999). Uncontrollability, depression, and the construction of mental models. *Journal of Personality and Social Psychology, 77*, 833–850.

Whitley, B. E. (1999). Right-wing authoritarianism, social dominance orientation, and prejudice. *Journal of Personality and Social Psychology, 77*, 126–134.

Wittenbrink, G., Judd, C. M., & Park, B. (1997). Evidence for racial prejudice at the implicit level and its relationship with questionnaire measures. *Journal of Personality and Social Psychology, 72*, 262–274.

CHAPTER 9

# ERP Time Course and Brain Areas of Spontaneous and Intentional Social Inferences

## Frank Van Overwalle
## Kris Baetens

### INTRODUCTION

In our daily interactions with other people, it is beneficial to have some sense of their immediate intentions and long-term personality traits in order to achieve smooth communication and mutual understanding. Detecting underlying personality traits—and especially the intentions of others—seems even more crucial when we have to make instantaneous decisions about whether they mean us good or bad, so as to approach or avoid them. Our immediate well-being and survival may depend on such critical decisions. For instance, is someone making a move to hit me or to shake my hand? Is a person carrying a gun or a mobile phone? Prior research in the social cognition literature has revealed that we can make such social inferences very spontaneously and almost automatically, including judgments on goals (Hassin, Aarts, & Ferguson, 2005) and traits (for a review see Uleman, Blader, & Todorov, 2005). However, this research tells us little about the underlying neurological processes by which we make such inferences, the timing at which these processes occur, and where in the brain they are computed. What are the neurological processes driving the detection of goals and traits of other

*Personality from Biological, Cognitive, and Social Perspectives* edited by Tomasz Maruszewski, Małgorzata Fajkowska, and Michael W. Eysenck. Eliot Werner Publications, Clinton Corners, New York, 2010.

people? How fast can we make goal and trait interpretations from behavioral information?

To answer these questions, this chapter briefly reviews prior neurological evidence on social processes, presents novel evidence on the timing of inferences like goals and traits, and shows how several brain areas are involved in sustaining these computations. In particular, to study the naturalness of these social processes, we focus on processing differences between spontaneous social inferences (SSI) and intentional social inferences (ISI). Spontaneous inferences reflect that we make social judgments without intention or awareness—for instance, while being busy doing other things. In contrast, intentional inferences reflect that we have the explicit goal to deliberately create impressions of others, such as (for example) while gossiping. This idea is prominent in dual-process models of person perception and social neuroscience, which propose that social information processing involves either spontaneous associative processes or controlled symbolic reasoning (Keysers & Gazzola, 2007; Satpute & Lieberman, 2006; Smith & DeCoster, 2000). Past behavioral research on spontaneous inferences in social psychology has focused mainly on traits of other persons. It has been demonstrated time and again that trait inferences can be made spontaneously, in the sense that if an actor's behavior is diagnostic of a trait, inferring that trait requires almost no intention or awareness, involves only little mental effort, and is difficult to suppress or modify (see Uleman et al., 2005). Only very recently have researchers begun to explore other types of spontaneous inferences, such as on the goals of someone's actions (Hassin et al., 2005; Van Duynslaeger, Coomans, & Van Overwalle, 2008; Van Duynslaeger, Timmermans, & Van Overwalle, 2008).

This earlier social cognition research, however, was limited to behavioral tasks, which does not allow for the exploration of the type and timing of the underlying neural circuits related to the identification of social inferences. At the neural level, we do not know whether goals and traits are identified at the same time and recruit the same brain areas, and to what extent spontaneous or intentional inferences modulate this neural process. In fact, we know little about the timing of spontaneous and intentional social inferences in general, and only somewhat more about their localization.

To provide more insight into these matters, this chapter describes two recent studies using event-related brain potentials (ERPs) derived from electroencephalographic (EEG) measurements that afford millisecond accuracy on the timing of brain processes. These brain waves also allow localizing the source of these ERP signals, so that the relevant brain regions involved in this process can be identified. Before embarking on this, we first provide an overview of the brain areas involved in social judgments—for example, goals and traits—on the basis of research using functional magnetic resonance imaging (fMRI), and then introduce the methodology and relevant social research on ERPs. We conclude this chapter with a discussion of the assumed process of social inference.

## BRAIN AREAS RECRUITED FOR SOCIAL JUDGMENTS

A recent meta-analysis of fMRI evidence by Van Overwalle (2009) suggests that two brain areas are predominantly involved in the understanding and attribution of mental states, such as goals and traits of others. As depicted in Figure 1A, inferences of goals (i.e., intentions and desires) and goal-directed behaviors by others mainly involve the temporo-parietal junction (TPJ). For instance, when viewing animations of simple objects that move in a human-like fashion, observers have an immediate sense of intentionality (e.g., a triangle "chases" a square) that activates the TPJ (Martin & Weisberg, 2003; Ohnishi et al., 2004; Schultz, Imamizu, Kawato, & Frith, 2004). When seeking or reacting to an appropriate ending for a story presented in a verbal or cartoon format, the TPJ is more strongly activated for stories involving behavioral intentions than mere physical events (Blakemore, den Ouden, Choudhury, & Frith 2007; den Ouden, Frith, Frith, & Blakemore, 2005; Saxe & Wexler, 2005; Völlm et al., 2006; Walter et al. 2004). When reading stories, the TPJ is recruited more often when these stories involve beliefs and reasoning by the actors than their physical appearances (Saxe & Powell, 2006) or when these stories involve moral dilemmas as opposed to impersonal decisions (Greene, Nystrom, Engell, Darley, & Cohen, 2004; Greene, Sommerville, Nystrom, Darley, & Cohen, 2001; Moll, de Oliveira-Souza, Brmati, & Grafman, 2002; Moll, Eslinger, & de Oliverira-Souza, 2001).

In a recent study (Spiers & Maguire, 2006), participants were immersed in a virtual reality of taxi driving in central London from a first-person perspective, and immediately afterward they reported (without advance warning) what they were thinking while viewing a video of their performance during scanning. It was found that the TPJ was engaged every time they thought about other agents' behaviors and intentions (e.g., customers, drivers, and pedestrians). In sum, these tasks elicit the TPJ irrespective of the visual or verbal format of the material. Many of these tasks do not focus explicitly on the goal underlying the behaviors and these inferences are thus relatively spontaneous.

In contrast, as depicted in Figure 1B, the medial prefrontal cortex (mPFC) is predominantly recruited for attributing enduring traits and attributes of others and the self (e.g., Mitchell, Banaji, & Macrae, 2005; Todorov, Gobbini, Evans, & Haxby, 2007). As can be seen, trait inferences of unfamiliar other people seem to activate the dorsal (superior) part of the mPFC, while trait inferences of familiar others (e.g., mother, siblings) and the self mainly recruit the ventral (inferior) part of the mPFC. Note that these trait studies mostly involve intentional judgments. A recent study by Mitchell, Cloutier, Banaji, and Macrae (2006) compared intentional with spontaneous (i.e., memory) instructions while participants were scanned using fMRI and found equally strong activation of the dorsal mPFC for trait-diagnostic sentences. However, these instructions were alternated between trials and it is doubtful that the "spontaneous" trait inferences were made without any awareness and intention.

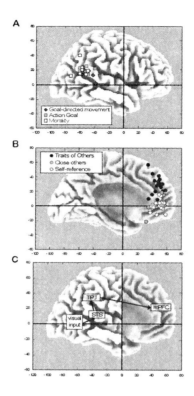

**Figure 1.** Brain locations of social judgments. The brain maps are oriented from the posterior to the anterior cortex and display either a medial view of the left hemisphere or a lateral view of the right hemisphere. Axes are set according to the Talairach atlas. [A] The TPJ involved in social inferences of intentionality: lateral view of the right hemisphere. [B] The mPFC involved in social inferences of traits (other and self). [C] The goal-trait processing stream: visual input in the superior temporal sulcus is propagated to the TPJ where the goal is identified, and then further propagated to the mPFC where trait inferences are made. Adapted from "Social Cognition and the Brain: A Meta-Analysis" by F. Van Overwalle, 2009, *Human Brain Mapping, 30*, p. 832. Copyright 2009 by John Wiley & Sons. Reprinted with permission.

Taken together, all these recent fMRI findings—as well as single cell-cell recordings of macaques (Keysers & Perret, 2004)—have contributed to the view that the TPJ implements prereflective, intuitive, and empathic representations about other people's intentions and beliefs. In contrast, the mPFC is involved in more deliberative reasoning (Keysers & Gazzola, 2007). In addition, the mPFC supports more integrative and abstract representations, like trait inferences (Van Overwalle, 2009). According to Van Overwalle (2009), this seems to suggest a processing sequence or neural pathway from automatic goal inference that informs later processing of traits. This pathway forms the hypothetical framework of this chapter and is illustrated in Figure 1C.

Briefly put, as depicted in the figure, visual input of human behaviors leads to the activation of the superior temporal sulcus, which is sensitive to human movement. From there visual processing (as well as verbal processing; not shown) further continues to the TPJ, where the direction or endpoint of the movement is identified. Although little is known about the underlying processes in the TPJ, most likely the information on observed behavioral endpoints is compared with one's own knowledge of behavioral orientations and associated goals, enabling the identification of ordinary goals of others. Evidence on this comes in part from single-cell recordings with macaques, which reveal that some neurons react to the end-location of the movement (reflecting its goal)—such as bringing food to the mouth (to eat) or to another location (to displace)—rather than the movement itself (Keysers & Perrett, 2004). Similarly, recent evidence with humans (Decety & Lamm, 2007; Mitchell, 2008) suggests that the TPJ area identifies the orientation or directionality of movement and behavior across different content domains. Hence this area is involved in the orientation of behaviors in space and beyond—that is, at a more abstract level reflecting the behavior's functional finality or goal. Once the intentions of others are inferred, this may lead to inferences of traits of the other persons. Because the mPFC can incorporate information over longer periods of time, it is ideally suited to process stable trait attributes of self and others (see Van Overwalle, 2009), especially if the behavior from which the trait is inferred is repeated over time.

In sum, based on past fMRI research, it appears that goal inferences are quickly inferred in the TPJ, while trait inferences require more processing in the mPFC. Note that many of the goal-directed behaviors that typically engage the TPJ also elicited the mPFC to a substantial degree (Van Overwalle, 2009). This may be due to spontaneous trait inferences after goals are inferred. Because fMRI offers a time resolution in the range of a few seconds, it does not allow separating goal and trait inferences at different stages of the process. To provide more accurate evidence on the timing of social judgment processes, we now turn to research using ERPs.

## ERP COMPONENTS OF SOCIAL STIMULI

As illustrated in Figure 2, ERPs are averages from the brain's EEG waves, time-locked at the onset of a specific stimulus (denoted by 0 ms) and typically stretching several hundred milliseconds before and after that onset. The prestimulus time window serves as a baseline to study the changes after the stimulus is presented. These ERP waveforms therefore reflect electric activity of the brain while responding to specific stimuli and their size or amplitude is expressed in μV (see Figure 2). To elicit ERP responses to particular stimuli, researchers typically use an "oddball" paradigm, in which infrequent or inconsistent information is provided among otherwise frequent and consistent information. Such inconsistent stimuli often result in a deflection of the ERP waveforms—that is, an increase in their peak amplitudes. The timing of an ERP deflection reveals the processing stage at which the brain reacts to inconsistencies, and at minimum indicates that an inconsistency is detected and that its identification has begun. Different timings of ERP deflections are associated with different functions or manifestations of information-processing activities, and research has revealed two main ERP types that index inconsistency detection (see also Figure 3). The first type is the P200, which reacts to early and automatic feature encoding and classification (Peters, Suchan, Zhang, & Daum, 2005). The second type is the P300, which occurs later and responds to inconsistencies in task-related comprehension. These characteristics make the P200 and P300 ideally suited for exploring the neural correlates of early (automatic) and late (intentional) social inferences, respectively.

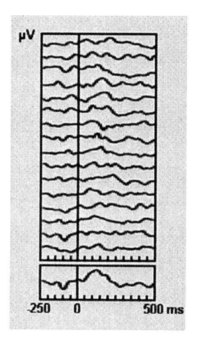

**Figure 2.** An illustration of ERP averaging. The EEG waveforms are time-locked at the onset of the stimulus (denoted by 0 ms) given a time window of −250 to 500 ms, and are then averaged into the waveform shown at the bottom.

## P200 and P300 as Indices of Inconsistency

The P200 is an early positive waveform that peaks at about 200 ms after the critical stimulus. There is evidence that the P200 indexes early sensory stages of feature detection (Luck & Hillyard, 1994), encoding and classification (Dunn, Dunn, Languis, & Andrews, 1998; Raney, 1993). In an oddball paradigm, the P200 reflects increased attention due to unexpected or improbable stimuli such as words (Peters et al., 2005). Research on lexical access indicates that low-frequency words lead to increased ERP amplitudes in comparison with high-frequency words as early as ~130 ms (Dambacher, Kliegl, Hofmann, & Jacobs, 2006; Sereno, Rayner, & Posner, 1998). More importantly, this research also revealed that a preceding sentence fragment may prime the appropriate meaning of an ambiguous word during a 130–200 ms window (Sereno, Brewer, & O'Donnell, 2003). This suggests that a preceding sentence context may "direct early, lexical selection of the appropriate meaning" (Sereno et al., 2003, p. 328). These findings have led to the view that the P200 and earlier ERP components index the selection or beginning of comprehension in response to preceding information.

The P300 is a late positive peak that typically initiates around 300 ms after the critical stimulus and continues until 600 or 1000 ms (and is therefore also termed the late positive potential). Research using the oddball paradigm has documented that there is a relationship between the P300 and the processing of anomalous, inconsistent, or infrequent stimuli presented in a context of otherwise normal or frequent information, as long as this information is relevant for the task. The amplitude of the P300 increases as a function of the amount of discrepancy between the stimulus and the preceding context, and correlates with later recall of the discrepant stimuli, especially when elaborate rehearsal strategies are minimized (Fabiani & Donchin, 1995; Fabiani, Karis, & Donchin, 1986). These findings have led to the view that the P300 is an index of online updating of working memory after inconsistency detection.

## P200 and P300 During Social Impressions

Social processes occur very rapidly. Several researchers found enhanced positive ERPs in response to emotional images—for example, angry, fearful, or happy human faces or armed persons in comparison to neutral faces or unarmed persons—leading to a P200 or P300 (Carretié, Mercado, Tapia, & Hinojosa, 2001; Correll, Urland, & Ito, 2006; Eimer & Holmes, 2002; Eimer, Holmes, & McGlone, 2003; Keil et al., 2002; Kubota & Ito, 2007). The P200 is sensitive to outgroup versus ingroup racial and gender differences, and this has been explained by the idea that outgroup members are often seen as more negative or threatening than ingroup members. Ito and colleagues found that black or male outgroup faces evoke larger P200s than white or female ingroup faces (Correll et al., 2006; Ito & Urland, 2003, 2005; Kubota & Ito, 2007). The P200 race divergence occurs even when tasks direct attention away from race and the judgment is made spontaneously (Ito & Urland, 2005). Figure 3A illustrates a stronger P200 and P300 for black faces in an inconsistent white context as opposed to black context (note that downwards reflects a more positive amplitude; Ito & Urland, 2005). These findings suggest early attention allocation to more emotional or distinctive social stimuli, and therefore reflect an automatic vigilance effect in which attention is quickly and spontaneously directed to stimuli with potentially negative implications.

More evidence on person inferences is available on the P300. Cacioppo and coworkers (Cacioppo, Crites, Berntson, & Coles, 1993; Cacioppo, Crites, Gardner, & Berntson, 1994) found that an evaluative inconsistency between a trait word and previously presented trait words (e.g., a negative trait after a sequence of positive traits) elicited a large P300 between 500 and 1000 ms. More pertinent to the present issue of deriving inferences from behavior, Bartholow and associates (Bartholow, Fabiani, Gratton, & Bettencourt, 2001; Bartholow, Pearson, Gratton, & Fabiani, 2003) asked their participants to form intentional trait impressions about actors described in short behavioral sentences. The behaviors were either consistent with traits implied during preceding behaviors (e.g., a friendly act after a sequence of courteous behaviors) or were opposite in valence with the implied traits (e.g., an impolite act). As shown in Figure 3B, the results showed significantly greater P300 activation in a 300–650 ms time window after presenting a critical word at the end of a behavioral description that revealed an inconsistent trait as opposed to a consistent trait. This result implies that intentional trait inferences are made at a late processing stage at ~400 ms poststimulus, but note that this tells little about the timing of trait inferences during spontaneous conditions.

## AN INCONSISTENT BEHAVIORAL INFORMATION PARADIGM OF GOAL AND TRAIT INFERENCES

This overview suggests that goal inferences lead to an early and automatic activation of the TPJ, whereas trait inferences are slower and mainly recruit the mPFC. Especially during that latter processing stage, differences between spontaneous or intentional instructions may potentially show their greatest impact. In the remaining part of this chapter, we describe two recent studies comparing for the first time the neural timing and localization of spontaneous and intentional social inferences. One study explored goal inferences (Van der Cruyssen, Van Duynslaeger, Cortoos, & Van Overwalle, 2009) while the other investigated trait inferences (Van Duynslaeger, Van Overwalle, & Verstraeten, 2007). In order to make the similarities and differences between goal and trait inferences more apparent, some of the results presented here were newly computed from these data and were not reported earlier.

### The Oddball Paradigm

How can we explore the timing and localization of social processes? To do so, we borrowed the oddball paradigm as applied by Bartholow et al. (2001, 2003) to trait-implying behavioral descriptions of other persons and extended this paradigm to goal inferences and spontaneous processing instructions. Specifically, we provided short behavioral descriptions that were consistent with, inconsistent (opposite) with, or irrelevant to the goal or trait implied during preceding behav-

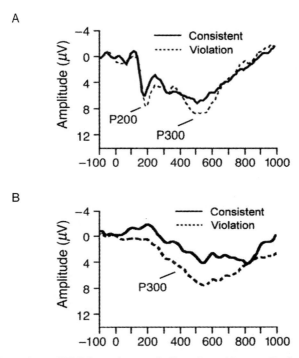

**Figure 3.** Illustrations of ERP inconsistency findings (a positive amplitude is shown downward). [A] A full line denotes a black face in a black context; a broken line denotes an inconsistent black face in a white context. Adapted from "The Influence of Processing Objectives on the Perception of Faces: An ERP Study of Race and Gender Perception" by T. A. Ito and G. R. Urland, 2005, *Cognitive, Affective, and Behavioral Neuroscience, 5*, p. 23. Copyright 2005 by the Psychonomic Society. Reprinted with permission. [B] A full line denotes an inferred trait that is consistent with preceding behaviors and a broken line a trait that is inconsistent. Adapted from "A Psychophysiological Examination of Cognitive Processing of and Affective Responses to Social Expectancy Violations" by B. D. Bartholow, M. Fabiani, G. Gratton, & B. A. Bettencourt, 2001, *Psychological Science, 12*, p. 201. Copyright 2001 by the American Psychological Society. Reprinted with permission of Blackwell Publishing Ltd.

iors. We instructed our participants either explicitly to infer the goal or trait of each target person (ISI) or to read the stimulus material carefully, without mentioning anything about a person's goals or traits (SSI). Table 1 illustrates the kind of sentences that were presented to the participants.

Social research has shown that negative inconsistencies in social inference give rise to more prominent responses (Cacioppo, Gardner, & Berntson, 1999; Reeder & Brewer, 1979; Ybarra, 2002) and stronger ERP deflections (Bartholow et al., 2003; Cacioppo et al., 1999). The reason is that negative violations of morality are more diagnostic. For instance, when an honest person is caught lying or stealing, this is much more diagnostic and revealing about the person than

TABLE 1. Goal and Trait Implying Descriptions in the Introductory Sentences in Function of Consistency Conditions

| Sentences | Goal<br>Washing a car | Trait<br>Friendly | Observations<br>Spring |
|---|---|---|---|
| Introductory | Takes the long<br>green hose | Gives his brother<br>a hug | Sees dew on the flowers |
| | Drives his family<br>car outside | Gives his father a<br>compliment | Smells a very fresh scent |
| | Searches for the<br>powerful soap | Gives his sister<br>a kiss | Hears the young<br>birds sing |
| Consistent | Rubs softly with<br>his *sponge* | Gives his mother<br>a *rose* | Sees a completely blue<br>sky |
| Inconsistent | Rubs softly with<br>the *mud* | Gives his mother<br>a *slap* | Sees large and big *flakes* |
| Irrelevant | Rubs softly with<br>his *hands* | Gives his mother<br>a *spoon* | Sees a very small *pimple* |
| Competence | — | Received an *F* in math | — |
| No-goal | Sees a completely<br>blue sky | — | — |

*Note.* The order of the introductory sentences was kept fixed for goal sentences. Consistent sentences describe behaviors that are consistent with the implied goal or trait from the introductory sentences, inconsistent sentences are opposite in valence, and irrelevant sentences describe neutral behaviors. Competence-inconsistent sentences imply a trait that is opposite in valence as well as different in personality content. No-goal sentences are part of observation stories depicted in the last column (i.e., observation-consistent sentences). These sentences are taken from Van der Cruyssen et al. (2009) and Van Duynslaeger et al. (2007) and were translated from Dutch with slight adaptations in order to obtain six words in each sentence (including the actor name; not shown), with the critical word at the end.

when a criminal pays a bill (e.g., a thief is not always stealing). Likewise, Van Duynslaeger et al. (2007) presented negative trait implications followed by positive trait violations and did not find significant ERP differences. Therefore we focus on positive goal or trait implications followed by the more diagnostic negative violations, as shown in Table 1. If the ERP waveforms show greater deflections following an inconsistency, this indicates that the participants identified the basic semantics of the inference and allocated early attention to it (for the P200), or dedicated more processing resources to identifying and understanding the implications of the inconsistency (for the P300).

## Manipulating Behavioral Consistency: The Oddball Paradigm in Action

How was the oddball paradigm of Bartholow et al. (2001, 2003) applied in our research? Participants read several sentences that described the behavior of a fictitious target actor and from which a strong goal or trait could be inferred or not (see Table 1). Each set of sentences was introduced by showing the name of the actor on the computer screen for two seconds. For each target actor, a series of behavioral sentences was presented, each consisting of six words shown in the center of the computer screen. Every word was presented during 300 ms followed by a 350-ms blank (Osterhout, Bersick, & McLaughlin, 1997). Critically, the last word of the last sentence determined the degree of consistency with the previously implied goal or trait: consistent, inconsistent, and irrelevant. These sentences had been pretested so that a majority of people spontaneously inferred the same implied goal or trait (> 70%), the opposite inference (> 70% for inconsistent sentences), or no inference at all (< 30% for irrelevant sentences). This was further verified using scales in which the goal or trait was explicitly rated on an 11-point rating (0 = less applicable to 10 = more applicable) as well as its valence (0 = negative to 10 = positive).

Apart from these standard consistency conditions, we also added some extra inconsistency conditions. For goal inferences we included descriptions containing observations of phenomena from nature that involve no intention or goal-directedness from the actor. Our question was whether these no-goal events would elicit stronger effects than goal-related events because they involve no intentionality at all. For trait inferences we added inconsistent sentences that implied, instead of an opposite trait, a trait that involved a completely different personality content. In particular, we provided behavioral descriptions implying high moral traits, followed by inconsistent sentences that implied the low competence of the actor. Our question here was whether such greater inconsistency, not only in valence but also in content, would be identified with the same ease and speed as behaviors implying only opposite (moral) traits.

## Spontaneous and Intentional Instructions and EEG Recording

To manipulate spontaneous versus intentional processing goals, the participants were informed that they would read stories about several persons before they were presented with the stimulus material. Next they received the instruction to "familiarize yourself with the material of the experiment" (SSI) or to "infer the goal that the person wants to reach/infer the personality trait of that person" (ISI; see also Todorov & Uleman, 2002). During reading the EEG was recorded from nineteen scalp sites according to the international 10–20 electrode system. In discussing the ERP results, we focus on the most meaningful results of one central midline (i.e., between hemispheres) site, termed Cz. For computing the localization of brain activity, however, all nineteen sites are used.

## DID SPONTANEOUS INFERENCES OCCUR? MEMORY VALIDATION

After the experiment the participants were given two memory tasks typically used in behavioral research to measure and validate spontaneous social inferences. The first, a cued recall task (Winter & Uleman, 1984), requested participants to recall all information presented with the aid of a cue word that reflects the implied goal or trait. When observing or reading about a behavior, the implied goal or trait is assumed to be stored in memory together with the behavioral information from which it is inferred. As can be seen in the top panel of Table 2, the results revealed the predicted pattern of greater recall for consistent sentences after cuing with the implied goal or trait (Van der Cruyssen et al., 2009; Van Duynslaeger et al., 2007). As a consequence, this suggests that while reading the material, the implied goal and traits were inferred and memorized under spontaneous as well as intentional instructions.

The second memory measure, a sentence completion task (Bartholow et al., 2001, 2003), asked participants to complete the last critical word of the original sentences. Memory effects on this measure depend on the assumption that inconsistent information receives more cognitive processing and is memorized better—at the word level—than consistent behavior (Stangor & McMillan, 1992). However, this measure might be less diagnostic for goals because goals are adaptive to new circumstances, so that inconsistent behavior may suggest a change of proximal means in the pursuit of the same distal intention (e.g., buying an "inconsistent" gun for a party suggests a surprise party for Halloween or carnival) rather than a real discrepancy. As shown in the bottom panel of Table 2, the pattern of

**TABLE 2. Proportion of Correct Memory as a Function of Instruction and Consistency**

|  | Spontaneous | | | Intentional | | |
|---|---|---|---|---|---|---|
|  | Consistent | Inconsistent | Irrelevant | Consistent | Inconsistent | Irrelevant |
| Cued Recall |  |  |  |  |  |  |
| Goals | $14_a$ | $04_b$ | $01_c$ | $15_a$ | $07_b$ | $02_c$ |
| Traits | $07_a$ | $00_c$ | $00_c$ | $09_a$ | $01_c$ | $00_c$ |
| Sentence Completion |  |  |  |  |  |  |
| Goals | $29_a$ | $23_a$ | — | $27_a$ | $24_a$ | — |
| Traits | $05_c$ | $08_b$ | — | $08_b$ | $10_b$ | — |

*Note.* Means in a row of the Spontaneous or Intentional condition not sharing the same subscript differ significantly from each other according to a Fisher LSD test ($p < 0.05$). Correct memory was scored on the basis of verbatim accuracy of the sentences (without the actor's name) in cued recall or of the last word in sentence completion, although synonyms were allowed. The means on goals are taken from Table 2 in Van der Cruyssen et al. (2009, p. 178) and on traits are taken from Table 2 in Van Duynslaeger et al. (2007, p. 183).

results was as expected. There were no memory differences between consistent and inconsistent words for goal-implying sentences (Van der Cruyssen et al., 2009), but there was stronger memory for inconsistent than consistent words from trait-implying sentences, although the difference was only significant for SSI (Van Duynslaeger et al., 2007).

In summary, the memory measures confirm that goals and traits were indeed inferred under both SSI and ISI instructions. There were no substantial differences in memory performance between SSI and ISI, indicating that SSI were made to the same degree as ISI and are stored in memory to a similar degree. Having validated the social inferences processes under study, we can now turn to the results of the ERP measures.

## ERP TIMING

For goal inferences a P200 deflection emerged that was substantially stronger for sentences that were inconsistent or irrelevant with the induced goal or involved no goal at all, in comparison with goal-consistent sentences, and this effect was observed irrespective of instruction (Van der Cruyssen et al., 2009). Figure 4A depicts the ERP waveforms of the most important conditions at the Cz midline site. As can be seen, no-goal behaviors (dashed line) and irrelevant behaviors (light line) elicited a larger positive ERP than goal-consistent behaviors (dark line) starting at ~200 ms (see arrows). These findings suggest that after goal expectations were developed during the introductory sentences, goal discrepancies were detected at a very early and automatic processing stage. The difference with the irrelevant—and especially the no-goal—condition was generally stronger than with the inconsistent condition, and continued until one second poststimulus. This further confirms our suspicion that inconsistent goals imply a change of means or type of the same distal goal rather than real discrepancies, whereas irrelevant or absent goals imply a more drastic departure from goal-directed behavior.

Turning to trait inferences, a P300 deflection emerged that was substantially stronger when a moral actor performed an inconsistent immoral as opposed to a moral behavior, irrespective of SSI or ISI instructions (Van Duynslaeger et al., 2007). Figure 4B shows that when trait inferences (dark line) are violated by negative behaviors (light line), this elicits a larger positive ERP at the Cz scalp site starting at ~600 ms (see arrows) and continuing over a second. These results suggest that after trait expectations were induced during the introductory sentences, inconsistent trait implications were detected considerably later as indexed by the P300. A similar pattern of results was found for competence-inconsistent sentences, although these discrepancies led to an earlier P300 at ~400 ms. In another study by Van Duynslaeger, Sterken, Van Overwalle, and Verstraeten (2008) that investigated spontaneous trait inferences, a significant P300 was found for trait inconsistencies, also at an earlier ~400 ms. This late onset of trait detection

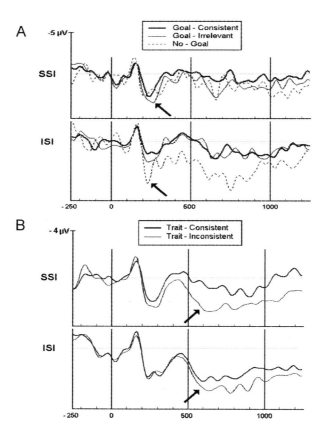

**Figure 4.** Effects of inconsistency on grand-averaged ERP waveforms showing early (P200) and late (P300) positive deflections at the central midline (Cz) scalp sites given spontaneous and intentional instructions. The timeline is given in ms. A positive amplitude is shown downward. [A] Goal inferences: the arrows indicate the onset of a P200 for goal-irrelevant and no-goal words, which are significantly different from goal-consistent words (*p* < 0.05). Adapted from "ERP Time Course and Brain Areas of Spontaneous and Intentional Goal Inferences" by L. Van der Cruyssen, M. Van Duynslaeger, A. Cortoos, and F, Van Overwalle, 2009, *Social Neuroscience, 4*, p. 174. Copyright 2009 by Psychology Press. Reprinted with permission of Taylor & Francis Ltd. [B] Trait inferences: the arrows indicate the onset of a P300 for trait-inconsistent words, which are significantly different from trait-consistent words (*p* < 0.05). Adapted from "Electrophysiological Time Course and Brain Areas of Spontaneous and Intentional Trait Inferences" by M. Van Duynslaeger, F. Van Overwalle, and E. Verstraeten, 2007, *Social Cognitive and Affective Neuroscience, 2*, p. 180. Copyright 2007 by Oxford University Press. Reprinted with permission.

beginning no sooner than 400–600 ms suggests that, in contrast to goal inferences, longer and more processing is involved in trait inferences.

## Memory Validation

To further validate that these ERP components are indicative of goal and trait identification, we computed correlations with cued recall and sentence completion. As can be seen in Table 3, there were significant correlations of at least one memory measure with early (P200) and late (P300) ERP waveforms, for goals as well as traits. There are also differences between spontaneous and intentional instructions, as shown in stronger correlations of memory with intentional goals and spontaneous traits. This may suggest that a minimal amount of focused attention or deliberation during goal inferences is necessary to develop a memory trace of them, because goal inferences are made very quickly and automatically. In contrast, reflective thought during deliberative trait inferences can be more extensive (since they occur later). Because these additional thoughts may differ between participants, these individual differences may hamper adequate memory measures of the participant's (relevant) thoughts, as well as undermine potential correlations between memory and ERP measures (see also Fabiani & Donchin, 1995; Fabiani et al., 1986). Taken together, the significant correlations with traditional behavioral memory tasks indicate that the ERP deflections are valid indicators of goal and trait inferences.

## ERP LOCALIZATION

The localization of electrical activity in cortical brain areas was computed with the LORETA inverse solution method (Pascual-Marqui, Michel, & Lehmann,

TABLE 3. Pearson Correlations (Across Participants) Between Memory Measures and Positive ERP-Deflections at Cz at Different Time Segments as a Function of Inference and Instruction

| Inference | Interval | Cued recall | | Sentence completion | |
|---|---|---|---|---|---|
| | | SSI | ISI | SSI | ISI |
| Goals | 50–300 ms | -0.14 | 0.55** | -0.19 | 0.48* |
| | 300–450 ms | 0.13 | 0.41* | -0.08 | 0.48* |
| Traits | 50–300 ms | 0.21 | 0.23 | 0.46* | 0.06 |
| | 300–450 ms | 0.25 | 0.22 | 0.11 | 0.22 |

Note. *p < 0.05; **p < 0.01. The % correct memory for goal-consistent and goal-inconsistent sentences was averaged before correlations (across participants) were computed with the P200 and P300 peaks in each interval. The correlations on goals are taken from Table 3 in Van der Cruyssen et al. (2009, p. 179) and on traits are computed from the raw data of Van Duynslaeger et al. (2007).

1994), which is a reliable method that estimates the EEG localization with fairly low errors "at worst in the order of 14 mm" (Pascual-Marqui, 1999, p. 85). This method has previously been applied to social interpretations of emotions (Esslen, Pascual-Marqui, Hell, Kochi, & Lehmann, 2004), and although the spatial resolution of ERP waves is poorer than fMRI, a prime advantage is that their high time resolution allows for the localization and imaging of brain activity in a millisecond range. Nevertheless it should be noted that this solution is not unique and should be confirmed by alternative methods such as fMRI. We focused our analyses on the consistent conditions and subtracted an irrelevant baseline from these, in order to eliminate irrelevant electric activation due to mere sentence reading and comprehension. As baseline, we chose the no-goal condition that showed the most robust ERP differences with the consistent condition; for traits we chose the trait-irrelevant condition. We computed LORETA brain maps in a broad 100–700 ms time interval. To obtain robust results with less noise, these solutions were averaged over time intervals of 50 ms each (except for the critical 200–250 ms interval for goal inferences, where averages were taken for each 25 ms). When subsequent intervals did not show substantial changes, they were collapsed (i.e., averaged) together.

Figures 5 and 6 display LORETA brain maps marking the brain areas of maximum activation relative to other areas in the brain in dark gray. As can be seen, these "hot spots" fall at the two predicted brain areas (TPJ and mPFC) as well as at some other brain areas, including the medial paracentral cortex extending to the posterior medial prefrontal cortex (pmPFC) or dorsal anterior cingulate cortex, which is typically recruited during conflict monitoring (e.g., Stroop task; see Van Overwalle, 2009). Activation in this latter area may suggest that participants were aware of the inconsistencies embedded in the stimulus material and reacted to it, which is consistent with the finding that this activation appears under intentional instructions only. The figures display the brain maps for SSI (left panels) and ISI (middle panels). The activation of the TPJ was mainly at the right hemisphere and is therefore shown on that surface, whereas the activation of the mPFC and the pmPFC is shown on the medial surface. The time sequence is shown from top (100 ms) to bottom (700 ms), with the relevant fMRI locations of goal inferences in the TPJ, trait inferences in the mPFC, and Stroop tasks in the pmPFC on the top (adapted from the meta-analysis by Van Overwalle, 2009).

As can be seen for goal inferences depicted in Figure 5, the TPJ is more involved during SSI while the pmPFC is more involved during ISI. This general pattern is interrupted by the onset of goal identification. During goal identification and shortly afterward (~225–300 ms), the TPJ was most active under both SSI and ISI processing modes. After some more time and beginning at ~350 ms, the mPFC activation was strongest for both processing modes, perhaps reflecting deliberative thoughts related to the initial goal identification or other thoughts. These results were largely confirmed by statistical tests as shown in the right column of Figure 5. The only exception is a short upsurge between 300 and 350 ms of more TPJ during ISI, which at first glance may seem surprising since the left

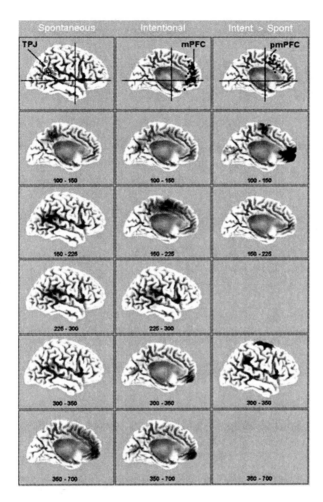

**Figure 5.** LORETA source analysis of goal inferences. The first two columns depict the amplitudes of the goal-consistent condition minus the no-goal baseline condition under spontaneous (left) and intentional (middle) instructions, averaged during consecutive poststimulus time segments. The maps are scaled with respect to their maximum amplitude. The last column depicts maps of t-values, with black indicating greater activation in intentional than spontaneous maps ($p < 0.025$). The brain maps are oriented from the posterior to the anterior cortex and display either a medial view of the left hemisphere or a lateral view of the right hemisphere. The top row shows the relevant brain regions according to the meta-analysis by Van Overwalle (2009). Computed from raw EEG data of Van der Cruyssen et al. (2009).

(SSI) versus middle (ISI) panels show rather an opposite difference. Note, however, that the activation under SSI and ISI is shown in terms of their local maxima (which may differ between brain maps), while the statistical tests calculate these differences directly.

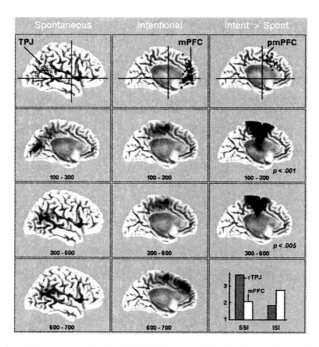

**Figure 6.** LORETA source analysis of trait inferences. The first two columns depict the amplitudes of the trait-consistent condition minus the trait-irrelevant baseline condition under spontaneous (left) and intentional (middle) instructions, averaged during consecutive poststimulus time segments. The maps are scaled with respect to their maximum amplitude. The last column depicts maps of t-values, with black indicating greater activation in intentional than spontaneous maps ($p < 0.025$ unless noted otherwise). The t-map at the bottom right shows no significant differences, and instead a table shows the mean μV for the right TPJ (rTPJ) and mPFC. The brain maps are oriented from the posterior to the anterior cortex and display either a medial view of the left hemisphere or a lateral view of the right hemisphere. The top row shows the relevant brain regions according to the meta-analysis by Van Overwalle (2009). Computed from raw EEG data of Van Duynslaeger et al. (2007).

As can be seen for trait inferences depicted in Figure 6, the TPJ (as well as posterior midline structures such as the cuneus) is generally more involved in SSI while the pmPFC is more involved in ISI, and t-tests confirm greater activation of the pmPFC under ISI. This pattern is interrupted at the onset of trait identification (~600 ms), after which the TPJ is most active under SSI, while the mPFC is more active under ISI, as predicted. However, this difference fell short of significance and the table at the bottom right explains why. Although the activation in the right TPJ is maximal for SSI and reduces (nonsignificantly) during ISI, the activation in the mPFC is quite similar under both conditions.

Considering the two inferences together (Figures 5 and 6), it is evident that there is a general tendency for the TPJ to be more active during SSI, while prefrontal midline structures (mPFC and pmPFC) tend to dominate ISI. However, the onset of social inferences disrupts this pattern. During and shortly after the onset of goal identification, the TPJ is most active and during trait identification and shortly afterwards, the mPFC is quite active (although the TPJ is more active under spontaneous trait inferences). This is consistent with prior brain imaging research implicating the TPJ in goal-directed judgments, and the mPFC in inferences of traits and stable attributes (see Van Overwalle, 2009). Being aware of inconsistencies and monitoring their occurrence may explain the additional activation of the pmPFC during ISI.

## Memory Validation

To validate these LORETA localizations, we also computed correlations with the memory tasks. For goals we did this for the critical 200–250 ms poststimulus interval (of the P200), and for traits we did this for the critical 600 ms poststimulus time (of the P300). The correlations surpassing the significance levels shown in Figure 7 for goals (A–B) and traits (C–D) are depicted in dark gray. As can be seen, the results suggest that when people are spontaneously making social inferences (left column), better recall cued by the implied goal or trait is associated with more processing in the TPJ (and additionally in the mPFC for trait inferences). By contrast, during intentional instructions (right column), more activation in the mPFC is associated with a stronger memory for inconsistencies (but only for goals and not for traits, which may be due to the fact that this region is always active for trait inferences). These correlations confirm that the TPJ is involved in spontaneous goal and trait inferences, while the mPFC is involved in deliberation about goal inconsistencies.

## IMPLICATIONS AND CONCLUSIONS

By using state-of-the-art neuroscientific ERP methodology, these results have advanced our understanding of the underlying neural processes involved in detecting and identifying goals and traits of others. We are now able to determine, when goals and traits of others are detected, which brain areas are implicated in their identification and whether spontaneous versus intentional processing influences the underlying dynamics of this neural circuitry. Note that these results were obtained when reading short sentences (which may reflect what is going on during gossiping and so on), but that more evidence is needed to generalize to (visual) observations in real-life situations.

## Timing of Social Inferences

The results showed an early P200 component at ~200 ms indexing increased neural activation when an expected goal changed or was missing, and presumably reflects increased attention and processing of the behavioral information elicited by the discrepancy with the goal inferred from the preceding behaviors. A later

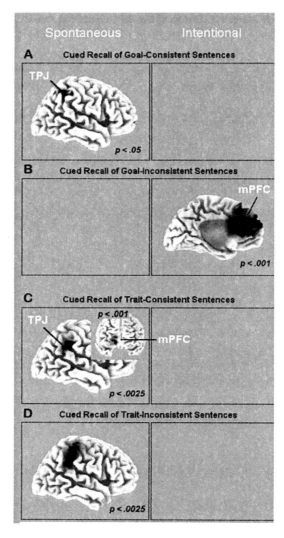

**Figure 7.** LORETA maps of significant correlations (across participants) between cued-recall memory measures and mean source amplitude [A–B] at 200–250 ms poststimulus for goals and [C–D] at 600 ms poststimulus for traits. Dark gray denotes correlations surpassing the significance levels indicated at each map. The brain maps display a lateral view of the right hemisphere or medial view of the left hemisphere oriented from posterior to anterior. The inset displays a frontal view. [A–B] are adapted from "ERP Time Course and Brain Areas of Spontaneous and Intentional Goal Inferences" by L. Van der Cruyssen, M. Van Duynslaeger, A. Cortoos, & F. Van Overwalle, 2009, *Social Neuroscience, 4*, p. 180. Copyright 2009 by Psychology Press. Reprinted with permission of Taylor & Francis Ltd. [C–D] are computed from raw EEG data of Van Duynslaeger et al. (2007).

P300 component at ~600 ms was found for trait inferences and is consistent with earlier research indicating that this component reflects the brain's response to diagnostic and potentially threatening social interaction, when negative behaviors violate an actor's high morality implied during preceding behavioral descriptions (Cacioppo et al., 1999; Reeder & Brewer, 1979; Ybarra, 2002). The fact that the P300 was even faster at ~400 ms—when also the content of the personality trait changed—rules out negative affect or valence as an alternative explanation for these findings, because both inconsistent conditions were similar with respect to valence (although valence may potentially play an additional role). Instead the P300 component presumably reflects a deliberative updating process by which an interpretation of the other person is adjusted and consolidated in long-term memory (Fabiani & Donchin, 1995; Fabiani et al., 1986).

The early P200 component for goal inferences is a surprising finding, because such early inconsistency deflections were not expected on the basis of earlier trait inference research (e.g., Bartholow et al., 2001, 2003). This early timing strongly suggests that goals are inferred automatically. In comparison with earlier research on lexical access showing that a preceding sentence phrase may influence the semantic interpretation of ambiguous words as soon as 130 ms post-stimulus (Sereno et al., 2003), it is intriguing to see how fast goals are identified, requiring a mere extra 50 ms of processing time. The fact that the P200 was strongest for goal-irrelevant or no-goal sentences, which are relatively neutral to positive in affective content, again rules out negative affect or valence as an alternative explanation for these P200 effects (e.g., Correll et al., 2006; Eimer & Holmes, 2002; Eimer et al., 2003; Keil et al., 2002; Kubota & Ito, 2007). Instead the fast identification of goals is consistent with the growing evidence that goal identification on the basis of behavioral information is part of an automatic system involving the TPJ (cf. Van Overwalle, 2009). Behavioral studies have also demonstrated that people can infer goals automatically without awareness or intent (Hassin et al., 2005) and make goal inferences more rapidly than trait inferences (Van Duynslaeger, Coomans, & Van Overwalle, 2008).

## Localization of Social Inferences

The ERP timings discussed above show little evidence of timing differences between spontaneous and intentional processing modes. However, these processing differences become more evident when the activation in the different brain areas is considered. In general, spontaneous inferences tend to activate the TPJ more strongly, while intentional inferences lead to more mPFC (and pmPFC) activation. Perhaps this differential activation reflects different attentional mechanisms or attentional boosts in different brain areas during preparatory or concluding phases when searching for some meaningful information (given spontaneous instructions) or specific details for deliberation (when making intentional judgments). Crucially, these general tendencies are interrupted during particular time windows, when goal or trait inferences are made and specific brain areas are maximally activated. During the 225–300 ms interval, after goal inferences have been identified, the most active brain area irrespective of instruction is the TPJ. This is consistent with the prediction that the TPJ dominates during early and automatic goal processing and therefore reduces differences between spontaneous or intentional mind sets. During the 600–700 ms interval, when trait inferences are made, one of the most active areas is the mPFC, although the TPJ is maximally active during spontaneous trait processing.

Overall these results are consistent with earlier fMRI research documenting that the TPJ is recruited during implicit goal identification when observing human-like, goal-directed movement (Martin & Weisberg, 2003; Ohnishi et al., 2004; Schultz et al., 2004) or goal-directed behavior (Blakemore et al., 2007; den Ouden et al., 2005; Saxe & Powell, 2006; Saxe & Wexler, 2005; Völlm et al., 2006; Walter et al. 2004), whereas the mPFC is implicated in trait inferences (e.g., Mitchell et al., 2005, 2006; Todorov et al., 2007) and the pmPFC is involved in conflict monitoring and controlled processing (Gilbert et al., 2006; Miller & Cohen, 2001).

## Implications

Dual-process models in person perception typically suggest that spontaneous associative processes occur quickly and subserve and inform later intentional thoughts (e.g., Smith & DeCoster, 2000). However, we saw little evidence for such a sequential process of inference making, because the timings of spontaneous and intentional inferences were largely similar. Moreover, each inference recruited a specific brain area during its critical time window for identification, irrespective of a spontaneous or intentional processing mode.

Consequently, the present results seem compatible with a more elaborate framework proposed by Van Overwalle (2009; see also Keysers & Gazzola, 2007), who argued that goal inferences are quickly and automatically inferred, and further guide trait inferences that require more processing mainly subserved by the mPFC, even under a spontaneous processing mode. Outside the critical time window in which goals and traits were inferred, we saw a general tendency for spontaneous instructions to activate the TPJ, whereas intentional instructions recruit the mPFC (or pmPFC). The selectivity of brain areas recruited for social inferences, but at different timings and areas for goals and traits, is a unique contribution of recent neurophysiological research. Further studies may uncover the circumstances under which these timings and activations may vary, such as when goals and traits are combined or when other social inferences—such as causal attributions or beliefs by others—are inferred. We still have a long way to go to fully unravel and understand the neural correlates of social judgments. Perhaps one future outcome may be to help uncover the origins of pathologies of person inference, such as in autism and paranoia.

# REFERENCES

Bartholow, B. D., Fabiani, M., Gratton, G., & Bettencourt, B. A. (2001). A psychophysiological examination of cognitive processing of and affective responses to social expectancy violations. *Psychological Science, 12*, 197–204.

Bartholow, B. D., Pearson, M. A., Gratton, G., & Fabiani, M. (2003). Effects of alcohol on person perception: A social cognitive neuroscience approach. *Journal of Personality and Social Psychology, 85*, 627–638.

Blakemore, S-J., den Ouden, H., Choudhury, S., & Frith, C. (2007). Adolescent development of the neural circuitry for thinking about intentions. *Social Cognitive and Affective Neuroscience, 2*, 130–139.

Caccioppo, J. T., Crites, S. L., Jr., Berntson, G. G., & Coles, M. G. H. (1993). If attitudes affect how stimuli are processed, should they not affect the event-related brain potential? *Psychological Science, 4*, 108–112.

Caccioppo, J. T., Crites, S. L., Jr., Gardner, W. L., & Berntson, G. G. (1994). Bioelectrical echoes form evaluative categorizations: I. A late positive brain potential that varies as a function of trait negativity and extremity. *Journal of Personality and Social Psychology, 67*, 115–125.

Caccioppo, J. T., Gardner, W. L., & Berntson, G. G. (1999). The affect system has parallel and integrative processing components: Form follows function. *Journal of Personality and Social Psychology, 76*, 839–855.

Carretié, L., Mercado, F., Tapia, M., & Hinojosa, J. A. (2001). Emotion, attention, and the "negativity bias," studied through event-related brain potentials. *International Journal of Psychophysiology, 41*, 75–85.

Correll, J., Urland G. R., & Ito, T. A. (2006). Event-related potentials and the decision to shoot: The role of threat perception and cognitive control. *Journal of Experimental Social Psychology, 42*, 120–128.

Dambacher, M., Kliegl, R., Hofmann, M., & Jacobs, A. M. (2006). Frequency and predictability effects on event-related potentials during reading. *Brain Research, 1084*, 89–103.

Decety, J. & Lamm, C. (2007). The role of the right temporoparietal junction in social interaction: How low-level computational processes contribute to meta-cognition. *The Neuroscientist, 13*, 580–593.

den Ouden, H. E. M., Frith, U., Frith, C., & Blakemore, S-J. (2005). Thinking about intentions. *NeuroImage, 28*, 787–796.

Dunn, B. R., Dunn, D. A., Languis, M., & Andrews, D. (1998). The relation of ERP components to complex memory processing. *Brain and Cognition, 36*, 355–376.

Eimer, M., & Holmes, A. (2002). An ERP study on the time course of emotional face processing. *NeuroReport, 13*, 427–431.

Eimer, M., Holmes, A., & McGlone, F. P. (2003) The role of spatial attention in the processing of facial expression: An ERP study of rapid brain responses to six basic emotions. *Cognitive, Affective, and Behavioral Neuroscience, 3*, 97–110.

Esslen, M., Pascual-Marqui, R. D., Hell, D., Kochi, K., & Lehmann, D. (2004). Brain areas and time course of emotional processing. *NeuroImage, 21*, 1189–1203.

Fabiani, M., & Donchin, E. (1995). Encoding processes and memory organization: A model of the von Restorff effect. *Journal of Experimental Psychology: Learning, Memory, and Cognition, 21*, 224–240.

Fabiani, M., Karis, D., & Donchin, E. (1986). P300 and recall in an incidental memory paradigm. *Psychophysiology, 23*, 298–308.

Gilbert, S. J., Spengler, S., Simons, J. S., Steele, D., Lawrie, S. M., Frith, C. D., et al. (2006). Functional specialization within rostral prefrontal cortex (Area 10): A meta-analysis. *Journal of Cognitive Neuroscience, 18*, 932–948.

Greene, J. D., Nystrom, L. E., Engell, A. D., Darley, J. M., & Cohen, J. D. (2004). The neural bases of cognitive conflict and control in moral judgment. *Neuron, 44*, 389–400.

Greene, J. D., Sommerville, R. B., Nystrom, L. E., Darley, J. M., & Cohen, J. D. (2001). An fMRI investigation of emotional engagement in moral judgment. *Science, 293*, 2105–2108.

Hassin, R. R., Aarts, H., & Ferguson M. J. (2005). Automatic goal inferences. *Journal of Experimental Social Psychology, 41*, 129–140.

Ito, T. A., & Urland, G. R. (2003). Race and gender on the brain: Electrocortical measures of attention to the race and gender of multiply categorizable individuals. *Journal of Personality and Social Psychology, 85*, 616–626.

Ito, T. A., & Urland, G. R. (2005). The influence of processing objectives on the perception of faces: An ERP study of race and gender perception. *Cognitive, Affective, and Behavioral Neuroscience, 5*, 21–36.

Keil, A., Bradley, M. M., Hauk, O., Rockstroh, B., Elbert, T., & Lang, P. J. (2002). Large-scale neural correlates of affective picture processing. *Psychophysiology, 39*, 641–649.

Keysers, C., & Gazzola, V. (2007). Integrating simulation and theory of mind: From self to social cognition. *Trends in Cognitive Sciences, 11*, 194–196.

Keysers, C., & Perrett, D. I. (2004). Demystifying social cognition: A Hebbian perspective. *Trends in Cognitive Sciences, 8*, 501–507.

Kubota, J. T., & Ito, T. A. (2007). Multiple cues in social perception: The time course of processing race and facial expression. *Journal of Experimental Social Psychology, 43*, 738–752.

Luck, S. J., & Hillyard, S. A. (1994). Electrophysiological correlates of feature analysis during visual search. *Psychophysiology, 31*, 291–308.

Martin, A., & Weisberg, J. (2003). Neural foundations for understanding social and mechanical concepts. *Cognitive Neuropsychology, 20*, 575–587.

Miller, E. K. & Cohen, J. D. (2001). An integrative theory of prefrontal cortex function. *Annual Review of Neuroscience, 24*, 167–202.

Mitchell, J. P. (2008). Activity in right temporo-parietal junction is not selective for theory of mind. *Cerebral Cortex, 18*, 262–271.

Mitchell, J. P., Banaji, M. R., & Macrae, C. N. (2005). The link between social cognition and self-referential thought in the medial prefrontal cortex. *Journal of Cognitive Neuroscience, 17*, 1306–1315.

Mitchell, J. P., Cloutier, J., Banaji, M. R., & Macrae, C. N. (2006). Medial prefrontal dissociations during processing of trait diagnostic and nondiagnostic person information. *Social Cognitive and Affective Neuroscience, 1*, 49–55.

Moll, J., de Oliveira-Souza, R., Bramati, I. E., & Grafman, J. (2002). Functional networks in emotional moral and nonmoral social judgments. *NeuroImage, 16*, 696–703.

Moll, J., Eslinger, P. J., & de Oliveira-Souza, R. (2001). Frontopolar and anterior temporal cortex activation in a moral judgment task. *Arq Neuropsiquiatr, 59*, 657–664.

Ohnishi, T., Moriguchi, Y., Matsuda, H., Mori, T., Hirakata, M., Imabayashi, E., et al. (2004). The neural network for the mirror system and mentalizing in normally developed children: An fMRI study. *NeuroReport, 15,* 1483–1487.

Osterhout, L., Bersick, M., & McLaughlin, J. (1997). Brain potentials reflect violations of gender stereotypes. *Memory & Cognition, 25,* 273–285.

Pascual-Marqui, R. D. (1999). Review of methods for solving the EEG inverse problem. International *Journal of Bioelectromagnetism, 1,* 75–86.

Pascual-Marqui, R. D., Michel, C. M., & Lehmann, D. (1994). Low-resolution electromagnetic tomography: A new method for localizing electrical activity in the brain. International *Journal of Psychophysiology, 18,* 49–65.

Peters, J., Suchan, B., Zhang, Y., & Daum, I. (2005). Visuo-verbal interactions in working memory: Evidence from event-related potentials. *Cognitive Brain Research, 25,* 406–415.

Raney, G. E. (1993). Monitoring changes in cognitive load during reading: An event-related brain potential and reaction time analysis. *Journal of Experimental Psychology: Learning, Memory, and Cognition, 19,* 51–69.

Reeder, G. D., & Brewer, M. B. (1979). A schematic model of dispositional attribution in interpersonal perception. *Psychological Review, 86,* 61–79.

Satpute, A. B., & Lieberman, M. D. (2006). Integrating automatic and controlled processes into neurocognitive models of social cognition. *Brain Research, 1079,* 86–97.

Saxe, R., & Powell, L. J. (2006). It's the thought that counts: Specific brain regions for one component of theory of mind. *Psychological Science, 17,* 692–699.

Saxe, R., & Wexler, A. (2005). Making sense of another mind: The role of the right temporo-parietal junction. *Neuropsychologia, 43,* 1391–1399.

Schultz, J., Imamizu, H., Kawato, M., & Frith, C. D. (2004). Activation of the human superior temporal gyrus during observation of goal attribution by intentional objects. *Journal of Cognitive Neuroscience, 16,* 1695–1705.

Sereno, S. C., Brewer, C. C., & O'Donnell, P. J. (2003). Context effects in word recognition: Evidence for early interactive processing. *Psychological Science, 14,* 328–333.

Sereno, S. C., Rayner, K., & Posner, M. I. (1998). Establishing a time-line of word recognition: Evidence from eye movements and event-related potentials. *NeuroReport, 9,* 2195–2200.

Smith, E. R. & DeCoster, J. (2000). Dual-process models in social and cognitive psychology: Conceptual integration and links to underlying memory systems. *Personality and Social Psychology Review, 4,* 108–131.

Spiers, H. J., & Maguire, E. A. (2006). Spontaneous mentalizing during an interactive real world task: An fMRI study. *Neuropsychologia, 44,* 1674–1682.

Stangor, C., & McMillan, D. (1992). Memory for expectancy-congruent and expectancy-incongruent information: A review of the social and social developmental literatures. *Psychological Bulletin, 111,* 42–61.

Todorov, A., Gobbini, M. I., Evans, K. K., & Haxby, J. V. (2007). Spontaneous retrieval of affective person knowledge in face perception. *Neuropsychologia, 45,* 163–173.

Todorov, A., & Uleman, J. S. (2002). Spontaneous trait inferences are bound to actors' faces: Evidence from a false recognition paradigm. *Journal of Personality and Social Psychology, 83,* 1051–1064.

Uleman, J. S., Blader, S. L., & Todorov, A. (2005). Implicit impressions. In R. R. Hassin, J. S. Uleman, & J. A. Bargh (Eds.), *The new unconscious* (pp. 362–392). New York: Oxford University Press.

Van der Cruyssen, L., Van Duynslaeger, M., Cortoos, A., & Van Overwalle, F. (2009). ERP time course and brain areas of spontaneous and intentional goal inferences. *Social Neuroscience, 4*, 165–184.

Van Duynslaeger, M., Coomans, D., & Van Overwalle, F. (2008). Co-occurring trait and goal inferences. Manuscript submitted for publication.

Van Duynslaeger, M., Sterken, C., Van Overwalle, F., & Verstraeten, E. (2008). EEG components of spontaneous trait inferences. *Social Neuroscience, 3*, 164–177.

Van Duynslaeger, M., Timmermans, B., & Van Overwalle, F. (2008). Automatic goal inferences: Are direct and hidden goals alike? Manuscript submitted for publication.

Van Duynslaeger, M., Van Overwalle, F., & Verstraeten, E. (2007). Electrophysiological time course and brain areas of spontaneous and intentional trait inferences. *Social Cognitive and Affective Neuroscience, 2*, 174–188.

Van Overwalle, F. (2009). Social cognition and the brain: A meta-analysis. *Human Brain Mapping, 30*, 829–858.

Völlm, B. A., Taylor, A. N. W., Richardson, P., Corcoran, R., Stirling, J., McKie, S., et al. (2006). Neuronal correlates of theory of mind and empathy: A functional magnetic resonance imaging study in a nonverbal task. *NeuroImage, 29*, 90–98.

Walter, H., Adenzato, M., Ciaramidaro, A., Enrici, I., Pia, L., & Bara, B. G. (2004). Understanding intentions in social interaction: The role of the anterior paracingulate cortex. *Journal of Cognitive Neuroscience, 16*, 1854–1863.

Winter, L., & Uleman, J. S. (1984). When are social judgments made? Evidence for the spontaneousness of trait inferences. *Journal of Personality and Social Psychology, 47*, 237–252.

Ybarra, O. (2002). Naive causal understanding of valenced behaviors and its implications for social information processing. *Psychological Bulletin, 128*, 421–440.

# Index

## A

Adolescents, 6, 105, 131

Affective perspective, 2, 132

Affective specialization hypothesis, 65–67

Aggression, 44–45, 138

Aging, 87–114
  cognitive functioning and, 5–6, 87–103, 104, 108
  information processing and, 91, 97–98, 100–103

Agreeableness, 137, 138, 165

Alertness, age-related decline in, 93–96, 102–103
  *see also* Attention

Allelic associations, 43–44

Anger, 59

Antireductionism, 14, 23
  reductionism *vs.*, 15–22, 24
  *see also* Reductionism

Antireductivism, 14, 23, 25
  *see also* Reductivism

Anxiety, 34, 39, 41, 58, 136, 137, 138

Approach behavior, 35, 42

Arousability, 34, 36*t,* 39–40

Arousal
  cortical, 38, 39
  determinants of, 31*f*
  genetic differences in, 133, 134, 136
  levels of, 34
  visceral, 37

Artificial intelligence (AI), 18, 19, 20–22, 24

*see also* Classic AI systems; Connectionist paradigm of AI; Embodied mind paradigm of AI

Atoms, 16

Attention
  age-related decline in, 90–91, 93–96, 98–99, 101–102, 103, 108
  intelligence related to, 106
  mismatch negativity related to, 118
  prejudice's effects on, 151, 157–158, 160

Attitudes, concept of, 130*n*
  *see also* Sociopolitical attitudes

Attractor, reconstructed, 107

Authoritarianism, 130, 132, 136, 164–165

Automatic integration mechanism, 5

Autonomic nervous system (ANS), 31*f,* 32, 35–37, 118

Autonomy, 60, 67

Average-intelligence individuals (AIIs), 104–107

Avoidance, 44, 45, 60

## B

Basin of attraction, 107

Behavior
  biological influences on, 31–32
  brain area responsible for, 177, 193
  consistency *vs.* inconsistency in, 18, 180–183, 185, 186*f*
  discrimination thresholds of, 119–120
  personality traits and, 1, 2, 3, 7, 30, 34, 45